Instructor's Manual
for
ENGLISH WORDS
from Latin and Greek
Elements

INSTRUCTOR'S MANUAL

for the Second Edition of
Donald M. Ayers's

English words

from Latin and Greek elements

R. L. Cherry

The University of Arizona Press
TUCSON

About the Author

R. L. Cherry has worked actively in the field of lexicography for twenty years. His experience has included work with the *Oxford English Dictionary* (*New Supplement*), *Doubleday Dictionary,* and with the Houghton Mifflin and the Funk and Wagnalls dictionaries. He has also taught English as a Second Language at the University of Arizona, English at the secondary level in the United States, and English through the Advanced Level in England, where he also taught Latin. He assisted with and edited the second edition of Saxton's *Papago/Pima—English; English—Papago/Pima Dictionary,* published by the University of Arizona Press in 1983. He also wrote the *Instructor's Manual* to the first edition of this Ayers text and assisted with the revised edition.

NOTE

Words used in this text that the author has reason to believe constitute trade names have been designated as such. However, neither the presence nor the absence of   h designation should be regarded as affecting the legal status o   ιy trademark.

Third printing 2003
THE UNIVERSITY OF ARIZONA PRESS

This book was set in Linotron Times Roman.
Manufactured in the U.S.A.
♾ This book is printed on acid-free, archival-quality paper.

ISBN 0-8165-0980-8

CONTENTS

The numbering of all lessons and exercises in the *Instructor's Manual (IM)* corresponds to the numbering in *English Words (EW)*. Some of *EW*'s topical subjects are not treated or even listed in *IM* because they are discussed in full in *EW.*

PART I: WORD ELEMENTS FROM LATIN

PART II: WORD ELEMENTS FROM GREEK

REFERENCES

The American Heritage Dictionary. 2d ed. Boston: Houghton Mifflin, 1982.

The Australian Pocket Oxford Dictionary. Edited by Grahame Johnston. Melbourne: Oxford University Press, 1976.

Barnhart, Clarence L., Sol Steinmetz, and Robert K. Barnhart. *The Second Barnhart Dictionary of New English.* Bronxville, New York: Barnhart/ Harper & Row, 1980.

Chambers Twentieth Century Dictionary. Edited by E. M. Kirkpatrick. Edinburgh: W. & R. Chambers, Ltd., 1983.

The Chicago Manual of Style. 13th ed. Chicago: University of Chicago Press, 1982.

Collins Dictionary of the English Language. Edited by Patrick Hanks. London: Collins, 1979.

A Dictionary of Canadianisms on Historical Principles. Edited by Walter S. Avis. Toronto: W. J. Gage, Ltd., 1967.

A Greek-English Lexicon. 2 vols. Compiled by Henry George Liddell and Robert Scott. A New Edition revised and augmented by Sir Henry Stuart Jones. Oxford: Clarendon Press, 1925.

Harper's Latin Dictionary, A New Latin Dictionary. Edited by A. E. Andrews. New York: American Book Company, 1879.

Morris, William and Mary. *Harper Dictionary of Contemporary Usage.* New York: Harper & Row, 1985.

Oxford English Dictionary. 13 vols., with new supplement edited by Robert L. Burchfield. Oxford: Clarendon Press, 1888–1933, 1972, 1976, 1982.

Oxford Latin Dictionary. Edited by P. G. W. Glare. Oxford: Clarendon Press, 1968–1982.

The Random House College Dictionary. Editor in Chief, Jess Stein. Revised Edition. New York: Random House, 1982.

The Random House Dictionary of the English Language, The Unabridged Edition. Editor in Chief, Jess Stein. New York: Random House, 1966.

Simpson, D. A. *Cassell's New Latin Dictionary.* New York: Funk & Wagnalls, 1960.

Stratmann, Francis Henry. *A Middle-English Dictionary* (1891). Revised edition by Henry Bradley. London: Oxford University Press, 1940.

Webster's New Collegiate Dictionary. Editor in Chief, Henry Bosley Woolf. Springfield, Massachusetts: G. & C. Merriam Company, 1981.

Websters Ninth New Collegiate Dictionary. Springfield, Massachusetts: Merriam-Webster, Inc., 1984.

Webster's Third New International Dictionary. Editor in Chief, Philip Babcock Gove. Springfield, Massachusetts: G. & C. Merriam Company, 1976.

The Winston Dictionary of Canadian English. Edited by Thomas Pinkeday. Toronto: Holt, Rinehart & Winston of Canada, Ltd., 1970.

The World Book Dictionary. 2 vols. Edited by Clarence L. Barnhart and Robert K. Barnhart. New York: Doubleday & Company, 1976.

ABBREVIATIONS

English Dictionaries

AHD	*American Heritage Dictionary*
Collins	*Collins English Dictionary*
OED	*Oxford English Dictionary*
RHD	*Random House College Dictionary*
W3	*Webster's Third International Dictionary*
WBD	*World Book Dictionary*
WNCD	*Webster's New Collegiate Dictionary*

Languages

AF	Anglo-French (the dialect of French introduced into England during the Norman Conquest)
Du	Dutch
E	English
F	French
Ger	German
Gk	Greek (classical, used until about A.D. 200)
It	Italian
L	Latin (the Latin of ancient Rome)
LL	Late Latin (Latin from about 300 to 700)
Late Gk	Late Greek (Greek from about 300 to 700)
ME	Middle English (English from about 1100 to 1500)
MF	Middle French (French from about 1400 to 1600)
ML	Medieval Latin (Latin during the Middle Ages, from about 700 to 1500)
ModE	Modern English (English from about 1500 to the present)
New L	New Latin (Latin after 1500, also called Modern Latin)
OE	Old English (English before 1100)
OF	Old French (French from about 800 to 1400)
Sp	Spanish
VL	Vulgar Latin (the popular form of Latin, the main source of the Romance languages)

Other

EW	*English Words from Latin and Greek Elements, Second Edition*
IM	this *Instructor's Manual*

The slash is used conventionally to show pronunciation as in the orthographic 'c' which is pronounced as /k/ in Latin.

TO THE INSTRUCTOR

This *Instructor's Manual* for the second edition of Donald M. Ayers's *English Words from Latin and Greek Elements,* as revised and expanded by Thomas D. Worthen with my assistance, is intended as a guide to accompany Ayers's classroom text. Material in the *Manual* that is not in the text includes the following:

- answers to all exercises in the text
- the Latin and Greek origin of all prefixes, suffixes, combining forms, and bases that are used in the text
- several hundred additional example words using the prefixes, suffixes, combining forms, and bases presented in the text, together with the derivation of many of these
- examples of orthographic similarities that will help to avoid confusion with English words from different bases
- additional material, often in the form of exercises, that can be used for extra assignments
- occasional suggestions for presenting material
- recommendations for specialized books that could help broaden the scope of various lessons
- extensive information throughout the *Manual* on variances among current desk dictionaries.

Users of the text who are familiar with the first edition will notice in the revised text a considerable overhauling of topical sections that open most lessons. Some of these have been expanded with further clarifying material, as in the background of the English vocabulary, assimilation of prefixes, combinations of bases, hybrids, doublets, and semantic change. Other sections have additional, updated examples (clipped words, blends, doublets, euphemisms), or have otherwise been fleshed out with additional exemplificative material (the history; words from Greek mythology, history, and philosophy; homonyms; and semantic change). Some topical sections are completely new (abbreviations and acronyms; back formations, apheresis, and aphesis; dissimilation and other sound changes; hyperbole; taboo deformation; circumlocution; metathesis; reduplication and onomatopoeia; loan words; and combining forms). Some of these topical sections, as with some in the first edition, have nothing in particular to do directly with the study of words that come from Latin and Greek elements. The expansion of the revised text in this area is, however, an effort to help make the book even more of a study in language, in vivid contrast to the many "vocabulary" books on the market. Depending upon time, level of instruction, and other considerations, the instructor can use this material or not. Some of the topical sections are, of course, essential to the understanding of the material at hand and should be gone over very thoroughly with the students, such as the sections on the Latin bases (most especially the material on -*at*- and -*it*-), assimilation of prefixes, combinations of bases, suffixes, and various others.

Latin and Greek source words are not given in EW because, as Ayers states in his preface, the book has been presented insofar as possible from the point of view of English. Sources are, however, offered in the *Manual* as there will always be some students at all levels who will have a natural curiosity about language and who, it must always be hoped, will ask questions. By having from the instructor just a little bit more than the rote material presented to them, although they may not remember all of it, they will nevertheless come away from the course with a richer and deeper understanding of English words. For those instructors who have not had any Latin or Greek background, a brief sketch of Latin accidence, that part of grammar that treats of the inflections of words, is also offered here. Greek grammar is much the same. Diacritics on Latin and Greek words are not used in IM except for the macron for 2nd declension Latin infinitives to distinguish them from 3rd declension infinitives.

If all of the material in the text is used, the students will have given definitions to over a thousand words—and to a thousand or so more if the additional example words are used, words that are of varying difficulty, familiarity, and specialization that can be used in accordance with the level of instruction. The definitions given in the *Manual* as answers to the exercises in the text are taken or adapted from one or more of the several dictionaries listed in the Abbreviations list a few pages back.

The numbering system and the general style and format of the *Manual* follows that of the text. In both, Latin and Greek bases are presented in all capitals, and prefixes and suffixes are in italics. The *Manual* also uses italics for foreign words and stems not included in the text but arbitrarily forgoes the convention of italicizing English words under discussion.

It will be seen that a few Latin and Greek bases are identical in form. Those that have different meanings—such as the Latin LATER-side, and the Greek LATER- to worship; or the Latin BI -two, and the Greek BI- life—will, of course, have to be kept separate, and this should be easy to do once the students become familiar with English words that derive from these orthographic similarities. A few of these similarities are noted in EW in the Word Analysis sections (Part I, Lesson IX, and Part II, Lesson VIII). In cases where meanings are the same—as in GEN- to produce. PATR- father,

GEN- race, kind, OCT- eight—it would seem ultimately unnecessary at most levels to insist that students separate the English words deriving from the two bases. However, their ability to distinguish between the two will, in many cases, sharpen as they become familiar with other Latin and Greek bases that combine with such as PATR-. For example, in patricide, the *-cide* is Latin, and therefore so is PATR-; in patronym, the -NYM is Greek, and so is PATR-. With other words this cannot be done so easily, as with patron, gender and genre (both from French), gene, octal (the *-al* is used on both Latin and Greek words), octet, etc. The instructor must choose the depth of study here.

A great many of EW's bases, especially in the Greek section, are recorded as combining forms in dictionaries, and several of these have suffixal extensions and become listed as separate combining forms. For example, phil-, -phil, -phile, -philia, -philiac, -philous are all variously recorded as combining forms from EW's base PHIL- to love. After or during the presentation of suffixes, if students encounter these compound forms in their dictionaries, choose to use them in their answers to exercises and define them correctly, this procedure should be considered as acceptable as having them list the constituents separately (PHIL- + *-ia*, or PHIL- + *-ous*). One purpose of the course certainly is to teach students how to understand and use a dictionary—which will be with them long after the course is finished. Combining forms are discussed in EW at Greek Lesson XII, where they are first introduced. They could quite easily be discussed at any point in the course, especially at the early days of Part Two because so many of the Greek bases are listed in dictionaries as combining forms, or as part of combining forms, and it is quite possible the subject will arise before Lesson XII. The revised EW has left combining forms at Lesson XII for the benefit of those who might have started the text at the Greek section: to keep the concept of "bases" and "suffixes" going until the students had gained reasonable proficiency in analyzing words.

Finally, I would like to take the opportunity here of thanking Professor Thomas Worthen of the Classics Department of the University of Arizona for combing through the 1983 IM (to the 1965 EW) with me in our joint effort to transplant some of the material from the 1983 IM to the revised 1986 EW. I am also grateful for his excising my glaring mistakes as we went along. Any new errors that may have crept into this revised IM are, however, all mine.

R.L.C.

INTRODUCTION
to English Words
from Latin and Greek Elements

Many students respond well to charts and often remember information they see there in contrast to information they are exposed to in prose, which is often not immediately retained. For this reason it would be well to spend a few minutes on the chart opposite page 1, and also to encourage the students to refer back to the chart when a new language is introduced in their reading of this introduction to EW.

ASSIGNMENT

I. Languages Cognate with English

Hindi (1), Russian (4), and Portuguese (6). These are members of the Proto-Indo-European family. The other three are not.

II. Branches of the Proto-Indo-European Family

1. Bulgarian—Balto-Slavic
2. Romanian—Italic
3. Sanscrit—Indic
4. Spanish—Italic
5. Greek—Hellenic
6. Welsh—Celtic
7. Swedish—Germanic

III. Language of Ultimate Derivation

Because dictionaries sometimes vary in etymological analysis, the instructor can expect different answers here. Where found, differences are separated in this exercise by a semicolon. Still, other differences may appear on students' papers. For more information on etymology see Section IV in Lesson I following (in IM).

1. almanac—perhaps from Late Greek; probably from Arabic; from Spanish-Arabic; Late Greek.
2. bizarre—Basque; French, cognate with the Italian, suggesting the

1

Spanish came from the Basque; Italian, with ultimate etymology unknown; Italian.

3. boomerang—native name in Australia; native dialectal word in New South Wales.

4. chair—Greek; Latin (etymologized to Greek at the doublet cathedra).

5. cherub—Hebrew.

6. chocolate—Nahuatl (the language of the Aztecs, Toltecs, and other Central-American Indians); Aztec.

7. crag—Celtic (or Celt). There is another crag, in Scottish dialect, meaning neck or throat—Middle English; Middle Dutch.

8. dollar—from Low German or Dutch; German.

9. galore—Irish; Irish Gaelic. These two terms are often used synonymously.

10. geyser—Old Icelandic; Icelandic; Old Norse.

11. gingham—Malay (the Indonesian language of the people in the Malay Peninsula).

12. hominy—Algonkian (North American Indian language family); probably from Algonkian. Also spelled Algonquian.

13. horde—Turkic or Turkish; Mongolian (the language of the Mongols in Asia).

14. hurricane—Arawak or Arawakan (a language spoken in parts of Brazil, and, formerly, in the West Indies); Taino (a branch of Arawakan).

15. julep—Persian.

16. khaki—Persian.

17. magazine—Arabic.

18. mammoth—earlier Russian; Russian; Tartar (the language of the descendents of the Mongols and Turks who now live in parts of the Soviet Union).

19. paradise—Iranian; Persian. (These two terms are often used synonymously; also called Farsi or Farsee.)

20. robot—Czech; apparently a back formation from Czech *robotnik* serf; Czech, from *robota* work.

21. sapphire—Sanskrit; penultimately from Hebrew, ultimate etymology unknown; perhaps from Sanskrit.

22. sherbet—Arabic.

23. swastika—Sanskrit.

24. tungsten—Swedish.

IV. Complete Linguistic Routes

The instructor can expect different answers here. Some dictionaries skip steps and the grading of papers should accommodate this characteristic. Noteworthy variances are separated by a semicolon.

1. apricot—from earlier *abrecock* (with variant spellings; the 'b' was still found as late as the eighteenth century), from Portuguese *albricoque*, from Sp *albaricoque* ("or [directly] from the Spanish"—OED), from Arabic *al-barquq* (*al the* + *barquq* apricot), with the *barquq* from Late Gk *praikokion*, a borrowing from L *praecoquis* (or *praecoquum*, short for *persicum praecox* early-ripening peach), from *prae* before + *coquere* to ripen. Some dictionaries stop with the Arabic; the OED stops at Portuguese, deriving all the above from the It *albercocca*.
2. bishop—from ME *bisshop*, from OE *bisceop*, from VL *ebiscopus* (a variant of L *episcopus* bishop, overseer), from Gk *episkopos* overseer, from *epi-* over + *skopos* watcher (from *skeptesthai* to look). Used in Latin and Greek in the general sense, but "with the rise in Christianity it gradually received a specific sense in the Church"—OED.
3. butter—from ME *boter* (with variant spellings), from OE *butere*, through West Germanic from L *butyrium*, from Gk *boutyron*, from *bous* cow + *tyros* cheese. Some dictionaries stop at the Gk *boutyron*.
4. car—from ME *carre*, from AF (some say Old North French here) *carre*, from ML (some say LL) *carra*, from L *carrus* a four-wheeled cart ("of Celtic origin"—WNCD). Some dictionaries stop at the L *carrus*.
5. chemist—from New L *chimista*, short for ML *alchimia* (or *alchimista*) alchemist, from Arabic (which introduced the *al*, meaning 'the') *alkimiya*, from Late Gk *chymeia* art of alloying metals, from Gk *chyma* ingot, from *chein* to pour. Some dictionaries stop at ML; some simply call it a variant of alchemist, where it is etymologized.
6. orange—from ME *orange*, from OF *pomme d'orenge* (where it was influenced by *or* gold, "and the *n* was lost by misdivision of the article *un* "—WBD), from Sp *naranja* (some say Old Provençal *auranja;* Provençal, a language of the troubadours, was spoken in southeastern France bordering the Mediterranean), from Arabic *naranj*, from Persian *narang*, from Sanskrit *naranga*, of Dravidian origin. Some stop at Persian; some stop at Sanskrit. The Dravidians were a group of intermixed races in southern India and Ceylon (Sri Lanka).

PART I
Word elements
from Latin

THE DICTIONARY

Although dictionaries are updated every few years, they, along with many other reference books, inherently retain the distinction of being out of date the very day they are published. Some of these reasons are discussed in EW for the purpose of informing students that not all of the words they look up are necessarily going to be in their brand-new dictionaries. Also, owing to the varying degrees of meticulousness among dictionary editors and editorial staffs, dictionaries often vary considerably in quality. Each has its good and bad points and such variances in both quality and quantity will be reflected in students' answers. Variances will be pointed out throughout this *Manual* and should be taken into account in the grading of papers or responses in class. Several of these variances are discussed in this lesson, which refer specifically to the editions (generally to the early or mid 1980s) that were in print at the time this *Manual* was written.

As to a school- or college-office dictionary that could complement this course, *The World Book Dictionary,* which is frequently updated, is for many reasons about the best there is. It has some 2500 pages, as opposed to the customary 1500 or so pages in such as WNCD and RHD, and even though it is in two 8½x11 volumes, it is more manageable than *Webster's Third International* and would be a good dictionary for the instructor or the department. Its coverage is excellent, including idioms and figurative usage; definitions are full, clear, and uncluttered; etymologies are unabbreviated, generally self-contained (with the usual cross-referencing to save space), and are more than adequate for the purposes of this course.

There is currently a trend among some contemporary dictionaries to alter the nomenclature of what is traditionally called prefix, suffix, and combining form. AHD does not use the term combining form, for example, a subject which is treated in IM in the topical essay of Lesson XII in Part II. RHD uses the term in certain etymologies, showing that the element was also a combining form in the original language. EW and IM follow the general premise that if such an element contains a morpheme that carries inherent lexical meaning (such as *-phil-* in the element *-philia*), the element is a combining form, whether or not it has a suffix (*-ia*, *-iac*, *-ous*, etc.) attached to it. For this same reason *phil-* and *philo-* are also combining forms, and not prefixes as AHD calls them. As far as the purpose of EW is concerned—to wit, the improving of students' vocabulary—the quibbling over nomenclature should not be allowed much class time, but inquisitive students using AHD will surely stumble across the situation and may bring it up. RHD also uses the label "a formal element" for some prefixes.

I. Form of the Word

Students should not only learn to recognize variant spelling forms but know which ones are preferred. The form that is cross-referenced to another form or that is at the end of an entry ("Also spelled *theatre*") is the second choice. Sometimes the main entry will say, as in WNCD, "abscisin *also* abscissin," calling abscissin a "secondary variant." In "counselor *or* counsellor" WNCD calls counselor as being "slightly more common." Counsellor is predominantly British, as are other similar double-l words.

II. Pronunciation

Although pronunciation is generally standard enough among dictionaries, instructors should not expect all students' answers to look the same. This is especially true in the case of loan words. (See topical section on Loan Words in EW and IM in Part II, Lesson VII.) In some dictionaries table d'hôte is given a French pronunciation first and a kind of Anglicized French second. Other dictionaries will have these reversed, while others will have only one pronunciation. Even words like necessarily and muscatel are honored with two pronunciations in RHD but only one in most other dictionaries. With 'Celtic,' British and Australian dictionaries consistently give the initial C a /k/ sound in first place, with /s/ second (with *Oxford Advanced Learner's* calling the /s/ "U.S."), the notable exception being the Oxfords, which give /s/ first. American dictionaries offer the /s/ first, with /k/ second, with the exception of AHD which offers /k/ first. (Actually, the British use both, reserving /k/ for the ancient Gauls and Britons, and /s/, generally, for the Scottish football team.)

III. Grammatical Information

Dictionaries vary in the layout of material. For example, WBD and RHD have all three parts of speech (noun, verb, and adjective) for the word 'dream' under one entry. WNCD and *Webster's Ninth* have two separate entries for this word, one for the noun and one for the verb; it does not record an adjective, but says the noun is used "often attributively." AHD (1982) does not admit an adjective or attributive use.

As with all variances, the grading of papers should accommodate such variations where they occur.

IV. Etymology

Dictionaries vary, often considerably, in the treatment of etymology. EW explains some of this. Further, WNCD, for many of its technical words, gives in its etymology (regretably as it concerns this course) only "ISV," meaning International Scientific Vocabulary, which it defines as "a part of the vocabulary of the sciences and other specialized studies that consists of words of other linguistic forms current in two or more languages and differing from New Latin in being adapted to the structure of the individual languages in which they appear."

The etymology, or in some cases only the ultimate etymology, of many English words is uncertain. Such words are accompanied by "obscure," "unknown," "uncertain," or such, or if there is an etymology there will be an accompanying "?," "supposedly," "probably," "possibly," etc.

V. Definition

Depending on the quality of a dictionary company's research program and editorial staff, dictionaries will vary in the quality and amount of its definition material. They will also often vary considerably in procedure for defining words. For many words, some dictionaries (notably the Webster's group) will offer only a synonym for a meaning, in which case the user must go to that word for the meaning. At all levels of instruction it is probably advisable to insist upon full definitions to thwart any corner-cutting from students who will put down a synonym for a definition when they do not even know the meaning of the synonym they have offered.

Dictionaries also differ in the treatment of add-ons, or run-ons. For example, OED Concise, Collins, and AHD have happily and happiness as run-ons to happy, whereas Webster's and RHD have separate entries for these two words to show that, in their estimation, happily and happiness are not, as adverb and noun, used in all the senses that happy can be used, and/or vice versa. Grading of papers should accommodate such differences.

VI. Special Information

The information here in EW does little more than introduce the controversy over usage labels that has ensued since, to a large extent, the publication of W3. Many general users, students, and instructors feel that they need guidance in the use of certain words and will look for a dictionary that will give such guidance. Others feel that usage labels are prescriptive and didactic. A guided discussion of this in class could be worthwhile. Questions such as the following could be addressed: Do I now, at sixteen, nineteen, or twenty-three, have a wide enough reading experience and command of the language to be sufficiently skilled in the use of words on all occasions without guidance? I go to my doctor for medical advice, my lawyer for legal advice, why not to a dictionary for word advice? Where I come from this word is *not* archaic, slang or dialect; why should I have to tolerate someone else's judgment about it?

VII. Synonyms

In the 1970s thesauri came onto the market in the more familiar format of the dictionary, abandoning their previous format that was difficult for many users. These thesauri have come to be even more refined, the more recent ones giving synonyms, antonyms, related and contrasting words, phrases and idiomatic equivalents, and words that are considered vulgar or otherwise have limited use, such as slang. Students should become familiar with these books, for not only will thesauri help to increase vocabulary they will help to fine-tune shades of meaning.

Synonym usage notes that also separate shades of meaning and discuss usage are frequently found in dictionaries but they differ in what they consider important to discuss. RHD has usage notes at aren't, disease, and dislike; AHD does not, but has notes at area, dive (verb), and historic, which RHD does not.

VIII. Idiomatic Usage

There are so many idioms in the English language that no dictionary could ever hope to record them all, much less keep up to date. For example, the verb 'get,' alone and with its various prepositions and adverbs (or so-called particles), has produced, as a conservative estimate, some 500 meanings; of these WBD (1976) has about 150, RHD (1984) about 80, WNCD (1981) about 65, and AHD (1982) fewer than 50.

Even dictionaries of idioms fall short. One such records some 4500 idioms, and by no means does this book cover the whole waterfront. Laurence Urdang, through Gale Research (1983), has put out an index entitled *Idioms and Phrases Index* in three volumes. It is a "compilation of 32 sources," boasts 140,000 entries, and calls itself "an unrivaled collection of idioms, phrases, expressions, and collocations."

IX. Miscellaneous

The essays in the front matter of most contemporary dictionaries are informative and often provocative. Some of the subjects they cover are the background of English, pronunciation, contemporary English of other countries (such as England, Scotland, Canada, Australia), usage and what constitutes "good English," and other topics, by such noteworthies as Francis

Nelson, Raven McDavid, Jr., Arthur Bronstein, Henry Kučera, Albert Marckwardt, Rex Wilson, and others. At most levels, depending upon time available, as an assignment students could read the essays in their own dictionaries, then next day swap dictionaries for a night so that all of the students will have the opportunity of reading all the essays. Also, many of the essays in dictionaries of the 1950s and 1960s, often available in a good library, would be enlightening. All of this material would contribute toward their knowledge of language.

ASSIGNMENT

I. Variant Spellings

1. abridgement (EW is generally preferred American; IM generally preferred British).
2. advisor (EW is preferred by most dictionaries).
3. archeology (EW is generally used in academic books and is also the British spelling; IM is used in most American national magazines).
4. catsup (IM is American and preferred in WNCD; EW is American and preferred in WBD; also, ketchup, which is preferred British and also preferred in RHD and AHD).
5. fulfil (EW is preferred American; IM is second choice American and preferred British).
6. moveable (EW is preferred in most dictionaries).

II. Words That Are Separate, Hyphenated, or One Word

1. anti-Semitic (most prefixes are spelled solid, except when the base word is a proper noun or a number, as in anti-Bolshevism, non-Spanish-speaking, pre-1960).
2. antislavery (as above, except some dictionaries use a hyphen when the base word begins with a vowel, as in anti-evolution, anti-icer).
3. blacklist (both as a noun and a verb, as with blackmail).
4. black market (noun), black-market (verb).
5. folk dance (noun), folk-dance (verb) (as with folk music and folk tale).
6. folk-rock (two words of equal value).
7. folklore (as with folkways).
8. good-humored (as with good-looking, bad-tempered, cold-blooded).

III. Pronunciation

1. chiropodist—accent on second syllable; opens with /k/, with /sh/ in second place.
2. schedule—accent on first syllable; U.S. opens with /sk/, British opens with /sh/.
3. forbade—accent on second syllable; *a* as in bad is preferred, *a* as in shade in second place.
4. perfect—accent on first syllable as adjective, on second syllable as verb.
5. frappé—accent on second syllable (pronounced: pay) is preferred, with /frap/ (one syllable) in second place. WNCD and WBD also recognize *frappe*, as one syllable.
6. forecastle—pronunciation as two syllables (/fok-səl/, with accent on first syllable, *o* as in poke) given first place, with three syllables (/for-kas-əl/, with primary stress on first syllable and secondary stress on second, given second place.
7. heinous—accent on first syllable; *ei* pronounced as in hay.
8. chauvinism—primary accent on first of four (pronounced) syllables, secondary stress on third; *chau-* pronounced /sho/.
9. alumnae (plural of alumna)—accent on second syllable; third syllable rhymes with bee.
10. creek—first choice rhymes with reek, second place rhymes with trick.

IV. Plurals

1. analyses (originally a Greek word which picked up this plural in Latin).
2. antennae (Latin), antennas (English). The Latin is preferred meaning appendages; the English is preferred meaning aerials.
3. appendices (Latin), appendixes (English). The English is preferred in all senses.
4. grottoes (generally preferred), and grottos.
5. geese.
6. mongooses.
7. moose.
8. phenomena (Latin and Greek), phenomenons (English). The foreign plural is preferred in some senses, the English in others.

9. data (Latin), datums (English). The Latin is preferred in some senses, the English in others. RHD recognizes that *data* is often construed as singular. (Being asked if he would accept 'media' as singular, as in the sentence The White House requested the cooperation of all the medias, Isaac Asimov responded: Let's put out a few memorandas on the subject after collecting the necessary datas.)

10. news, "plural noun used with a singular verb" (AHD), "construed as singular or plural" (RHD), "noun plural but singular in construction" (WNCD).

V. Past Tenses and Participles

All of these verbs, with one exception, are either 'strong'—that is, the internal vowel is changed to form the past tense, and the past participle is altered in various ways, as in choose, cling, forget, hold, run, etc.; or they are 'irregular weak'—that is, the internal vowel does not change but they do not strictly follow the -ed rule of regular verbs either.* Regular weak verbs are like walk, walked (past tense), walked (past participle). Irregular weak verbs are like let, lose, bleed, creep, read, keep, with some having alternate regular forms, as dream (past tense and past participle, dreamed and dreamt, for both). Some weak irregularities have become only orthographical, as in dropped and dropt, or dressed and drest. Only awaken is completely regular in this list. The order given in the answers is: present participle, past tense(s), past participle(s), with semicolons separating each category.

1. abiding; abode or abided (no preference); abode or abided (no preference). Originally a strong verb that now has both forms.

2. awaking; awoke (generally preferred) or awaked; awaked (preferred in WNCD), awoke, awoken (preferred British). Originally a strong verb.

3. awakening; awakened; awakened. Originally weak.

4. bidding; bade (generally preferred), bid, bad (archaic); bidden, bid (no preference between these two), bade (a variant). Originally strong.

5. cleaving; cleaved (generally preferred), cleft, clove; cleaved (generally preferred), cleft, cloven. Originally strong; in OE *cleofan* (infinitive), *cleaf* (past), *cloven* (past participle)—a good example of a verb that really got messed up over the centuries and never became weeded out.

---

*In Old English, verbs were not 'regular' and 'irregular' as we call them today. Verbs then fell into different classes, as in Latin and Greek, of which the -ed class with its variations constituted only one of several. The tendency over the centuries has been to go 'regular.'

6. diving; dove or dived (no preference); dived.

7. dragging; dragged (preferred), drug; dragged (preferred), drug. Originally strong, with the strong 'drug' still popular in some regions of the U.S. but not generally recorded in contemporary dictionaries.

8. dwelling; dwelt or dwelled (no preference); dwelt or dwelled (no preference).

9. pleading; pleaded or pled (variant plead) (no preference); pleaded or pled (variant plead) (no preference). WBD calls pled "informal."

10. spitting; spit or spat (no preference); spit or spat (no preference). Originally weak, and one of the very few examples in which a weak verb picked up strong forms, which in this case happened around the sixteenth century.

VI. Origins

1. amethyst—through ME and OF from L *amethysus* from Gk *amethustos* not drunken, from *a-* not + *methuein* to make drunk, with reference to the belief that the stone could prevent drunkenness.

2. gerrymander—from Elbridge *Gerry* (1744 – 1814), a governor of Massachusetts, + sala*mander*, from the salamander shape of an election district formed during his governorship.

3. grog—supposedly short for grogram, nickname of Edward Vernon (1864–1757), a British admiral, who ordered his seamen to dilute their rum, so-called from his grogram cloak, grogram is a coarse cloth made of silk, or of wool, or of these two combined with mohair, often stiffened with gum.

4. guy—from *Guy* Fawkes, who instigated the Gunpowder Plot, an attempt to blow up the Houses of Parliament in 1605. The day is celebrated annually on November 5th in England with effigies of Guy, bonfires, and gatherings of family and friends for food and fireworks.

5. O.K.—origin uncertain; perhaps from the O K Club (a group of Van Buren supporters during his 1840 campaign for president), which derived its name from *O*ld *K*inderhook, Van Buren's New York birthplace; or perhaps from *o*ll *k*orrect, alteration of all correct, the OK meaning all was in order, as written on a box of incoming merchandise.

6. paraphernalia—from ML *parapherna* the personal possessions a woman brought to a marriage apart from the dowry, from Gk *para-* besides + *pherne* dowry, from *pherein* to bear.

VII. Usage or Status Labels

As pointed out earlier, usage labels will vary from one dictionary to another. Only three dictionaries were picked, at random, for IM for this exercise. It is not unlikely that students will come up with other labels. If IM offers only one label, the three dictionaries used all agree.

1. ain't—not standard; disapproved by many; should be shunned (as a contraction for *am not*), and substandard (for *have not*).
2. fake—no labels.
3. irregardless—nonstandard.
4. lave—archaic.
5. phony—slang; informal.
6. poke—dialect; chiefly South and Midland; Midland U.S. and Scottish.

VIII. Geographic Labels

The same procedure was followed here as with Exercise VII above. A familiar meaning follows in parentheses.

1. agley—Scottish; chiefly Scottish; chiefly Scottish and North England (= awry).
2. billabong—Australian (= a branch of a river coming to a dead end).
3. cayuse—Western U.S.; West (= a native Indian pony often used by cowboys).
4. pone—Southern U.S.; South and Midland (= bread made of maize). Also called corn pone and pone bread.
5. pub—British (= short for public house, a business establishment where alcoholic beverages are sold and consumed). Also Australian.
6. pukka—Anglo-Indian; especially in India (= properly done, authentic, first-class, very good). Variant spelling pucka.

IX. Synonyms

The synonyms for any word may vary from one dictionary to another; the instructor may therefore expect different answers here. Thesauri may list several others. The following are a random sampling, which in some instances accommodate the multiple senses and different parts of speech of the EW word.

1. claim: postulate, demand, challenge, exact, require, requisition, solicit.
2. gentle: balmy, faint, lenient, mild, smooth, soft, moderate.

3. inert: inactive, asleep, idle, passive, quiet, sleepy, sluggish.
4. monetary: fiscal, financial, pecuniary.
5. paramount: supreme, dominant, predominant, predominate, prevalent, overbearing.
6. sparkle: flash, gleam, glitter, glisten, shimmer, twinkle.

X. Distinguishing Between Synonyms

The point of this exercise is to show that however close in meaning two words may come, they do not always mean exactly the same thing. One word will often have a meaning, or a shade of a meaning or meanings, that the other word does not carry. Examples of usage follow the dash.

1. Both mean to start or do the first part of an action. **Begin** carries the additional meaning of to give origin to, bring into existence, create, as a dynasty or a town (which cannot be commenced); it also means to come anywhere near or make the best approach (usually with a negative preceding)—$3000 couldn't begin to cover my expenses at school. **Commence** has more formal associations with law and procedure, combat, divine service, and the ceremonial—Commence firing!

2. **Copious** means more than enough, plentiful, abundant—copious hair, copious evidence, copious supply of grain for winter; also (of a language) having a large vocabulary. **Ample** means extending far and wide—an ample forest; also, of large volume or capacity—an ample heart, an ample kitchen; also, enough to satisfy all demands —There is ample time for the meeting, ample food for the picnic.

3. Both mean having an interest in others' concerns. **Curious** also means strange, odd, novel—a curious manner; it also carries the sense of being a little out of bounds socially, too eager to know, prying—a curious interest in their neighbor's affairs. **Inquisitive** suggests a delicate curiosity tempered by good manners; it also means inclined to ask questions—She has an inquisitive nature.

4. Both mean treating equally, not biased. **Fair** carries a sense of involvement—Parents should be fair with their children. **Impartial** does not carry this sense of involvement—an impartial judge. **Fair** also has several other meanings: beautiful, pleasing—fair weather; applied to women—the fair sex; average, nothing special—a fair speaker, etc.

5. **Faithful** means firm in adherence to promises or observation of duty—a faithful commander; also, given with strong assurance, binding—a faithful promise; also, steadfast in affection—a faithful

husband; also, accurate in detail—a faithful translation. **Loyal,** which can be used only of people, means true and unswerving in allegiance to one's leader(s) or one's government—a loyal soldier; also, true to an ideal, cause or custom—loyal adherents of the New Left.

6. **Meaning** is the thing one intends to convey, that which is meant, the denotation of a word or phrase—Tell me the meaning of that word. **Significance** also means something conveyed, but often obscurely or indirectly; also, importance, consequence, weight—Tell me the significance of this line in the poem.

7. A **riddle** is a misleading or puzzling question posed as a problem to be solved or otherwise understood. An **enigma** is a baffling or puzzling problem, situation, or person, one that cannot be figured out or solved.

8. **Specific** means restricted or set apart by nature to a particular individual or situation—a disease specific to elm trees; also, accurate, free from ambiguity—a specific statement; also, exerting a distinctive influence—specific antibodies. **Special** means distinguished by some unusual quality—a special person or friend; also, in some way superior or different—a special bus for the handicapped, a special room for dancing; also, distinguished from others of the same category—a special day of thanks; also, designed for a particular use or occasion—special silver.

9. **Sudden** means happening or coming unexpectedly—a sudden shower; also, made or brought about in a short time—a sudden decision or conclusion. **Abrupt** means brusk or brief in speech or manner, curt—an abrupt remark; also, steep or precipitous—an abrupt drop-off into the ocean.

10. **Timely** means well-timed, carrying a sense of an arranged convenience—a timely visit to his dying father. **Opportune** means suitable or convenient for a particular purpose, but carries a sense of chance—When the children went out to play was an opportune time for a nap.

11. Both **value** and **prize**, as verbs, mean to think highly of because of worth, importance, or some other quality. **Value** has the added sense of to fix the financial or material worth of something—jewels valued at $50,000. As nouns, the differences in meaning are more immediately apparent.

12. Both mean current among the common people or lower classes. In other senses **vulgar** is stronger than common, when it means offensive in language—a vulgar word; also, morally crude or gross—a vulgar remark. **Common** also means falling below ordinary stan-

dards, second-rate, lacking refinement—a common man, a common restaurant; also, familiar or known to most—a common word, a common car.

XI. Idiomatic Expressions

Idiomatic expressions fall into different categories. Some expressions have lost their original meaning which is now shrouded in history or fable, as dog in the manger. Others have lost their literal meaning (if there ever was one) and are now used only figuratively, as in stamping ground, and down at the heel. Others are used in a restricted sense only, as in to pop the question. Still others are strictly idiomatic, as make away with. Numbers 1, 3, 6, 7, and 8 in this list are also called phrasal verbs. Some phrasal verbs have different meanings depending on transitivity, such as check out (v.t., ...the new applicants; ...this job advertisement; ...your groceries; ...his story) (v.i., to leave, as a hotel, and pay your bill; to leave; to die), as with carry on. Examples of usage follow the dash in the following.

1. do for: to convict of a crime or an offense—They did him for burglary; also, to attend to one's needs—He did for himself until he was 87. In the sentence He did housework for his neighbor, do for is not idiomatic.
2. dog in the manger: one who prevents others from using something he himself has no use for (from the fable of the dog who would not allow an ox to eat hay he himself did not want).
3. let on: to allow it to be known—Don't let on that you saw me here; also, pretend—If I wanted to...'let on' what had occurred in the remote past...what an opportunity is here! (Mark Twain)
4. down at the heel: shabby; worn; scruffy; slovenly.
5. fill the bill: to fulfill all necessary requirements.
6. carry on: to manage or conduct (such as a business); also, to behave in an excited, foolish, or indiscreet manner; also, to continue (with) —Carry on with your game, don't let me stop you; also, to persevere or persist, even in the face of obstacles or danger.
7. make away with: steal; carry off; abduct; kill; get rid of; destroy.
8. get over: to make or become understandable—He just couldn't get his point over to the crowd (also equals get across); also, to recover from (an illness, a friend's death); also, (in negative) be startled or stunned by—I couldn't get over how rude he was to the principal.

LESSON II

LATIN ACCIDENCE AND EW'S BASES

In all the Latin lessons the ultimate source of all bases is given in IM as additional information, some of which, with a simple explanation from the instructor, will further illuminate the material without making it complicated.

Latin nouns and verbs, whereas generally regular enough as Latin goes, are not as simple as English regular nouns and verbs (e.g., dog, dogs; walk, walked, walked). Inevitably the added variation in Latin forms has allowed for more variation in English derivatives, some of which are shrouded in inflections. For example, art and part are derived from *ars* and *pars*, respectively. "Where is the 's'," your students may ask, "and why the 't'?" Consider the declension, here in singular only:

Nominative	*ars*	*pars*	(subject case)
Genitive	*artis*	*partis*	('s and 'of')
Dative	*arti*	*parti*	(indirect object and benefactive 'to' and 'for')
Accusative	*artem*	*partem*	(direct object and some prepositional phrases)
Ablative	*arte*	*parte*	(most prepositional phrases)

English words derived from the head words, the *ars* and *pars* of the nominative case, are rare. For *ars*, see Discussion of Bases following. For *pars*, there is the English verb parse. Art, artistic, etc., all come from *arti-*, the stem derived from the genitive of *ars*. Part, partial, partition, particle, particular, partisan, and party derive ultimately from *parti-*, the stem derived from the genitive of *pars*. Usually, however, EW's bases appear without the final vowel, hence its ART- and PART-, with the *i* being considered a connective vowel for reasons that are discussed on the opening page to Lesson VI in EW.

There are several classes of nouns in both Latin and Greek, as there are regular and irregular nouns—e.g., dog, dogs; man, men; moose, moose—in English. In order to identify the particular class that a noun is in, Latin and Greek dictionaries, and many English dictionaries, are accustomed to giving the stem derived from the genitive right after the nominative form. In its etymologies, WNCD puts the derived stem before the nominative, as with the following example:

18

vocation ...*n* [ME *vocacioun,* fr. L *vocation-*, vocatio* summons, fr. *vocatus,*
pp† of *vocare* to call ...].
*stem
†past participle

Some nouns in Latin spin off other Latin words, as the noun *mater*
(genitive *matris*) brought forth the adjective *maternus* of a mother, maternal.
When there are English words deriving from both of these Latin words, EW
presents both bases, here MATR- and MATERN-. Similarly, many Latin
words derive from adjectives, such as *malignus* ill-disposed, malicious,
wicked, which derives from the adjective *malus* bad, evil. Hence EW's two
bases here, MAL- and MALIGN-.

As there are regular and irregular verbs in English—e.g., walk, walked,
walked; swim, swam, swum; put, put, put—there are different classes of
verbs in both Latin and Greek. All Latin verbs are identified by their four
principal parts.

1. *voco*   I call   (first person singular, present indicative)
2. *vocare*   to call   (infinitive)
3. *vocavi*   I called   (first person singular, past tense)
4. *vocatus*   called   (past participle)

Vocal and its derivatives (vocally, vocalize, etc.) and vocabulary, for example, are all ultimately connected with the infinitive *vocare,* but vocation,
avocation, vocative, etc., are connected with the past participle *vocatus.* The
word inspect comes from the infinitive *spectare,* and spectator comes from
the past participle *spectatus.* These differences in the principal parts of verbs
and the case endings of nouns account for nearly all of EW's bases where
there are two or more forms to one base. Other differences are spelling
variants or forms that came in through French. EW accommodates irregular
past participles such as *quisitus* from *quaerere* to seek, and *missus* from
mittere to send, by offering the bases QUIR-, QUISIT- and MITT-, MISS-.
It does not, however, accommodate past participles of the first conjugation
such as *vocatus* and *spectatus* above, offering as bases for these two verbs
only VOC- (with the variant VOK-) and SPEC(T) (with the variant SPIC-).
It was felt that to add this predictable *-at-* for all the first conjugation verbs,
of which there are many in EW, would unnecessarily clutter the text. It has
therefore been discussed in detail in Lesson II under the heading Latin
Bases. The importance of going over this material with the students cannot
be stressed strongly enough. It should not take them long to spot this recur-
ring *-at-* in such as avocation, interrogate, and spectator; as well as in the
adjective (Lesson X) and the noun (Lesson XV). The *-it-* of other conjugations, as in *auditus* from *audio,* is also offered at Lessons II and X as a
predictable element.

Latin prepositions and adverbs often tack on to other Latin words to form new words, as the preposition *inter*, meaning between, attached to the verb *mittere* (EW's base MITT- to send), giving the new word *intermittere*, which produced the English intermittent, and which, through its past participle *intermissus*, produced intermission.

Latin adjectives agree with nouns in gender, number and case, and are declined like nouns.

ASSIGNMENT

I. Discussion of Bases

ALIEN- from OF *alien*, from the L adjective *alienus* (as an adjective: that which belongs to or relates to another; as a noun: a stranger), from *alius* (adjective and pronoun) another, other, different. Also, alienate, alienist, inalienable.

ART- from OF *art*, from the stem *art-* of the L noun *ars. Ars* appears mainly in set borrowings as *ars gratia artis* and *ars longa, vita brevis.* Also, artifact, artifice, artificial (ART- + FAC- to do, to make), artillery, artisan, artist. The basic meaning of this base is 'fit together.' Compare the related (English) arm, (Latin) armor and article (lit. little joint), (Greek) harmony (lit, a joining [of sounds]), and the Greek combining form ARTHR- joint.

FIN- ultimately from the noun *finis* boundary, limit, border, end. Also, define, definite, affinity, finis, finish, finite, finitude, fine, final, finale, finance, infinite, infinity, refine.

FIRM- from It *firma* signature, from the L infinitive *firmare* to make firm, strengthen, from the adjective *firmus* firm, stout, strong. Also, affirm, confirm, infirm, firmament, reaffirm.

FORT- from F *fort*, noun use of the OF adjective, from the L adjective *fortis* strong, robust, stout. Also, effort, enforce, force, fortalice and its doublet fortress, forte, fortify, fortis, fortitude. Compare fortuitous and fortune from the noun *fors* (stem *fort-*) chance, luck.

GRAND- from OF *grand*, from the L adjective *grandis* full-grown, great, large. Also, grande (as in the F borrowings grande armée, grande dame), grandeur, grandiflora, grandiloquent (GRAND- + LOQU- to speak), grandiose, grandstand, all grand- compounds (as grandmother, etc.), and in set expressions, as grand larceny, grand march, grand master, Grand Old Party, grand piano.

GRAV- ultimately from the adjective *gravis* heavy, weighty, serious. Also, gravitate, graviton, gravity, grieve (through F, as grief). Compare the homonym grave with its derivatives (as engrave), gravel, gravy (GRAN- grain), and gravure (short for photogravure), all from different roots.

LINE- a fusion in both spelling and sense of ME *ligne* line, borrowed from L *line-* through F, and of OE *line* rope, line, which was early borrowed from L by several Germanic dialects.

NIHIL- the indeclinable noun *nihil* (and its contraction *nil*) nothing.

NUL(L)- from MF *nul* not any, from the L adjective *nullus* (*ne-* not − *ullus* any). Also, nullify, nullipara, nullity, annul.

PART- from OF *partir,* from the L infinitive *partire,* which derived from the stem *parti-* of the noun *pars* part, portion, piece, share. The Afrikaans (South African Dutch) apartheid is the OF *a part* to one side + *-heid* (= English -hood).

VERB- ultimately from the noun *verbum* word, verb. Also, adverb, proverb, verbal (through LL), verbiage, verbicide, verbify, verbigeration, verbose. Note that 'word,' from OE, is related to this base. Compare reverberate, from the noun *verber* a lash.

VEST- from F *veste,* from It, from L *vestis* a covering or garment, clothing. Some words came in through *vestire* to clothe, from *vestis.* Also, vestment, vesture, devest, divest, invest, investiture. Compare investigate, from *vestigare* to track, from *vestigium* footstep.

II. English Derivatives

The examples in Exercise I above should adequately serve as a foundation for this exercise, although the lists there are not meant to be complete. In order to become familiar with derivatives, students should be encouraged to enter these in their lists. For the examples of GRAND- offered here in EW, grand- is called a combining form. RHD is the only dictionary I have seen that records this, which for some reason they call a prefix. EW introduces prefixes in Lesson III, but nowhere in EW will grand-, or even this type of form, be termed a prefix. Combining forms are introduced in EW at Greek Lesson XII. See IM's discussion of combining forms at Greek Lesson XII. Grand- as in grandmother and grandniece, as well as great- (which the 1984 RHD does not record) as in great-uncle, are both special uses of grand and great.

III. Analysis and Definition of Words

All verbs in these exercises are defined in the infinitive form since that is the way they are defined in dictionaries. Participles in such as passive constructions and reduced clauses are defined as infinitives also. Similarly, countable nouns are defined in singular, and attributive nouns are defined as nouns. Participles that do not admit a finite form, such as appetizing, are defined as adjectives. To align their thinking with dictionary procedure, students should follow this pattern.

1. FIN- end, limit: immeasurably small.
2. NIHIL- nothing: to destroy; ruin; reduce to nothing. (Also, though not requested, the -at- might be pointed out here, as well as in sentences 3, 15, and 16.)
3. GRAV- heavy: the state of being irritated or annoyed.
4. NULL- nothing: to deprive of effectiveness; destroy; wipe out.
5. ALIEN- of another: that cannot be taken away or given away.
6. VERB- word: too many hard-to-understand or useless words in proportion to sense or content.
7. VEST- garment: a formal service, often accompanied with the donning of a robe, giving a person authority, power, dignity, office, etc.
8. VERB- word: in exactly the same words; word for word.
9. FORT- strong: one's strong point, or whatever one does very well.
10. GRAND- great: the act or process of making more powerful; an increase in power or rank; etc.
11. NULL- nothing: a nobody; a nonentity.
12. PART- part: the act of treating in detail.
13. GRAND- great: the quality of being impressive, awesome, or magnificent; majesty; splendor.
14. FIN- end, limit: a state of being unlimited in (here, temporal) extent.
15. FIRM- firm, strong: a declaration of asserting (a statement, etc.) as being valid or truthful.
16. ALIEN- of another: to turn from friendliness or affection to hostility or indifference.
17. LINE- line: an outline, feature, or contour.
18. VEST- garment: a mockery or parody (through the F *travestir* to disguise, from L *trans-* across + *vestire* to dress; compare transvestism).
19. LIGN- line: here, figurative, the condition of adjusting and bringing into line (such as mechanical parts in a literal definition) for a coordinated situation or performance. (Aline is a variant spelling.)
20. PART- part: the act of showing no more favor to one side than to the other.

IV. Correction of Definitions

1. diffident—incorrectly defined as a noun; should be an adjective definition: distrustful, reserved, lacking in self-confidence.
2. raceme—given in specialized botanical language; could be in plainer language, as in WBD: "a simple flower cluster having its

flowers on nearly equal stalks along a stem, the lower flowers blooming first."

3. supine—unnecessarily defined in negative; should be: lying on the back face upwards.

4. perjury—too general; should be related to violating an oath or vow.

5. impervious—defined in terms of the root word; should be: not capable of being damaged, affected, disturbed, etc.

6. dog—a whimsical statement about the word and not a definition (a four-legged, flesh-eating mammal, etc.).

7. redundancy—defined in terms of the root word*; should be: the quality or state of being unnecessary, superfluous, etc.

8. mutton—too general; should be related to sheep.

9. carnivorous—misleading when put in a sentence ("He is carnivorous" = "He is eating human flesh"); also, human flesh is too restrictive; should be: subsisting on animal flesh.

10. benign—unnecessarily defined in negative; should be: of a gentle disposition, showing kindness, etc.

11. chemist—too broad; should be related (in the U.S.) to chemistry, or (in England and Australia) to pharmacy.

12. vigilance—incorrectly defined as a verb; should be a noun definition: the quality or state of being watchful, etc.

13. poultry—too restricted in one sense (includes all fowl, not just chickens), and not sufficiently restricted in another (poultry is domesticated); should read: domesticated birds raised for their meat or eggs.

14. magnanimous—incorrectly defined as a noun; should be an adjective definition: generous and noble, showing greatness of mind, etc.

15. uncle—too restricted, since it is also the brother of one's mother.

16. introvert—this is a statement (effect or result) about the term and does not cover the essential characteristics of the term, as: one whose personality is characterized by predominant concern with and interest in one's own mental life.

17. calumny—too general; should be related to slander or misrepresentation with the view toward blackening another's reputation.

---

*Redundancy, and most such abstract noun derivatives like it, when offered as a main entry in dictionaries, will, however, in the interest of space, usually be defined as it is here in EW. In these cases, students will have to go to the root word—here, to redundant—for a full definition.

18. drunkenness—defined by a term generally less familiar than the word being defined; should be: excessive use of alcohol, or intoxication, etc.

19. patriotism—a whimsical statement about the word and not a definition; should be: devotion to one's country, etc.

20. improvident—improperly defined as an adverb; should be an adjective definition: heedless or incautious, not foreseeing and providing for the future, etc.

LESSON III

ASSIMILATION OF PREFIXES

Additional Exercise on Assimilation

The following list could be used as extra practice in assimilation.

1. *com-* + -laborate
2. *in-* + -licit
3. *dis-* + -fer
4. *ob-* + -tensible
5. *ob-* + -casion
6. *sub-* + -gest
7. *ex-* + -loquent
8. *dis-* + -gress
9. *ad-* + -locate
10. *com-* + -rupt

1. collaborate—assimilated to *collaboratus,* past participle of *collaborare* to labor together, from *com-* with + *laborare* to work.

2. illicit—assimilated to *illicitus,* from *in-* not + *licitus* lawful, the past participle of *licēre* to be allowed.

3. differ—assimilated to *differre* to set apart, differ, from *dis-* apart + FER- to carry (Lesson VII).

4. ostensible—assimilated to *ostensus,* past participle of *ostendere* to show, from *ob-* toward + TENS- to stretch (Lesson VIII).

5. occasion—assimilated (originally) to *occasus,* past participle of *occidere* to fall, from *ob-* down, away + CAS- to fall (Lesson XII).

6. suggest—assimilated to *suggestus,* past participle of *suggere* to suggest, supply, from *sub-* under + GEST- to bring, carry (Lesson XVIII).

7. eloquent—assimilated (originally) to *eloqui,* from *ex-* out + LOQU- to speak (Lesson III).

8. digress—assimilated to *digressus,* past participle of *digredi* to deviate, from *dis-* apart + GRESS- to step, go (Lesson V).

9. allocate—assimilated to *allocatus,* past participle of *allocare,* from *ad-* to, at + LOC- to place (Lesson XX).

10. corrupt—assimilated to *corruptus,* past participle of *corrumpere,* from *com-* (an intensive) + *rumpere* to break, shatter, burst open.

ASSIGNMENT

I. Discussion of Prefixes

ab-, a-, abs-   from the same prefixes that occur on L words. All are from the preposition *ab* away. The *a-* form is a reduction that appears before m, p, and v (as in amentia, aperture, avert, avocation). The *abs-* is an expansion that is used before c and t (as in abscess, abscond, abstain, abstract). Most contemporary dictionaries enter only the *ab-* form. Compare the assimilated *ab-* under *ad-* (below).

ad-, ac-,   etc. from the preposition *ad* to, toward, at. It appears in several assimilated guises: *ab-* (before b, as in abbreviate); *ac-* (before c, k, or q, as in accede, acknowledge, acquire, acquisitive); *af-* (before f, as in affect); *ag-* (before g, as in aggravate); *al-* (before l, as in allocate); *an-* (often before n, as in annex, announce, annul); *ap-* (before p, as in appreciate, approach); *ar-* (often before r, as in arrest, arride, arrive, arrogant); *as-* (often before s, as in assimilate, assist, associate); *at-* (before t, as in attain). The *ad-* form appears before all other sounds, and sometimes before one of the consonants listed above, as in adsorb, adrenal, adnate. Also reduces to *a-* in amortize, amount, amuse.

ambi-   from the L prefix *ambi-,* from *ambo* both. Variously called a prefix and a combining form. Compare the amb- in ambulance and ambulate, from L *ambulare* to walk.

ante-   from the preposition *ante* before, in front of. Compare the Gk suffix *anti-* against.

circum-   from the preposition *circum,* which was apparently adapted from the accusative (i.e., object) case of the noun *circus* ring, circus*. Most of the 30-odd English words with *circum-* were lifted from compounds in Latin, which boasts close to a hundred.

---

*The British used the word in such as Picadilly Circus and Oxford Circus when these intersections were originally traffic circles. Such traffic circles, popular in some states, as New Jersey, are called roundabouts in England, especially in the provinces.

con-, com-, co-   from the preposition *cum* with. Appears in various assimilated forms: *co-* (before vowels, h, and gn, as in coagulate, cohabit, cognate); *col-* (before l, as in collide), *con-* (before n and other consonants except b, l, m, p, r, w, as in connect, concur, conduct, confide, congregate, conjure, conquer, consent, contemplate, convert); *cor-* (before r, as in correlate); elsewhere *com-*.

contra-, contro-   from the preposition *contra* against, opposite.

de-   from the preposition *de* away from. This also carries other senses in English: removal or separation (dehumidify, decontaminate); negation or the reverse (demerit, de-emphasize); an intensifier (deny, denigrate).

dis-, di-, dif-   from the prefix *dis-* apart. *Di-* appears before, b, d, l, m, n, r, s, v, and sometimes before g and j (as in digress, dilate, dimidiate, direct, disciple, divulge); *dif-* before f (as in differ, diffract). Compare the Gk base DI- twice, double.

II. Discussion of Bases

In this and the following exercise only, the additional English words offered here that derive from verbs are separated into those that derive from the infinitive and those that derive from the past participle.

CED-   from the verb infinitive *cedere* to go, withdraw, depart, yield, happen. Also, cede, exceed, proceed, recede, secede. CESS- from the past participle *cessum,* as in procession, recession, secession.

DUC-   from the verb infinitive *ducere* to draw (as into the body, or as from place to place), to lead. Also, adduce, deduce, produce, seduce. DUCT- from the past participle *ductus,* as in duct, adduct, deduct, ductile, conduit (a doublet, from OF via ML, of conduct), product, production, seduction.

JUDIC-   from *judicium* (*iudicium*) judgment, from *iudex* judge. See note on *j* and *i* at JUR- following. Also, judiciary, judicious, prejudicial.

JUR-   from *iur-,* the stem of *ius* right, law (older dictionaries and classical texts printed a 'j' when 'i' was used as a consonant). Also, jurisdiction (JUR- + DICT- to say), jurisprudence (JUR- + *prudens* present participle contraction, ultimately from *providere* to see at a distance, look forward to), injury (*in-* not + JUR- right, law, justice).

LEV-   from the adjective *levis* light, not heavy. Also, lever, levy, levee. Compare levigate, from *levis* smooth.

LOQU-   from the deponent verb infinitive *loqui* to speak. Also, loquacious, colloquy. LOCUT- from the past participle *locutus,* as in elocution, interlocutor, circumlocution (*circum-* around + LOCUT-).

LUD-   from the verb infinitive *ludere* to play, sport, mimic, imitate. Also, allude, elude, ludicrous, postlude, prelude. LUS- from the past participle *lusus,* as in allusion, elusion, elusive.

PREC- from the deponent verb infinitive *precari* beg, invoke, request, pray, ultimately from the genitive singular *precis* of the noun *prex* a request, an entreaty. Also, imprecate. Compare other prec- words, as precious, appreciate, depreciate (*de-* away + *pretium* price), precipitate, precipice, precis, precise (*pre-* in front + CIS- to cut), and other pre- words with 'c' following.

TRUD- from the verb infinitive *trudere*, as in intrude, extrude, obtrude. TRUS- is from the past participle *trusus*, as in intrusion, extrusion, obtrusion, intrusive, etc.

VEN- from the verb infinitive *venire*, as in advene, contravene, convene. VENT- is from the past participle *ventus*, as in advent, adventitious, adventure, convention, intervention. Compare *ven-*, *vener-*, love, charm, as in Venus, venerate, venereal; also, *venen-* poison, as in venom; also, *vent-* wind, as in ventilate, also, ventricle (etc.) and ventriloquism, both from L *ventr-* belly.

III. Analysis and Definition of Words

1. *ab-* from + JUR- swear: to abstain from; reject; avoid.
2. assimilated to *alleviatus,* past participle of *alleviare,* from *ad-* to + LEV- light: to partially remove; lessen.
3. *abs-* from + TRUS- to push, to thrust: difficult to understand; esoteric.
4. *circum-* around + LOCUT- to speak: the use of several or too many words in expressing an idea; evasion in speech.
5. *ad-* to + VEN- to come: an arrival or coming (often one that is awaited).
6. *de-* off, from + LINE- line: to describe with detail and precision. (Point out the *-ate* verbal suffix here.)
7. *contra-* against + VEN- to come: to contradict or come into conflict with.
8. assimilated to *affinis* bordering on, from *ad-* to + FIN- end, limit: a natural attraction or liking.
9. *con-* together + VEN- to come: to come together.
10. assimilated to *accessus,* past participle of *accedere,* from *ad-* to + CED- to go, to yield: the act of coming into a position of honor or power.
11. assimilated in ML to *divestire* to remove privileges, from *dis-* apart + VEST- to clothe (from *vestire*): to rid or free; strip.
12. *ad-* to + DUC- to lead: to offer as reason in support of an argument.
13. *ante-* before + CED- to go, to yield: coming before; previous.

14. assimilated to *collusio* a secret understanding, from *com-* together + LUS- to play, to mock: a secret agreement for an illegal purpose.

15. *de-* (here, negative/pejorative use) + LUD- to play, mock: to mislead (someone's) mind or judgment; trick; deceive.

16. *de-* from + DUCT- to lead: that is inferred; of or pertaining to a conclusion reached by reasoning.

17. assimilated in LL to *annulare*, from *ad-* to + NULL- nothing: to make inoperative.

18. *con-* together + DUC- to lead: tending to promote.

19. *circum-* around + VENT- to come: to defeat by trickery or ingenuity.

20. from *deprecatus*, past participle of the deponent infinitive *deprecari* to (try to) avert by entreaty or prayer, from *de-* from + PREC- prayer: to express disapproval of. (Point out the *-at-* verbal suffix here.)

IV. Assimilated Prefixes

1. allusion—assimilated to *allusus*, past participle of *alludere*, from *ad* + *ludere* (past participle *lusus*).

2. suffuse—assimilated to *suffusus*, past participle of *suffundere*, from *sub* + *fundere* (past participle *fusus*).

3. arrogate—assimilated to *arrogatus*, past participle of *arrogare*, from *ad* + *rogare* (past participle *rogatus*).

4. distract—from *distractus*, past participle of *distrahere*, from *dis* + *trahere* (past participle *tractus*).

5. effusive—assimilated to *effusus*, past participle of *effundere*, from *ex* + *fundere* (past participle *fusus*).

6. occlusion—assimilated to *occlusus*, past participle of *occludere*, from *ob* + *claudere* (also spelled *cludere*, past participle *clusus*).

7. irruption—assimilated to *irruptus*, past participle of *irrumpere*, from *in* + *rumpere* (past participle *ruptus*).

8. admonition—from *admonēre*, from *ad* + *monēre* (past participle *monitus*).

9. obtrusive—from *obtrusus*, past participle of *obtrudere*, from *ob* + *trudere* (past participle *trusus*).

10. corrosive—assimilated to *corrosus*, past participle of *corrodere*, from *com* + *rodere* (past participle *rosus*) to gnaw or nibble at.

LESSON IV

ABBREVIATIONS, INITIALISMS, AND ACRONYMS

Abbreviations (*ad-* to + *brevi-* + *-at-* to make—a doublet of abridge) take on various forms: an abbreviation can be (1) the first and last letters of a word, as Dr., Mr. (appearing as Dr and Mr in England, i.e., with no periods, a practice restricted to forms that end with the same letter the original word ends with); (2) the initial letter, as C. (= Catholic, Celtic, etc.); (3) the initial letters of the words of a phrase, as EST (or E.S.T. or e.s.t. = Eastern Standard Time), OTC (or O.T.C. = Officer's Training Corps); minor words such as preposition are often left out, as D.D.S. (= Doctor of Dental Surgery), but occasionally retained, as in MIA and POW; (4) the first few letters of a word, as Conn. (= Connecticut), illus. (= illustration); (5) a combination of (1) and (4), as mol. wt. (= molecular weight); (6) a shortened form based on substitution, as i.e. (= *id est*), P.M. or p.m. (= *post mortem* after death; also = *post meridiem* afternoon). There are other variations.

An initialism (from L *initialis,* from *initium* a beginning, from *in-* in + IT- to go—Lesson XVI) is only number 3 above. The word is not very popular and is infrequently recorded. In dictionaries I have examined of the 1970s and 1980s, only WBD and WNCD list it. WNCD calls it "an acronym formed from initial letters," which is misleading, since an acronym is pronounceable (NATO, SALT or S.A.L.T.; British Nato and Salt—and others that are listed in EW) and an initialism is not pronounceable (MIA, POW, OTC, ISBN). Initialism is not in W2 or W3. The OED calls it a nonce word.

Periods and capital letters are a general nuisance to dictionary editors. Some dictionaries avoid periods altogether whereas others attempt to record all the forms used.

ASSIGNMENT

I. Discussion of Prefixes

ex- from the preposition *ex* from, out of; with *e-* before consonants except, c, f, p, q, s, and t (as in ebulient, edit, egest, elude, emancipate, enunciate, evade) and *ef-* before f (as in efficient, effect, effete). This is identical in meaning with the Gk preposition *ek, ex.*

extra-, extro- from the preposition *extra* outside (of). The 'o' form is an alteration.

in-   from the preposition *in* in, with *im-* (before b, m, and p, as in imbecile, imbibe, immediate, impose, important), *il-* (before l, as illude, illusion), *ir-* (before r, as in irradiate, irrigate, irrupt). A variation of this suffix is *en-* or *em-* (before b, p, and sometimes m), which is found in words that came in through French, as emboss, employ, enamel, enamor, encounter. This variant prefix also carries the sense of to put in or put on, as in encircle and enthrone.

in-, im-   (etc., as with the above) meaning 'not.' Ignoble will be found analyzed in two ways: 1) *in-* not + *nobilis* noble; and 2) *i-* (variant of *in-*) + Old Latin *gnobilis*. Ignore is generally found as *i-* (= *in-*) + *gnar-* (= GNO- to know—Lesson XX; cf. Greek base GNO- at Lesson VI). Ignominy will be found analyzed the same as ignoble, with the OED reading the *g* form as **gnomen* (form not found but inferred). All of these are the negative prefix on the original Latin words. Other examples are indirect, illogical, immovable, imbalance, impossible, irrational.

infra-   from the preposition *infra* below, under. Also, infrahuman, infrasonic, infrared.

inter-   from the preposition *inter* among, between, during. Also carries the sense of between or among (members of) a group, as interscholastic, meaning between (members of) schools. Also means together or one with the other, as intercommunicate.

intra-, intro-   from the preposition *intra* within. Also sometimes defined as inside, on the inside. Other examples are intracranial, intradermal, intrafamilial, intranasal. Compare other words beginning with *intra-*, as intransigent (*in-* not + *trans-* across + IG- to do), intransitive (*in-* not + transitive).

non-   from *non* not. *Non-* may be used with any noun, adjective, or adverb. If there is a commonly used word of the same meaning that is formed with *un-, in-,* or *dis-,* that word is generally preferable.

ob-   from the L prefix *ob-*, from *ob* against. Also, *o-* (before m, as in omit), *of-* (before f, as in offend, offer—but not office, which is from *opus* work + FIC- to do), *op-* (before p, as in opponent, opportune, opposite), *os-* (in some cases before c and t, as in oscine and ostensible).

per-   from *per* through, on account of. Also has a chemistry definition, meaning the maximum, or a large amount of, as in peroxide. This is also used as a free-standing (loan) word, meaning for each or for every, as in four dollars per person, eighty cents per pound.

II. Discussion of Bases

CRUC-   from *cruci-*, the stem of *crux* cross (which gives the English crux). Also, excruciate, cruciate, crucial, crucifix.

GREG- from *gregi-*, the stem of *grex* flock. Also, gregarious, egregious.

HAB- from *habēre* to have, hold, with the 'h' (scarcely pronounced in Latin) dropping off in certain words. In 'able,' for example, OF was also dropping this 'h' as seen in their two forms *hable* and *able*. HIB- appears with prefixes, as in inhibit, exhibit, and prohibit. Inhabit and cohabit are from *habitare* to inhabit, dwell, a frequentative of *habēre*.

PED- from *pedi-*, the stem of *pes* foot. Also, biped, bipedal, expedient, impede, quadruped. Compare the Gk PED- child, as in pediatrics. The Gk base POD- foot is cognate with this L base.

PUNG- from the verb infinitive *pungere* to prick, puncture, or stab. Also, expunge, pungent. PUNCT- is from *punctus*, the past participle of *pungere*; also, punctuate, compunction.

SACR-, (SECR-) from the adjective *sacer, sacrum*, sacred, holy, consecrated. Also, sacral (= holy), sacrarium, sacrifice (SACR- + FIC- to do, to make— "to make holy"), sacrilege (SACR- + LEG- gather, choose, pick out— "the stealing of sacred things"), sacristry. Compare sacrum, from *os sacrum* the last bone of the spine; literally, the holy bone, which gives sacral and sacroiliac. The 'e' of SECR- is the result of vowel weakening. Compare secret, secrete, secretion, sectarian and other words that come from different roots.

SANCT- from *sanctus* holy, which also produced the OF and E saint. *Sanctus* derives from the verb *sancire* to consecrate, which is related to (the above base) *sacer*, holy.

SENT- from the verb infinitive *sentire* to feel, experience, realize, perceive. Also, sentence (from *sententia* a way of thinking, opinion, thought, meaning, from the present participle *sentens* feeling), assent (*ad-* + SENT-), dissent (*dis-* not), sentient, sententious (from the above *sententia*); SENS- from the past participle *sensus*, which gives insensate, sensation, sense, sensible, sensitive.

TURB- from the noun *turba* tumult, uproar, disturbance, mob, swarm, crowd. EW's 'to disturb' is a translation of the verb *turbo, turbare*, which is derived from the noun. Also, turbulent, perturb. The noun *turbo, turbinis* a movement in a circle, an eddy, which is connected with the noun *turba*, gives turbine and some fifteen words with its combining form turbo-, such as turbocharger, turbofan, turbogenerator, turbojet.

VERT- from the verb infinitive *vertere* to turn, turn around. Also, avert (*ab-* + VERT-), divert (*dis-* + VERT-), convert, obvert, pervert, vertex; VERS- from the past participle *versus*, giving inverse, diverse, diversity, diversify, converse, conversation ("keep company with"), averse, obverse, verse, versicle. *Vorto* is a variant form of *verto, vertere*, and from this comes vortex, vorticism and their derivatives.

VI(A)- from the noun *via* a way, a highway, a road, etc. Also, viaduct (DUCT- to lead), voyage (through OF), deviate, obviate, obvious. Compare viable, now much used as a figurative transfer, from F *vie*, from L *vita* life; and vial, from Greek.

III. Analysis and Definition of Words

1. *con- (com-)* together + GREG- flock, herd: a group of people gathered together in a crowd; an assemblage. Point out the *-at-* addition, also in sentences, 5, 6, 12, 14, 16, 18, and 19.

2. *ob-* in the way, against + TRUD- to push: to push out or thrust forward.

3. *per-* wrongly (*per-* has a pejorative force here, as in the English *for-*, to which it is connected, as in forswear, meaning perjure) + JUR- to take an oath: the violation of an oath by giving false information.

4. *ob-* against + LOQU- to speak: blame; public reproach.

5. *in-* not + CESS- to yield: continuing without interruption; continual; constant.

6. *per-* wrongly (see number 3 above) + VERS- to turn: improper; wrongheaded.

7. *im- (in-)* not + *per-* thoroughly + TURB- to disturb: not easily confused, disturbed, or upset; calm.

8. *a- (ad-)* to + LIGN- line: to bring into line.

9. *in-* not + JUST- right, law: lack of fairness or rightness.

10. *inter-* between + CESS- to go: the act of intervening between parties in order to reconcile differences.

11. *ex-* out, from + PUNG- to prick, to point: to strike out; mark for deletion.

12. assimilated to the deponent verb *imprecari* to invoke (harm, evil, etc.) upon, from *im-* on + PREC- prayer: a curse; evil.

13. *inter-* between + LOCUT- to speak: a female who takes part in a conversation or dialogue.

14. *con- (com-)* here, an intensive + SECR- sacred: to make or set apart as sacred or holy.

15. *in-* not + *per-* through + VI- way: the quality of not being open to argument or suggestion. (Dictionaries rarely send this back farther than *in-* + *pervius* pervious.)

16. *ex-* completely + (S)ECR- to curse (the unfavorable sense of the derivative *sacrare*): to feel intense loathing for; detest; abhor.

17. *in-* not + *ad-* toward + VERT- to turn: carelessly; needlessly; negligently; by mistake.

18. *inter-* between + LINE- line: material written between lines that are already written or printed.

19. *in-* not + SENS- to feel (into LL *insensatus*): senseless; foolish; brutal.

20. *in-* in + DUC- to lead: to bring about; cause.

IV. Reversal of Meaning Through Prefixes

1. persuasive—unpersuasive
2. militarize—demilitarize
3. enfranchise—disenfranchise
4. resistance—nonresistance
5. resistible—irresistible (assimilation of *in-*)
6. combustible—incombustible
7. inclination—disinclination
8. clockwise—counterclockwise
9. sensitize—desensitize
10. audible—inaudible

V. Meaning of Abbreviations

1. D.D.S.—Doctor of Dental Surgery.

2. F.R.S.—Fellow of the Royal Society.

3. Skt.—Sanskrit.

4. v.t.—transitive verb.

5. KGB (also K.G.B.)—*K*(omissija) *G*(osudarstvennoj) *B*(ezopasnosti), Russian, for Commission of State Security, is an official police agency of the Soviet Union in charge of state security.

6. q.—quart, quarts; quarter, one fourth of a hundredweight; quarterly; quarto; quasi; queen; query; question; quintal; quire. (Not all dictionaries record all of these).

7. a.m.—before noon (as in Class starts at 8 a.m.); the time from midnight to noon (L *ante meridiem*).

8. ca.—cathode; centiare(s). Also abbreviated *c* (L *circa* about), about or approximately (in reference to time), as in ca. 1986.

9. cf.—calf (of a bookbinding); center field (in baseball), also centerfielder; compare (L *confer*).

10. e.g.—for example, for instance (L *exempli gratia*).

11. i.e.—that is, that is to say (L *id est*).

12. lb.—pound (L *libra*, the Roman pound of twelve ounces).

VI. Meaning of Acronyms

1. flak—from German, *Fl*iege*r*abweh*r*kanone; literally, aircraft, defense gun; much used figuratively in current English.
2. laser—*l*ight *a*mplification by *s*timulated *e*mission of *r*adiation.
3. loran—*lo*ng-*ra*nge *n*avigation.
4. radar—*ra*dio *d*etecting *a*nd *r*anging.
5. rem—*r*oentgen *e*quivalent *m*an, with rem and rems as plurals.
6. SEATO—*S*outh*e*ast *A*sia *T*reaty *O*rganization.

LESSON V

BACK FORMATIONS, APHERESIS, AND APHESIS

Additional examples of back formations are scavenge (-er), sidle (v.) from sideling (adj.), safc-keep (-ing), callithump (-ian), tumesce (-nce), back mutate (-ion), thermoregulate (-ion), didact (-ic), electrophorese (-sis), and the verb duff (-er), meaning to perform (a bad shot) in golf, and in the transferred sense to botch, make a mess of. As of 1985, some of these words had not appeared in contemporary dictionaries. Like all fledgling neologistic efforts, they have to wait in the wings and prove themselves— through usage and time; generally they have a good purpose in life, have an open slot to fit into which apparently needed filling, and so live on.

Apheresis has been going on for centuries. In OE, dozens of words opened with prefixal elements, such as *a-*, *for-*, and *ge-*, all of which had special meanings. *For-*, for example, carried, among other meanings, a sense of completion with intensive force, as in *spillan* to spill, and *for-spillan* to waste, lose, or destroy; or *leosan* to lose, and *for-leosan* to abandon or destroy. See the OED for the long and complex history of this prefix. In some words *ge-* is generally considered cognate with L *cum* with (EW's prefix *con-, com-,* etc.), as in OE *gebedda* one who shares a bed 'with' someone else (from OE *bedd* bed); or *gefera* one who goes 'with' another (from OE *faran* to go); or OE *gerunnen* to run 'together.' Some of these elements have survived in a modified form, such OE *gefordian,* to ME *iford* (the consonant was generally the first to go) to ModE *afford.* But most of them fell away, and in order to retain the sense of the original, we had to put the preposition after the verb, and produce 'run with' (or 'run together'), 'share a bed with,' and 'go with,' just as when the OE infinitive endings fell away in ME, similar paraphrasis (i.e., 'to') had to be employed.

ASSIGNMENT

I. Discussion of Prefixes

post-   from the preposition and adverb *post* after, behind.

pre-   from the preposition and adverb *prae* before, in front (of). The Latin spelling survives in a few direct lifts as praetor, praetorium, praetorial, and in variant spellings as praedial (= predial), praefect (= prefect), etc.

pro-   from the preposition and adverb *pro* before, in front (of). Compare the Gk prefix *pro-* before.

re-, red-   from the prefix *re-* back, again. Usually does not take a hyphen except where there would be ambiguity, as in re-form, re-cede, re-act, and re-creation (as opposed to reform and recreation, etc.), or before capital letters as in re-Anglicize. Sometimes a hyphen also occurs before e, as in re-establish. *Red-* is used sometimes before vowels, as in redundant (*re-* + UND- wave), redeem (*re-* + *emere* to buy), redolent (*re-* + *olere* to smell).

retro-   from the adverb *retro* backwards, back, behind. Occurs in words from Latin, as retroflexion and retrograde, and in modern English formations, as retrofit and retrorocket (or retro-rocket).

se-, sed-   from the L prefix *se-* apart, from the older preposition *se, sed* without (this is the same L conjunction *sed,* meaning 'but'). Infrequently listed since it appears only in loan words. *Sed-* appears before vowels, as in sedition (*se-* + IT- to go). Also, seduce and select.

sub-   from the preposition *sub* under. Appears in various assimilated forms: *su-* (before sp, as in suspend, suspect), *suc-* (before c, as in succeed, succinct), *suf-* (before f, as in suffer, suffice, suffix, suffocate), *sug-* (before g, as in suggest), *sum-* (sometimes before m, as in summon; but more often not assimilated, as in submerge, submit), *sup-* (before p, as in supple, supplicate, supply), *sur-* (before r, as in surreptitious, surrogate; compare surround in the entry below under *super-*), *sus-* (sometimes before c, p, or t, as in susceptible, suspect, sustain). Compare the F prefix *sur-,* for which see next entry.

super- from the preposition and adverb *super* over, above. Appears in words from Latin, as supererogate, superficial, superfluous, superior, and much used in modern English formations as in supercold, supercontinent, supergene, superman, supernova, superpower. Became reduced to *sur-* in words that passed through F or AF, as in surround (*super-* + UND- wave), surrender, surcease, surtax. Also, supreme, where the 'e' is suppressed. Related to *super-* is the prefix *supra-*, meaning on, above, or beyond, which could also be introduced here; from the preposition and adverb *supra* above, over. Examples are supraliminal, supranational, suprarational; occasionally is simply a variant of *super-*, as in suprahuman and supramundane.

trans-, tran-, tra- from the preposition *trans* across. *Tran-* appears in words in which the base began with 's,' with one 's' suppressed, as in transpire (*trans-* + SPIR- to breathe), transect (SECT- to cut), and transilient (SIL- to leap), and in other words such as tranquil. *Tra-* appears in L, F, or It reductions, as traffic (*trans-* + *figere* to set), tradition, traduce (DUC- to lead), traitor, trajectory (JECT- to throw). Also, transform, transitive.

ultra- from the preposition and adverb *ultra* beyond, on the far side. Carries an intensive force (very, unusually, excessively) in English.

II. Discussion of Bases

CLUD- from the verb infinitive *cludere* to shut, close, bring to an end. This is a variant form of *claudere* (past participle *clausus*) which has produced clause (from ML *clausa* the close of a rhetorical period) and claustrophobia. CLUS- is from the past participle *clusus*, giving occlusion (*ob-*), inclusion, preclusion, inclusive, etc. Also, preclude, obclude.

CUR(R)- from the verb infinitive *currere* to run, hasten; CURS- from its past participle *cursum*. Also, concurrent, occur, cursive, cursory. Compare procure, secure, cure, from *cura* care, concern; and curse, which is English.

GRAD- from the deponent verb infinitive *gradi* to step, walk; GRESS- from its past participle *gressus*. Also, digress, grade, ingredient (from *ingredi* to step into, to enter), ingress, egress, regress, transgress.

PEND- from the verb infinitive *pendēre* to hang, or the related VL *pendere* to cause to hang down, to weigh, to pay; words with PENS- are from the past participle *pensus*. Also, compensate, expend, pendant, pendulum, impending, suspend, suspension, propend.

PLE- from the verb infinitive *plēre* to fill; PLET- from its past participle *pletus*; PLEN- from the adjective *plenus* full—supplying plenary, plenteous, plenipotentiary, plenum. Also deplete, replete. Compare the Gk *plethora* fullness, from *plethein* to be full, which gives the English plethora and plethysmograph.

SPEC- from the verb *specere* to look at, see; SPIC- is a variant form of this, found in words with prefixes, as conspicuous; SPECT- is from the past participle *spectum*. The verb *specere* whelped the frequentative verb *spectare* to watch, with a past participle *spectatus* from which the English spectator is derived. Also, aspect, Perspex (= a trade name for any of the various clear acrylic resins that are used chiefly as a substitute for glass, from *per-* through + SPEC-), perspective, perspicacious, prospect, spectacle, spectacles, and specks, suspect, suspicion. Also, special and species, from *species* a seeing, view, look, which derives from *specere*.

UND- from the noun *unda* water, water in motion, a wave.

VID- from the verb infinitive *vidēre* to see; VIS- is from its past participle *visus*. Also, advice and advise (from OF *avis*, a shortening of *ce m'est a vis* it seems to me, my view is, from L *mihi videtur* it seems to me), vision, visit, visage, visor, and the spate of words from the combining form video- (= I see), as video cassette, videodisc, videogenic, videophone, videotape, etc., and videoize.

VOC- from *vocare* to call, summon, from the stem *voc-* of the noun *vox* a voice, a cry, a call (as in the trade name Magnavox, and a few borrowings as vox humana, vox pop). From the past participle *vocatus* (VOC- + -at-) come vocation, avocation (*ab-* + VOC-), invocation, revocation, etc., where there is no vocate, etc. Also, voice (through OF, from *vox*). The 'k' in VOK- is an orthographical variant of the Latin 'c,' pronounced /k/, as in revoke, invoke, provoke, etc.

III. Analysis and Definition of Words

1. *red-* back + UND- wave: extra; superfluous; unnecessary.
2. *pro-* forward + TRUS- to push: sticking out; projecting.
3. *re-* back + GRESS- to go: an act of going back or returning to a previous condition.
4. *retro-* backward + SPECT- to look: directed backwards.
5. VID- to see: a brief, musical-theatrical production that is recorded usually on magnetic tape for transmission on a television set.
6. *com-* with (or, in addition) + PEND- to weigh: a brief summary of the main points or ideas of a larger, extensive work; abstract; precis; summary; abridgment; condensation.
7. *pre-* before + CLUD- to shut: to make impossible beforehand; prevent.
8. *retro-* backward + GRAD- to step, to go: moving backward; retreating.
9. *im-* in + PLE- to fill: to put into effect; carry out.
10. *se-* away, apart + CLUS- to shut: state of being apart or shut off from others.

11. *in-* not + *super-* above, over (or, SUPER- to rise above—see footnote in EW here): incapable of being passed over, overcome, or surmounted; insurmountable; invincible.

12. *pro-* forward + PENS- to hang: a natural tendency or inclination.

13. *con-* (*com-*) with + SPECT- to look: a comprehensive view.

14. *trans-* across + GRESS- to step, to go: an act of breaking a law or command; violation; offense.

15. *pre-* before + SENT- to feel: a sense that something (usually bad or evil) is about to happen.

16. *suc-* (*sub-*) up from under (i.e. up to) to + COR- to run—which in L combined into *succurrere* to run (up) to help: anything that helps, assists, or relieves; aid; assistance.

17. *con-* (*com-*) with, together + CUR- to run: to be of the same opinion; agree. (See the discussion of *gerunnen* in the opening notes in IM on apheresis).

18. *sub-* under + VERT- to turn: to cause the destruction of; ruin; overthrow.

19. *ir-* (assimilated from *in-*) + *re-* back + VOC- to call: incapable of being brought back, called back, or annulled.

20. *sup-* (assimilated from *sub-*) up from under + PLE- to fill: additional.

IV. Antonyms Formed Through Prefixes

1. assent—dissent
2. supersonic—subsonic
3. prelude—postlude
4. depreciate—appreciate
5. associate—dissociate (or disassociate)
6. ante-bellum—post-bellum
7. converge—diverge
8. persuade—dissuade
9. discord—concord (or accord)
10. inflate—deflate
11. retrogress—progress
12. accelerate—decelerate

V. Back Formations

1. spectate—spectator
2. emote—emotion
3. execute—executor
4. scavenge—scavenger
5. enthuse—enthusiasm
6. vaccinate—vaccination
7. pea—pease (erroneously construed as plural)
8. edit—editor
9. surreal—surrealism
10. preempt—preemption

LATIN LESSON V/VI • 39

VI. Apheretic or Aphetic Forms

1. lone—alone
2. mend—amend
3. state—estate
4. auger—nauger

5. umpire—(ME) *noumpere*
   (as with apron)
6. spite—despite

LESSON VI

COMBINATIONS OF BASES

Although 'i' is the standard connecting vowel, when bases are combined, so as to help prevent misspellings it should be pointed out clearly that any one of the five vowels can, for reasons explained in EW, be used as a link between two bases. Even in Latin, both 'i' and 'u' followed QUAD-, as in *quadrilibris* and *quadrupes* where both *quadri-* and *quadru-* are reduced (in Latin) from *quattuor*. The E quadriphonic is considered a variant of the preferred quadraphonic. As will be seen in Part II, 'o' is the standard connecting vowel in Greek.

ASSIGNMENT

I. Discussion of Numerical Bases

SEMI- is the same in L and is always spelled solid when used in English compounds. Compare semin-, from L *semen* seed, which gives seminal, seminar, seminary, semination. Also compare semiology from Gk *semeion* sign.

UN- from the adjective *unus*. Most English words beginning with un- come from other sources, such as: *un-* the E prefix meaning not, the opposite of; uncate and unciform (from *uncus* hook); uncle (from OF *oncle*, from L *avunculus* the brother of one's mother); unction (ultimately from *unguere* to anoint); ungula and ungulate (from *unguis* nail, claw).

PRIM- from *primus*. The prefix has also whelped the adjective primo, meaning unsurpassed, of the highest quality, or, as a noun, the best (specifically, marijuana).

DU- from *duo*. There are other words that may be mistakenly associated with this prefix, such as due and duty (both from OF *deu,* from L *debēre* to owe), durable, duress, duration (from OF, ultimately from *durus* hard), etc.

BI- from *bis* twice; BIN- from *bini* (plural form of the adjective *binus*) double, two at a time, two. BIN- appears in English words of Latin origin, as binary, binate, binocular, and in analogical constructions as binaural (aural = concerning hearing). Unfortunately, the meaning of both words melted into *bi-*, which, in words concerning time, means both twice a, and every two, as biweekly (= occurring twice a week, and occurring every two weeks), bimonthly, biyearly. Sense is separated in biannual (= occurring twice a year) and biennial (= occurring every two years). When *bi-* is to mean twice a, students are advised to use *semi-*, as semiweekly, etc.

TRI- from *tria* (from *tres*) three. Compare the Gk base TRI- three. It would seem unnecessary to separate the English words deriving from these two bases.

QUADR(U)- from the stem *quadr-* from *quattuor* four. Quadri- was the combining form in Latin, as it is in English, and is generally listed in contemporary dictionaries. Also appears as quadra-, as in quadraphonic, quadrasonic.

QUART- from *quartus*; QUINT- from *quintus*; SEXT- from *sextus* (from *sex* six; compare the L noun *sexus* sex); SEPT-, SEPTEM- from *septem*; OCT- from *octo*; OCTAV- from *octavus* (from *octo*); DECI-, DECIM- from *decimus*; CENT- from *centum*; MILL- from *mille*.

Sex, sexi (as in sexipolar); sept-, septi- (septisyllable); deci- (decibel, decigram); cent-, centi- (centimeter, centigrade); and milli- (millimeter, milligram, milliliter) are all generally recorded as combining forms for *sex, septem, decem, centum,* and *mille.*

II. Analysis and Definition of Words

1. CENT- hundred + *i* connecting vowel + PED- foot: a wormlike arthropod composed of from 15 to 173 segments, each with a pair of legs, the first pair of which is modified into poison fangs.

2. VIA- road + DUCT- to lead: a bridge over a canal, railroad, or (here) a road. (Compare the hybrid overpass.)

3. DU- two: a condition consisting of or involving two parts.

4. QUADR- four + *i* connecting vowel + PART- part: divided into or consisting of four parts.

5. SEXT- six + *-uple* -fold: one of six offspring born to the same mother at the same time.

6. *inter-* between + LOCUT- to speak: one who takes part in a conversation.

7. *con-* (*com-*) together + VOC- to call: an assembly. (Point out the -*at-* here and in sentences 14 and 16.)

8. *trans-* across + VERS- to turn: lying or passing across.

9. SACR- sacred + *o* (ablative) inflection (or connective vowel) + SANCT- holy. (Both of these bases are derivatives of *sacer* sacred, holy; with SANCT- coming from *sancire* to consecrate. The L compound *sacrosanctus* means "consecrated with religious ceremonies.")

10. *ac-* (assimilated from *ad-*) to + CED- to yield: to agree with or assent to.

11. TRI- three + PART- part: composed of three parts.

12. *in-* in + CURS- to run: a sudden attack, invasion, or raid.

13. CENT(i)- one hundred + GRAD- to step, go: having a thermometric scale on which the interval between the freezing point (0°) and the boiling point (100°) is 100 degrees.

14. *de-* the reversal of something + SECR- sacred: disregard for the sacredness of; violation of the sacred character of (a place or thing) by destruction or other sacrilegious action.

15. SEMI- half + FIN- end: one of two matches (as in a sports event) that determines who will play in the final match, which follows.

16. DECIM- tenth: to kill a large part of. (The original meaning was to select by lot and kill every tenth man of.)

17. from the past participle *elusus* of the verb *eludere* to delude, evade, from *ex-* out, away + LUS- to play, mock: tending to slip away or be unexplained.

18. from *pensare* to weigh carefully, estimate, ponder, consider, from PENS- (of *pendere* to weigh): seriously thoughtful, often in a sad way.

19. QUADRU- fourth + PED- foot: an animal that has four feet.

20. PRIM- first: (a) any of the highest (first) order of mammals (order *Primates*); (b) an archbishop (first among bishops).

III. Words With Numeral Bases

1. unicorn—the unicorn (UN- one) has a single horn in the middle of its forehead.

2. primer—(a) a first book in reading, or any first book or beginner's book; (b) a first coat of paint or oil on new wood, etc.; (c) a cap or cylinder containing a small amount of gunpowder, used for firing a charge (i.e., the first step in firing), from PRIM- first.

3. primeval—concerning the first age or ages (especially of the world); ancient, prehistoric ("first history"), from PRIM- first.

4. biscuit—from OF *pain bescuit* twice-cooked bread, from BI- twice + *coquere* to cook, prepare food.

5. trivial—from *trivialis* of the crossroads, ordinary, common, of the streets, trivial, from *trivium* a place where three roads meet, from TRI- three.

6. trillion—a million (the unit or first step in the -illion measurement) has six zeros; a billion (BI- the second step) has nine zeros; a trillion (TRI- the third step) has twelve zeros; quadrillion (QUADRI- the fourth step) has fifteen zeros; etc. The difference between the British and German system as opposed to the U.S., Canadian, and French system could be explained here.*

7. Septuagint—the Greek translation of the Old Testament (before the time of Christ), the Pentateuch (from the Gk PENTA- five) of which was translated from the Hebrew by seventy Jewish scholars; from LL *septuaginta* seventy, from SEPT- seven.

8. octogenarian—a person who is eighty years old, or between eighty and ninety, from *octogenarius* containing eighty, from OCT- eight.

9. centurion—in Roman times, an officer commanding a hundred men, from CENT- a hundred.

10. mile—from *milia passuum* a thousand paces, from MILL- a thousand.

IV. From Roman to Arabic Numerals

1. XVIII—18	7. xxxii—32
2. xlix—49	8. LVII—57
3. CVII—107	9. CCXIV—214
4. DCLX—660	10. MMXX—2020
5. DCCCXLIV—844	11. lxvii—67
6. MDCCXXXIX—1739	12. xcvi—96

---

*The difference begins at a billion, which in the U.S., Canada, and France, means a thousand million (9 zeros), a trillion means a thousand billion (12 zeros), and so on up the scale. A billion in England and Germany means a million million (12 zeros), a trillion means a million billion (18 zeros), and so on up the scale. The U.S. billion is usually called 'a thousand million' (occasionally milliard) in England, which in recent years has introduced confusion into its system by also using the U.S. sense of billion.

LESSON VII

HYBRIDS

It might interest some of your students to know that the L *hybrida* (for *hibrida*) was the label given to an offspring of a tame sow and a wild boar. In terms of humans it was still restricted to an offspring of a Roman male and a foreign woman. The term also later applied to plants. By the nineteenth century it was used to describe anything of heterogeneous elements—even words.

ASSIGNMENT

I. Discussion of Bases

ANIM-   two words are connected with this stem—*animus* the spiritual or rational principle of human life, as opposed to the body or physical life; and *anima* (the feminine form of *animus*) something breathing, the physical life, a living being. Most Latin and English derivatives come from *anima*. Also, animosity, animadversion.

ANN(U)-   from *annus* year, a circuit of the sun; the 'e' in ENNI- is the result of vowel weakening when certain prefixes are added, as in biennial (= occurring very two years) and perennial, but biannual (= occurring twice a year) and superannuation.

BENE-   from *bene* well, from *bonus* good (which gives the English word bonus), whence BON-. The comparative degree of *bonus* is *melior* (the) better, which gives meliorate, ameliorate, and their derivatives. The superlative degree is *optimus* (the) best, which gives optimum, optimize, optimism, etc. Also, beneficent, benevolent, beneficiary. Compare option, from L *optare* to desire.

CANT-, CENT-, [CHANT-]   from the verb *cantare* to sing, itself a frequentative of *canere* to sing. CENT- is the weakened form used with some prefixes. From *cantare* the OF produced *chanter*, giving chant, enchant, disenchanted, etc. Also, cantabile and cantata (through It), cant, cantus, canto (through It), cantor (-ate, -ial), cantilate. Compare cant (= a sloping, inclination), cantilever, cantina (= a saloon, through Sp and It), cantle (= a part of a saddle), canton (= a political division of a country), all from VL *cantus* a corner or edge.

CUR-   from the L noun *cura* care, charge. Also, insecure, incurable, curate (and its doublet curé from F), curette (or curet) from F *curer*, from OF,

43

from L *curare,* a derivative of *cura* (itself derived from *cavēre* to guard against, take care for, provide).

EQU- from the adjective *aequus* equal; the weakened IQU- after some prefixes. Also, egalitarian (alteration of equalitarian, influenced by F *egal*), equation, equator, equilateral, equilibrium, equinox, equitable, equity, equivalent. Compare equestrian from *equus* horse, and equip from OF *eschiper* to fit out (a ship).

FER- from the verb infinitive *ferre* to bear, bring, carry. LAT- to bear, carry (see listing below), comes from *latus* the irregular (borrowed) past participle of this verb. Also, circumference, differ (*dis-* in different directions), suffer (*sub-* under). Compare interfere, from *inter-* between + *ferire* to strike.

LAT- see FER- above. Also, collate, prelate ("one that is preFERred"). Compare late, from OE, and latitude and other words from *latus* wide.

MAGN- from *magnus* great, large. The Latin combining form for constructing words was *magni-* (the stem of *magnus*), or *magn-* before vowels as in the English magnanimous and magnate. Also, magnificent, magnicide, magniloquent, and magnum (= a bottle), which is the neuter form of the adjective *magnus.* The comparative degree of *magnus* is *maior*, which gives majesty and major (when 'i' is used as a consonant, it appears as 'j'). The superlative degree is *maximus*, which gives maximum (the neuter form of *maximus*), maxim, maximize. Compare magnesia, magnesite, magnet and magnesium, all from the Greek region Magnes which was rich in minerals.

MAL(E)- from *malus* bad, evil; MALIGN- from the derivative *malignus* (connected with *gigno,* the GEN- verb base of Lesson IX) ill-disposed, malicious, malignant, wicked. Also, malady, malapropism, malefactor (FACT- to make), malevolent (VOL- to wish), malice, malign. The superlative degree of *malus* is *pessimus*, whence pessimism. Compare male (through OF from L *mas* a male), a doublet of masculine.

MULT- from *multus* much, many. The combining form, usually listed in dictionaries, is mult- before some vowels as in multangular and multocular, and multi-, which is found in some sixty combinations. The comparative of *multus* is *plus* more, which gives plus and nonplus. The stem of *plus* is *plur-*, which gives plural (-ism, -ist, -ity, -ize), and the combining form pluri-, meaning hav⟶ more than one, or many, as in pluriaxial, and a few words where multi- is usually used in place of pluri-, as in pluricellular (= multicellular); also in the motto *e pluribus unum* (literally: out of many, one), the official motto of the U.S. until 1956 when "In God We Trust" took over.

OPTIM- see BON- above.

PLIC-, PLEX-, PLY- Two related verbs give these bases: *plectere* (past participle *plexus*) to plait, braid, interweave; and *plicare* (past participle *plicatus*, with the variant form *plicitus*) to fold (up), bend, coil. The combining form -plex (not often listed) gives duplex ("two fold"), triplex, fourplex, etc. Also, simple (*sem[el]* once + -PLE, i.e., one fold), ply, plait, (through OF *pleit*), plexus (as in solar plexus), pliant (through OF *pliant*), pliers, perplex, explicate, explicit, duplicity, duplicate. Compare the Gk base PLEX- stroke, and the trade name Plexiglass (*pl*astic + fl*exi*ble + *glass*).

VOL- from the past tense stem *vol-* of the infinitive *velle* to be willing, to wish. Also, volition, volunteer. Compare revolution and evolution from VOLUT- to roll; and volume and voluble, ultimately from the same verb.

II. Analysis and Definition of Words

1. MAGN- great + ANIM- mind, feeling: noble; generous; free from mean or petty feelings.
2. *in-* not + IQU- equal (or just): unjust; wicked; nefarious; unrighteous.
3. MAL- bad: a desire to inflict injury or suffering on another; active ill-will; spite; animosity; enmity.
4. MULT- many + *i* connecting vowel + PLIC- to fold: either a) a great many, or b) a great variety or diversity.
5. BON- good + BON- good: a piece of candy having a soft center of usually jelly with nuts, coated with creamed sugar.
6. *in-* not + ANIM- spirit, life: without life; lifeless.
7. MILL- thousand + ENNI- year (patterned on the English word biennium): (a) a period of one thousand years; (b) here, figurative, a period of happiness, peace, and prosperity.
8. *ad-* on + GRIEV- heavy: to injure unjustly. (Unlike its doublet aggravate, aggrieve is rare except in passive.)
9. *com-* with (here, more an intensive) + PUNCT- to prick: uneasiness of the mind because of a wrongdoing; regret; remorse.
10. *ex-* out + PLIC- fold: precisely and clearly expressed; leaving nothing to implication.*
11. *pro-* forward + *of-* (*ob-*) toward + FER- to carry: an offer made.
12. *cor-* (*com-*) together + *re-* back + LAT- to carry: the mutual relation of two or more things (concepts, parts, etc.); connection.

---

*This unusual situation might be pointed out to the students: *plico, plicare* had both *-atum* and *-itum* past participle forms. The *-at-* formed verbs (implicate, explicate, complicate, replicate); and *-it-* formed adjectives (implicit, explicit, and complicity where there was never a complicit).

13. *in-* against + CANT- to sing (or to chant): the set of words recited or chanted as a magic charm to cast a spell. (Point out the -at- for the -ion suffix.)

14. *se-* aside, away (or free from) + CUR- care: to make safe or protect.

15. (a) BI- two + ENNI- year: occurring every two years; (b) QUADR- four + ENNI- year: occurring every four years.

16. *suc-* (*sub-*) up + CESS- to go: in a manner coming one after another.

17. *com-* together + PLEX- to fold, interweave: an instance of a difficult or complicated condition. (This use is at least quasi-concrete; a definition as an abstract noun should not be accepted. Concrete and abstract concepts are discussed at Lesson XV.)

18. *inter-* between + VENT- to come: favoring the interfering in an affair, so as to affect its course or outcome.

19. EQU- equal + ANIM: mind: eveness of mind; composure.

20. OPTIM- best: to make the most or best of:

III. Derivation of Hybrids

1. television—from F *television*, from Gk TELE- afar + L VIS- to see.

2. anteroom—from L *ante-* before + OE *rum* room.

3. megaton—from Gk MEGA- large + OE *tunne* ton.

4. ill-tempered—from Old Norse *illr* ill + L *temperare* to exercise control, observe proper limits.

5. automobile—from F *automobile,* from Gk AUT- self + F *mobile* moving (ultimately from L MOV- to move).

6. speedometer—from OE *sped* luck, advancement + Gk *metron* a measure.

7. monorail—from Gk MON(o)- one, single + OF *raille* bar, beam (from L *regula* a straight length, a ruler, from EW L base REG-).

8. antibody—from a translation of the German *Antikorper*, from Gk *anti-* against + German *Korper* substance, body; body is from OE *bodig* body. (As this word is generally not etymologized, students will have to look under the individual components for their answer.)

9. aqualung—from L AQUA- water + OE *lungen* lung.*

10. monaural—from Gk MON- one, single + L *auris* ear.

---

*Some dictionaries main-entry the trademark Aqua Lung, Aqua-Lung, or Aqua-lung, without recognizing it as a common noun. Some main-entry aqualung, with Aqua-Lung as a second definition, or with Aqua-Lung not even mentioned.

LESSON VIII

SUFFIXES

It is appreciated that some instructors may wish to introduce all of the suffixes at one time, and to this end they can easily be abstracted from the next fourteen lessons and grouped together. However, now that suffixes are to be included in the analysis of words that are suffixed, the way EW is set up, no words are offered for analysis containing suffixes that have not already been studied; for example, endurance is not used until Lesson XVIII because -ance is not introduced until that lesson. This process does, however, work backwards (commodious is in Lesson XVII, with MOD- at Lesson XI, and -ious at Lesson VIII).

As a general rule, suffixes function to change the part of speech of a word, but occasionally they get involved in meaning, as of-FIC-ial and of-FIC-ious. Some of these pairs are to be discussed in Exercise III of this lesson.

ASSIGNMENT

I. Discussion of Adjective-Forming Suffixes

-al (-ial, -eal) from the L ending *-alis* having to do with; the noun suffix comes from the neuter form *-alia* of this suffix. The *-al* suffix when added to nouns gives genuine adjectives, as in natural. Others are generally referred to as substantive adjectives which have undergone function shift (for which see Latin Lesson XIII), but words such as numeral and pedal have been around for so long that we now think of them as full-fledged nouns. The noun suffix *-al* is added to verbs, giving words like arrival and refusal; in science it indicates aldehyde, as in butanal; and also indicates a pharmaceutical product, as phenobarbital. The 'i' and 'e' come in through derivatives, as in corporeal (from *corporeus,* from *corpus*) and substantial (from *substantia,* from *substare*). The *-eal* is a contraction of the L suffix *-e(us)* + *-al.*

-ane, -an (-ian; also -ean), [-ain] from *-anus* a suffix of L adjectives, as *urbanus* which gives both urban and urbane in English. As substantive- or noun-forming, it also means a person belonging to or coming from (as European and American), a person typical of (as Elizabethan), an adherent of (as Christian), a specialist in (as historian). Also in variant spellings, as Shakespearean and dietician. The *-ane* is also used in science to indicate a saturated carbon compound of

47

the methane series, as in butane and propane. The 'i' and 'e' came in through derivatives, as amphibian, humanitarian, Jacobean. RHD gives *-n* as a variant of *-an,* with Virginian as an example, as with Asian from Asia and Australian from Australia, with the *-ia* being a separate noun suffix meaning territory, as in Polynesia, Micronesia, and Rumania. EW's *-ian* would, of course, have to be used for Bostonian from Boston, Episcopalian from Episcopal, and Proustian from (Marcel) Proust, for both the adjective and noun, where there is no Bostonia, etc.

-ar from OF *-er,* from L *-aris,* replacing *-alis* (the *-al* suffix above) when there was dissimilation. (A topical section on dissimilation opens Lesson X, the second paragraph of which deals with this situation.)

-ose (*-iose*), from *-osus,* a Latin adjective suffix. Also used in chemistry to denote a type of sugar or other carbohydrate, as fructose, lactose.

-ous came in from two sources: (1) from adjectives ending in *-osus,* as *gloriosus* glorious (from *gloria* glory) and *famosus* famous (from *fama* fame); and (2) from adjectives ending in *-us* as *spontaneus* spontaneous (from *sponte* willingly), *gregarius* gregarious (from GREG- to flock)—with the 'i' and 'e' being introduced through the derivatives. The suffix also means having to do with, as in monogamous; committing or practicing, as in bigamous, larcenous; also, in chemistry, having a valence lower than in compounds ending in *-ic,* as mercurous/mercuric, stannous/stannic.

II. Discussion of Bases

AQU(A)- from *aqua* water. Also, aquacade, aquaculture (or aquiculture), aquafarm, aqualung (which sometimes appears as the trade name Aqua-Lung), aquamarine, aquanaut (NAUT- sailor), aquaplane, aquarium, aqueous, aquifer. (These various connecting vowels are discussed in the topical section at Lesson VI in EW.)

CORP(US)- from *corpus* body, producing the English words corps (through F), corpse (through OF *corps*), and corpus. CORPOR- (from the derivative adjective *corporalis* relating to the body) gives corporal, incorporation, incorporeal.

OMN- from the adjective *omnis* all, every, whole. Also, omniscience (SCI- to know—Lesson XIII), omnibus (your actual Latin—the dative plural of *omnis* for all) and its clip bus; and omnipotent, omnidirectional, and others. Omni- is offered as a combining form in most dictionaries, but called a prefix by AHD.

REG- from the verb infinitive *regere* to guide, direct, rule, govern. RECT- is from *rectus,* the past participle. RIG- is used in prefixed words. Dirigible is from *dirigere* (*dis-* apart + *regere*). Also, rectum, rector.

Linguistically, all three forms go together; however, the adjective *rectus,* a spin-off from the past participle, took on the additional meanings of straight and the transfered senses of correct, right, proper, which show in rectify, correct (com- + RECT), rectitude.

SIMIL- from *similis* similar; SIMUL- from its derivative *simulare* to make similar. Also, simile, similitude, simulacrum, simulant, simulate. Simultaneous is an analogical construction, from such as momentaneous. Note simulcast, a blend of *simul*taneous and broad*cast.*

TEMPER- from the verb *temperare* to set bounds, keep within limits, a derivative of *tempus, temporis* a division, section, a portion or period of time—whence TEMPOR-. Most TEMPOR- words passed through the adjective *temporarius* temporary, seasonable, adapted to time and circumstance. Also, temper, temperance, temperature, tempo (music). Tempest is from yet another derivative, *tempestas,* a space or period of time, weather, bad weather, storm.

TEN- from *tenēre* to hold, own, keep, restrain, hold back. TIN- is in prefixed words, as continent (from *continens, -entis,* the present participle of *continēre* to hold together, from *com-* together + *tenēre*). TENT- is from the past participle *tentus.* TAIN-, which came in through F, survives in pertain, maintain (through OF, from L *manu tenēre* lit. to hold by the hand), contain, entertain (through OF, from L *inter-*). This base and the next two are all related, but the next two went their own way semantically.

TEND- from the verb *tendere* to stretch, extend, spread, attempt, strive, contend, etc. TENS- is from the past participle *tensus,* and TENT- comes from the variant past participle *tentus.* With three L bases, there are often three related English derivatives—such as, tend, tent, tense (strained); intend, intent, intense; extend, extent, extensive (from the archaic extense); distend, distent, distensible; pretend, pretentious, pretense. In other cases, there are only two, as attend and attentive (from the archaic attent). Also, tension, tendon, tendency, content, tempt. Compare tense (time), from L *tempus* time, through F *tens;* and to tender, from the base TEN- to hold, through ME *tendre* to tender.

TENU- from *tenuis* thin, fine, slender, unimportant, weak.

III. Analysis and Definition of Words

Dictionaries frequently vary in the definition of adjectives, especially in the material that signals the part of speech. EW's blanket "pertaining to," "connected with," and some others, although in many instances completely adequate to the task, may not serve all words comfortably. When students use their dictionaries, the instructor can expect to be confronted with a variety of signals, such as "of," "concerning," "having," "involving," "consisting of," "relating to," "belonging to," "inclined to," etc. These signals do not have to be used in all instances; indeed, to do so in some cases would make for some clumsy definitions. To define dissimilar (No. 12 below) as "having the character of not (being) like," is awkward. The word means "different, unlike," even "not similar," and any one or all of these should serve as adequate answers. Students are encouraged to give full answers for definitions, but when these make for wordy or otherwise clumsy responses, recognizable synonyms are, of course, preferable and should be accepted. EW's tags can more often than not be used, but sometimes another expression might be better, as in sentence No. 8. To define verbose as "full of words" should not be accepted. RHD's "expressed in or characterized by the use of many or too many words" seems...verbose. Encourage students to be on their guard and use care in their definitions. Depending on the level of instruction, the instructor must choose the depth of refinement here.

1. *de-* off + VI- way + *-ous* full of: not sincere; deceitful.

2. *col-* (*com-*) with + LOQU- to speak + *-ial* pertaining to: used in common talk; conversational; informal.

3. *col-* (*com-*) together + LAT- to carry (or bring): to put together (such as the sheets of two or more copies of a manuscript) in proper order.

4. *dis-* apart + TEND- to stretch: to swell out or stretch out by pressure from within; expand.

5. TEMPOR- time + *-al* pertaining to: lasting for only a time; of this life only; transient (as opposed to eternal), hence, earthly or terrestrial.

6. TENU- thin + *-ous* having the character of: flimsy; weak; not substantial.

7. *con-* (*com-*) together + TIN- to hold + *u* connecting vowel + *-al* pertaining to: never stopping (but see ,.ercise 4, no. 4, following); very frequent.

8. VERB- word + *-ose* full of: full of or using too many words; wordy.

9. CORPOR- body + *-al* pertaining to: inflicted on the body; bodily. (Corporal punishment, offered as a main entry in some dictionaries, also includes, in the legal sense, imprisonment and death.)

10. AQU- water + *-eous* full of: watery.

11. PRIM- first + *-al* pertaining to: of early times; original.

12. *dis-* not + SIMIL- like + *-ar* having the character of: different; not similar.

13. CRUC- a cross + -ial pertaining to: very important; decisive; critical.*

14. in- not + JUDIC- judgment + -ious like + -ly in a (specified) manner (E adverb suffix): in a manner not showing good judgment.

15. per- through + ENNI- year + -al pertaining to: lasting for a very long time; enduring; perpetual; everlasting.

16. pre- before + TENS- to stretch: a false claim; the act of pretending or alleging falsely.

17. per- completely (an intensive) + TAIN- to hold: to be connected as appropriate or in some way related.

18. in- not + CORPOR- body + -eal; not made of any material substance.

19. RECT- straight + i connecting vowel + LINE- line + -ar pertaining to: forming a straight line; in a straight line.

20. con- with + TEMPOR- time + -an belonging to + -eous having the character of (characterized by): happening at or belonging to the same period of time; contemporary.

IV. Differences in Meaning Based on Suffixes

Examples of usage follow the dash.

1. **Official** means of or having to do with an office, or authorized by an authority. **Officious** means too eager to give service or advice, or tending to meddle.

2. **Aquatic** means growing, living, or taking place in the water. **Aqueous** means containing or made with water; produced by the action of water—aqueous rocks.

3. **Equal** means identical or the same in degree, intensity, amount, size, etc; the same throughout, uniform; evenly matched—equal opportunity. **Equable** means unvarying or changing little, even or uniform—equable temperature, an equable disposition.

4. **Continuous** means extending uninterruptedly in space or time—a continuous procession of floats in the parade. **Continual** emphasizes recurrence at regular or frequent intervals; often repeated—Dancing requires continual practice.

5. **Urban** means having to do with or characteristic of a town or city. **Urbane** means having the elegance, refinement, taste, sophistication, etc., characteristic of city life.

---

*See topical section of the following lesson in IM.

6. **Judicial** means having to do with law or the administration of justice. **Judicious** means wise, sensible, well thought out, having or showing good judgment.

7. **Imperial** means having to do with an empire, or the rule of one country over another or over colonies; befitting an emperor, majestic. **Imperious** means haughtily arrogant, overbearing, domineering.

8. **Funeral,** as an adjective, means suitable for a funeral—funeral march, funeral parlor. **Funereal**, which also means suitable for a funeral (as in funereal garb), carries the additional meaning of gloomy, melancholy, sad, suggesting a funeral—a funereal countenance.

9. **Human** means having the characteristics of, or relating to, human beings (as opposed to animals). **Humane** means characterized by mercy, sympathy, or kindness.

10. **Military** means relating to the armed forces, soldiers, or war—military training; also means suitable for war, warlike—military strength; also means dominated or supported by military force—military regime. **Militant** refers only to people and means aggressive or warlike—a militant spirit; also means active in serving a cause or in spreading a belief—a militant churchman, a militant pacifist.

LESSON IX

WORD ANALYSIS: ETYMOLOGICAL DEFINITION

This mini-essay on etymological definition in EW is the first of several topical sections concerned with meaning, changing meaning, transferred senses, metaphor, radiation, and other aspects of semantics. Students have, of course, already encountered situations where their etymological analysis of a word seems quite far away from the meaning of the word in the sentence at hand. In the previous lesson at sentence 13, "very important, decisive, critical" may not seem to have much connection with the etymological meaning of crucial, "a cross," until we learn that in this instance the cross refers to a cross signpost at a fork in a road. With this extra, good news we feel more comfortable with the connection. The bad news is that extremely few dictionaries take the trouble to offer just this little bit more. Just as EW cannot offer all the meanings or situations in which certain suffixes are found, neither can it cover all the meanings (general, specific, transferred, etc.) of all the bases in EW, especially when the meanings of all the derivatives are considered. A whole page, for example, could be devoted to GEN-, GENER- in this lesson. This is where a good unabridged dictionary comes in, and students should be encouraged to familiarize themselves with these larger dictionaries, such as Random House, W3, and the OED and its New Supplement, where they will encounter more refined and detailed information.

ASSIGNMENT

I. Discussion of Adjective-Forming Suffixes

-lent   from the adjective suffix *-lent(us)*, as fraudulent from *fraudulentus* (from the stem *fraud-* of the noun *fraus* cheating) and violent from *violentus* (from *vis* force), is preceded by either *o* or *u* as the connecting vowel. The *-ulent* is found listed more frequently than *-olent.*

-ic, -tic   variously etymologized to L *-icus* and Gk *-ikos* (this suffix is also used on Greek words, for which see Greek Lesson VII). Some *-ic* words came in through L from Gk, as phonetic, physic, Philippic, gnostic, historic. Honorific, horrific, terrific, rustic, domestic, civic, soporific, and a few others are consistently etymologized to L. Many *-ic* words are directly from Gk, as somatic, diagnostic, ceramic. Some came in through F, as democratic, republic. The 't' came in through derivatives, such as rustic, from L *rusticus,* from *rus, ruris,* or from stems, such as somatic, from Gk *somat-*, the stem of *soma* body. The suffix is also defined as consisting or being (as bombastic), containing (or, as a substantive, in this case, one addicted to) (as alcoholic), and made or caused by (as volcanic).

-ary   from the adjective suffix *-arius (-a, -um)*, as *litterarius* literary, etc. Many *-ary* words have also been handed down as substantives, and these are discussed at Lesson XVIII.

-ile, -il   from the adjective suffix *-ilis,* as juvenile from *juvenilis,* and fossil from *fossilis* (from *fossa* a cave). Not often recorded in dictionaries. Compare *-ile* in Lesson XI.

II. Discussion of Bases

DOM-   from *domus* house, with DOMIN- coming from the derivative *dominus* lord, master. Domain came in through F. Dome came in through

LL *doma* roof, house. *Domus* also had transferred senses, one being native country, whence the two meanings of 1) belonging to the house, and 2) native (as opposed to foreign) in the derivative *domesticus* (*-a, -um*) domestic. *Domus* generated upwards of fifteen derivatives in Latin.

FLAG(R)- from the verb *flagrare* to blaze, burn, glow, flame; to glow or burn with passion; to suffer from; (as a participial adjective) blazing, burning, glittering, passionate, ardent—a verb that is a good example of one with extended senses. FLAM(M)- is a derivative of the stem *flag-* (=*flag-ma*), itself related to *fulgēre* to flash, shine, as in effulgent, refulgent. FLAG- produces the E flagitate and flagitious.

FLAT- from the past participle *flatus* of the verb *flare* to blow (forth), to blow on (a musical instrument). Also, reflate and -ion in the financial sense.

GEN- from *genus* race, kind, stock, family; GENER- its stem *gener-*. General comes in through the adjective *generalis*. Compare Gk GEN-, which also means kind, race, and which is related to this L base. Genus (plural, genera or genuses), generation, generator, generic, generous, genre, and gender are all from this particular L noun base. The L noun *genus* was derived from the verb base GEN- to produce, give birth to, which is to be compared to the Gk base GEN-, of the same meaning. Since, at this lesson, in their perusal of gen- in their dictionaries, students are quite likely to stumble across genesis and gene (from this Gk verb base) as well as genocide and genealogy (from the Gk noun base), the instructor might wish to introduce briefly all four bases at once—if not to teach all four at once or at least to let them know that all four exist. It would seem for certain classes ultimately unnecessary to separate the English derivatives from the two nouns or the derivatives from the two verbs.

GEN- from the verb *gignere* (originally *genere*) to beget, bear, bring forth. *Gignere* directly or indirectly brought forth some 25 words in Latin, including *genus* kind, race (see topical section on Functional Change at Lesson XIII), most having to do with the origin of something, as congenial (*com-* together + *genialis* having to do with generation) and engine (through OF *engin* skill, from -*in* into + GEN- to produce). Also, congenital, ingenuous, disingenuous, progenitor, genitive. Compare the similar Gk base GEN(E)- to produce, giving hydrogen, genesis, gene. At most levels it would seem unnecessary to separate the English words deriving from these two verb stems.

LATER- from the *later-* of the noun *latus* side, flank. Also, uni-, bi-, tri-, etc. -lateral. Compare the Gk base LATER- to worship excessively.

LUC- is from the stem *luc-* of the noun *lux* light. Lucid, elucidate, etc. came in through the derivative *lucidus* full of light, clear, bright. Also,

Lucifer, and the trade name Lucite. LUMIN- from the stem *lumin-* of the noun *lumen* light. Also, lumen, luminance, luminary, luminosity, luminous, illuminate (*in-* in).

PAR- from *parare* to prepare, make ready, put in order, provide, furnish; procure, get, obtain. Preparatory, reparation, apparatus (4th declension loan) all picked up the *-at-* from the past participle. Repair (= restore, fix), from OF *reparer,* inherited the 'i' in ME. Repair (e.g., to the busom of your family) is from *repatriare* and is a doublet of repatriate (PATRI- Lesson XV). Also, apparel (*ad-*), pare (verb) with its doublet parry. *Parare* has also produced the combining form para- meaning a guard against or a protection from, as in parachute and parasol; and in the word paratrooper, para- even means parachute.

There are other *par-* stems that could be discussed here. *Parēre* to appear, come into sight, is related to *parare* and has produced apparent, transparent ("appear through"), apparition; also, appear (*ad-*), through OF, which in turn influenced the development of the verb 'to peer.' The noun peer (a doublet of par, in all its senses), derives, through OF *per,* from L *par* equal (as adjective and substantive), which also produced compare ("equal with") and pair (through OF). Impair is from *pejor* worse (comparitive of MAL- bad). Parent is from the verb *parere* to bring forth. A great many English words opening with *par-* are from the Gk prefix *para-* of Greek Lesson VI.

SEN- from the adjective *senex, senis* old. Senior is from *senior,* the comparative degree of this adjective; senate through *senatus*; senator through *senator.* Also, senile, from *senilis.*

SERV- from the adjective *servus* serving, servile (and a noun, a slave). The verb *servare* to serve, gives the meanings to watch, keep, preserve, protect. Also, reserve, reservation.

III. Analysis and Definition of Words

1. SEN- old + *-ile* having the character of: characteristic of old age.
2. UN- one + *i* connecting vowel + LATER- side + *-al* pertaining to: proceeding from only one of two or more sides (here, nations), in a contract, agreement, transaction, etc.
3. GENER- kind + *-ate* verbal suffix (to produce): to bring into being; produce.
4. LUMIN- light + *-ary* having the character of: here, a figurative substantive, a famous person; celebrity.
5. TURB- to disturb + *u* connecting vowel + *-lent* disposed to (or *-ulent*): disorderly; unruly.

6. AQUA- water + -*tic* pertaining to: taking place in or on water.

7. CORP- body + *u* connecting vowel + -*lent* full of (or -*ulent*): large or bulky of body; obese; fat; stout.

8. PREC- prayer + -*ar* pertaining to + -*ious* belonging to (from *precarius* depending on another's will, uncertain): not secure or safe; uncertain; risky.

9. *in*- on + VOK- to call: to call or bring into effect; implement.

10. QUADR- four + *i* connecting vowel + LATER- side + *al* pertaining to: here, substantive, a plane figure having four sides and four angles.

11. GREG- a flock + -*ar* belonging to + -*ious* like: enjoying the company of others (i.e. like one belonging to a flock).

12. *de*- from (here, do the opposite of) + FLAT- to blow + -*ed* E past tense suffix: to injure or destroy the conceit or confidence of. (Most dictionaries etymologize this as *de*- + (in)*flate*.)

13. *re*- back + TAIN- to hold + -*ed* E past tense suffix: to employ (as a lawyer) by payment of a fee.

14. GENER- kind + -*ic* pertaining to: pertaining to a whole class of similar things.

15. *in*- in ("in" must be accepted here, although the *in*- prefix in this case is simply a verb-formative with no special force or meaning) + FLAM- flame + -*ed* E past tense suffix: to excite; stir up; arouse; kindle.

16. LUMIN- light + -*ous* full of: radiatir̹ ɡht; glowing.

17. *con*- together + TEMPOR- time + -*ary* pertaining to: occurring (here, written) in the present time; also, modern, in the sense of using or conforming to current ideas, techniques, style, etc., as in music and art.

18. SERV- to serve + -*ile* pertaining to: submissive; like a slave.

19. *en*- against + CHANT- to sing + -*ed* E past participial suffix: here, figurative, to delight or charm.

20. *in*- in + FER- to bring: to derive or find out by reasoning; arrive at a conclusion by premises or evidence.

IV. Divide by Etymology and into Syllables

1. (a) lumin-ary—(b) lu-mi-nar-y
2. (a) aqu-eous—(b) a-que-ous
3. (a) pre-car-ious—(b) pre-car-i-ous
4. (a) con-tempor-an-eous—(b) con-tem-po-ra-ne-ous

5. (a) greg-ar-ious—(b) gre-gar-i-ous

6. (a) un-i-later-al—(b) u-ni-lat-er-al

The difference between the Americans and British systems of dividing words might be mentioned here. The British syllabify words largely on the basis of derivation as de-mo-cra-cy, know-ledge, am-bi-val-ent, am-bi-gu-ous, de-sper-ate. Americans divide words by pronunciation, as de-moc-ra-cy (but dem-o-crat), knowl-edge, am-biv-a-lent, am-big-u-ous (but am-bi-gu-i-ty), des-per-ate.

Note that it is not considered acceptable to split a word so as to have only one letter either at the end of a line (not a-queous, but aque-ous) or at the beginning of another line (not luminar-y, but lumi-nary). It is also considered bad style to carry over two-letter word endings onto a new line: slack-en, real-ly, loss-es, etc., should not be broken.

LESSON X

DISSIMILATION

Dissimilation never took place on the grand scale that assimilation did. Only a handful of words were altered by the former compared to the many hundreds that underwent assimilation. Contrast the fact that the majority of dissimilated words affected the liquids *l* and *r* (especially in the endings -*lar* and -*ral*) with the several consonants that were involved in assimilation, such as the many guises of just the one prefix ad-: ab-, ac-, af-, ag-, al-, an-, ap-, ar-, as-, and at-.

Concerning sound change and differences, students always find pronunciation that is different from their own to be interesting, especially those differences between American English and English of other countries. The front matter of several dictionaries, some of which are now out of date but can often be found in larger libraries, have excellent essays on Australian, New Zealand, British, and Canadian English. Many books are, of course, also available on this subject. This would also be a good excuse to bring a native Brit or Aussie or a skilled dialectitian into the classroom for some good conversation.

ASSIGNMENT

I. Discussion of Adjective-Forming Suffixes

-ine   from the L adjective suffix *-inus,* as *caninus* canine, from *canis* dog. Coming from the same source (as well as from Gk), *-ine* can also be a noun-forming suffix used in various chemical senses, for which see EW Lesson XXIV of the Greek section.

-ate   from *-atus,* the past participle inflection of 1st conjugation verbs, which end in *-are.* The *-ite* is from *-itus,* the past participle inflection of 2nd, 3rd, and 4th conjugation verbs, ending in *-ēre, -ere, -ire,* as composite, opposite (*ob-*), erudite (*ex-*), requisite. This is the same *-at(e)* of Lesson II. Favorite came in through Italian. The *-ate* is also a noun suffix (from *-atus,* of 4th declension nouns), meaning the jurisdiction or office of, as caliphate.

-ant   and *-ent* are the stems *-ant-* and *-ent-* of present participles from verbs of the 1st conjugation and the 2nd, 3rd, and 4th conjugations respectively. This suffix carries the sense of having, causing, performing, showing, exhibiting, exercising, as in confident (= having or showing confidence) and competent.

II. Discussion of Bases

CUMB-   from the verb *cumbere* to lie down, occupy, lie hidden. Also, recumbent, decumbent, accumbent, incumbent, procumbent. Compare encumber and cumbersome, from OF *encombrer,* from *combre* barrier. CUB- words are from the verb infinitive *cubare* to lie down, recline, as in cubicle ("bedroom"). Compare cube, cubic, and cubism from *cubus* die, cube, from Gk *kybos* a cube.

FEDER-   is from the stem *foeder-* of the noun *foedus* compact, league, agreement, a law.

FID-   from *fidere* to trust, believe, confide in. Also, perfidy and perfidious, confide (*com-*), fiduciary.

FIDEL-   is from *fidelis* steadfast, true, faithful; this adjective derives from *fides* faith, which derives from *fidere* (above), giving fidelity, infidel, and high fidelity (faithful reproduction) and its clip hi-fi.

HER-   from the verb *haerere* to stick, cleave, adhere. HES- is from its past participle *haesus.* Compare herald, of Germanic origin.

ORD(IN)-   The basic stem is ORD- from the noun *ordo* a series, line, row, order; in transferred senses, an order, rank, or class. *Ordo* derives from the deponent verb *orior* to rise. Also, ordain (through AF and OF), order, coordinate (*com-* together + *ordinare* to set in order), inordinate ("not set in order"), ordinal, ordinance, ordinate, subordinate.

POT- from *potis* able, capable, which combined with the irregular verb *esse* to be, to give *posse* to be able to, can, whence POSS- as in possible and posse (but not in possess, from *sidēre* to sit down, settle). Potent, impotent, potential, etc., spring from *potent-*, the stem of the present participle of *posse*.

SAL- from the verb *salire* to spring, leap, jump, bound. SALT-, as in saltatorial, is from *saltus* the past participle of *saltare* to dance, a frequentative verb from *salire*. SIL- appears in prefixed words, as resilient, from *resilire* to leap back, spring back, rebound, the past participle of which is *resultus,* whence SULT-; as in consult, insult. Assault (*ad-* at + SALT-), assail (*ad-* + SAL-), both from OF, and somersault (from MF, ultimately from L *supra* over) should also be mentioned here. Compare silent, from *silēre* to be still or quiet.

SED- from the verb *sedēre* to sit, (of things) to lie still or be fixed. Reside is from *residēre* (*re-* back). SESS- is from the past participle *sessum* of this verb. Sedate and sedative, though related to *sedēre*, come from another verb, *sedare* to settle, soothe, calm, allay. SID- before suffixes, as in assiduous, insidious (from *insidiosus* cunning, deceitful, from *insidiae* [a plural noun] an ambush, from *insidēre* to sit in), preside ("to sit before"), subside, subsidy.

TERRA- from *terra* land, earth. Terrestrial is from the derivative *terrestris* earthly, worldly. Also, terrier, terrain, terrace, terrene, terrella, terrazzo (from It), terradynamics (analogically patterned on aerodynamic), terraqueous (AQU- water). Compare *terr-* and *terror-*, stems of *terrēre* (to frighten, terrify) and *terror* (fright, fear, alarm, dread, terror) respectively.

III. Analysis and Definition of Words

1. from *diffidere* to distrust, from *dis-* not + FID- faith + *-ent* -ing: shy; timid; lacking self-confidence.

2. *-in* not + *sub-* under + ORDIN- order + *-ate* being: not submissive to authority; disobedient.

3. from *concumbere* to lie down with, have sexual intercourse with, from *con-* with + CUB- to lie down + *-ine* pertaining to: a woman who lives with a man without being married to him. (This is a substantive use of this *-ine* adjective prefix.)

4. from *supersedēre* to be superior to, from *super-* above + SED- to sit + *-ed* E past participial suffix: to take the place of; displace; replace.

5. *in-* in, into + HER- to stick + *-ent* -ing: belonging to a person as a permanent quality or attribute; inborn; innate (NAT- to be born).

6. SAL- to leap + *-ient* -ing: standing out; prominent.

7. PLEN- full + *i* connecting vowel + POT- to have power + *-ent* -ing (+ *i* through the derivative *potentia* potency) + *-ary* pertaining to: (of a diplomatic agent) having full power and authority.

8. SED- to sit + *-ent* -ing + *-ary* characteristic of: sitting still too much of the time; inactive.

9. *sub-* under + SID- to sit (+ *i* from the derivative *subsidium* aid, reserve troops) + *-ary* pertaining to: subordinate or secondary.

10. from *aggregare* to add to, from *ad-* to + GREG- flock + *-ate* possessing, being: here, substantive, the sum of separate units; combined mass.

11. TERR- land + *-ain* pertaining to: here, substantive, any tract of land especially considered with respect to its natural features.

12. PUNG- to prick, sting + *-ent* -ing: having a sharp smell.

13. UN- one + *i* connecting vowel + VERS- to turn: the entirety of existing things; everything there is; the whole of reality.

14. *re-* back + SIL- to leap + *-ient* -ing: here, a figurative extension, readily recovering, bouyant, or cheerful.

15. *in-* not + ORDIN- to put into order + *-ate* being: much too great; excessive.

16. FLAGR- to burn + *-ant* -ing: outrageously noticeable; blatantly offensive; scandalous.

17. OMN- all + *i* connecting vowel + POT- to have power + *-ent* -ing: having all power.

18. *ex-* out, from + PED- foot + *-ient* -ing: advantageous rather than fair or just; suitable.

19. *in-* on + CUMB- to lie down + *-ent* -ing: resting (on a person) as a duty.

20. *con-* with + GEN- to produce + *-it-* verbal suffix + *-al* pertaining to: existing as a result of faulty development at birth; inborn, inherent.

IV. Connection Between the Base and Current Meaning

1. annals—from ANN- year: a yearly record of events.

2. ordinance—ORDIN- to put in order, arrange, regulate: a law or regulation made by authority.

3. confinement—from FIN- end, limit: the act of keeping within limits.

4. impediment—from PED- foot—literally, something that shackles the feet: something that hinders or obstructs.

5. impend—from PEND- to hang: to hover threateningly.

6. incorporate—from CORPOR- body: to unite into or as one body.

7. incubate—from CUB- to lie down: (of a fowl) to sit (i.e., lie down) on (eggs).

8. invent—from VENT- to come: to produce for the first time (i.e., to come into being).

9. jury—from JUR- to swear: a body of people sworn in to give a verdict.

10. magnate—from MAGN- great: a person of great power, influence, or distinction.

11. obvious—from VI- way: easily seen or understood (i.e., in the way or sight of one's vision, etc.).

12. prejudice—from JUDIC- judgment: a preconceived judgment or opinion. Can also be a verb.

13. punctuate—from PUNCT- to point: to mark (written work) with points (i.e., punctuation marks).

14. segregate—from GREG- herd, flock: to set apart from a group.

15. senate—from SEN- old: a governing body, assembly, or council of (generally) older, mature people.

16. travesty—through F *travestire* to disguise, from *tra-* across + VEST- garment: a burlesque (figurative, of wearing extravagant clothing, or removing the clothing, as an entertainer) translation or imitation of an artistic or literary work, usually grotesquely incongruous in style, conception, etc. Compare the doublet transvestism ("cross dress").

LESSON XI

SEMANTIC CHANGE

Students should understand that there is generally no explaining why words, such as those in the additional exercise following, have undergone semantic change. It is simply a fact of life that change takes place, in the meaning of words as elsewhere, and all that descriptive lexicography can do is simply to record semantic change. Some changes are the result of the extension of an already existing meaning, many of which show up in the sciences, for example: in electronics, the familiar socket, plug, charge, battery, distributor, terminal, and the more recent bus, grid, solid-state, pin, probe; in space sciences, the capsule, probe, vehicle, booster, nozzle; in computer science, the floppy disk, disk drive, disk pack, hard copy, hardware, environment, the acronym bit, and the whimsical nibble; in medicine, respirate (discussed in Lesson II); and hundreds of others. Other examples open Lesson XVII in IM.

Some words slide in quickly as slang (hustle, -er; crash = to sleep, or reside temporarily at; pad = one's living quarters; streak = to run naked through a public place; cruise = to go out looking for a sexual partner; suck = to be, or to be considered to be, unfair, dishonest, immoral, etc.; sick = disgusting, revolting), some of which fall just as quickly into oblivion—as some of these examples have done. Slang is discussed in detail in IM at Latin Lesson XVIII. Some words are condemned by association: one critic says because of its association with homosexuality it is "impossible to use the word *gay* anymore in any sense without hearing snickers and titters" and that "the word should be eliminated from the language." Other words demand caution in their use, or even replace   nt, such as relationship or involve/involvement, which, in the 1980s, in their infancy surreptitiously suggested sexual fooling around, shortly thereafter to graduate to overt denotation of this.

Contemporary dictionaries usually list most of the meanings that a word has had in its history but are often slow to pick up on new meanings, especially those (such as slang) that are feared may not be around very long. For thorough and detailed documentation of semantic change, the OED is the primary tool.

Additional Exercise on Semantic Change

The following words have undergone semantic change or have etymological meanings different from current meanings. The list could be used as extra practice on semantic change.

1. concert—from L *con-* with + *certare* to strive.
2. effrontery—from OF *esfronte* shameless, from L *effrons* bare-faced, from *ex-* out + *frons* (genitive *frontis*) brow.
3. panel—from OF *panel* piece, from L *pannus* piece of cloth.
4. pansy—from F *pansee* pansy, ultimately from L *pensare* to weigh, consider.

5. quick—from OE *cwic* alive.

6. slop—from ME *sloppe* a mud hole.

7. smear—from OE *smeoru* grease (a noun).

8. solemn—ultimately from L *sollemnis* established, festal, religious.

9. uncle—penultimately from L *avunculus* one's mother's brother, from *avus* one's maternal grandfather.

10. vertical—from LL *verticalis* vertical, from *vertex* highest point.

11. vest—from It *vesta, veste* vest, from L *vestis* garment.

Figurative Usage with Additional Examples

Figurative language has invaded the American language scene with such force that it is usually impossible to read a paragraph in many national magazines without encountering one or two or even several metaphors. Students' early skirmishes with metaphors are often blocked because they do not know the literal meaning of the word at hand or because they have had inadequate practice in the intellectual skill of transferring a meaning. The subject has been touched upon in Lesson I (topic VIII, Idiomatic Usage) but could be elaborated upon here.

The words in the following list, all popular in the 1970s and early 1980s, are from national magazines. Because some dictionaries are not quick (or even eager) to record a lot of figurative language, some of these words may not be in students' dictionaries. One approach to the list would be to have students check their dictionaries for coverage of some of them and then have them use the words in sentences of their own. Or the instructor could choose a few, incorporate them into short sentences or phrases and present them to the students with a request for definitions of the words as they are used. Students could also be asked to determine the original territory proper to these words from which their transferred meaning is derived.

Some of the words are used as simple similitudes and hence transfer quickly with little or no hesitation on the part of the reader, such as crutch, which means, figuratively, anything like a crutch in shape or use, or support, as in the sentence She used another student's notes as a crutch to get through the assignment. Here the figurative meaning is not that far away from the literal meaning. However, in 'to take to the cleaners' (= to cause to lose one's money or property) the connection is not so obvious, as in He was taken to the cleaners at the races because of a false tip; i.e., he was cleaned out. This is a true metaphor. Here are a few other examples of metaphorical usage:

1. He had to use his home as collateral for a loan to keep his business *afloat.*
2. ... to *anchor* the news at five o'clock.
3. Sex and politics make strange *bedfellows.*
4. A summit conference *defused* an impending war on the continent.
5. The democratic President's *honeymoon* with his new republican Congress was short-lived.
6. The city's economy received a *face-lift* when new jobs were created after previously taking a *nosedive* during the depression.
7. ... the *lion's share* of the praise.
8. The free counseling program ceased after government funding *dried up.*

afloat	drawing board	rekindle
anchor (n. and v.)	dress rehearsal	reshuffle
anesthetize	dry up	roadblock
arsenal	dry out	sacred cow
give or get the ax	easy street	salvo
backdrop	face-lift (n. and v.)	send up
battleground	field (v.t.)	sew up
bedfellows	freewheeling	shockwave(s)
beef up	fuel	shot in the arm
belt out	gear up	showcase (n. and v.)
bench mark	grab-bag	shopping list
bible	hemorrhage (n. and v.)	springboard
blizzard	honeymoon	take a bath
boiling point	tip of the iceberg	take to the cleaners
brownnose (v.)	insurance policy	tailor (v.t.)
caldron	launder	top dog
catalyst	lion's share	trademark
churn out	major league(s)	transfusion
cottage industry	nickel-and-dime (v. and adj.)	unglued
crazy quilt	nosedive	U-turn
crutch	nuts and bolts	volcanic
defuse	one-way street	wind down
derail	pay dirt	wrap up

Figurative use often involves simple prepositional phrases. Following is a list of a few which the students could be asked to give formal definitions for.

1. at (home, stake)
2. below (the belt, the salt)
3. down (the drain, the tubes)

4. in (the bag, the black, the clear, clover, the doghouse, the pink, the red)

5. off (one's nut, one's rocker, one's chest, one's back, the shelf, the wall)

6. on (the ball, the blink, the button, the carpet, the cuff, the make, the QT, the skids, the rocks, target, the town, the up and up, the wagon, one's back)

7. over (a barrel, the counter, the hill)

8. out (of the blue, to lunch, of tune)

9. under (the counter, the table)

10. up (front, one's alley, the creek)

11. with it

Depending on the level of instruction, time, etc., another exercise students might enjoy is to have them make a list of figurative expressions involving body parts, an exercise which could involve family and friends. Head (e.g., bite one's head off, come to a head, go to one's head, hang one's head, head and shoulders, head off, head over heels, head up, keep one's head, lose one's head, headhunter, headmaster, head money, headquarters, head shop, head-shrinker, etc., etc.), ear, eye, nose, tooth/teeth, arm, armpit, hand, finger, hip, leg, foot, heel, toe, even 'life' itself, all have collectively generated dozens of expressions, mostly figurative with a few having a literal meaning in use, as head over heels. This would be a good out-of-class assignment with the results shared orally in class.

A reading assignment in any national magazine should also turn up several figurative expressions. Magazines with broad, general scope usually produce many more results than specialized magazines, which generally tend to be conservative in language. Students could also be assigned to take notes during a TV news broadcast or test out their local newspaper.

There is fad and fashion in contemporary language just as there is in clothes, cars, and (other) status symbols. We throw away last year's words as we throw away last year's dress or shirt. High-schoolers (and even many college students) in certain echelons, or anyone seeking social promotions, have been quick to learn the language of their group or clique, or of the group or clique they aspire to join. Reaffirmation of status is contingent upon, among other things, the ability to recognize change when it happens and to go with it; and this means change in language as well as in attitude, clothes, gait, and whatever else it takes to gain or cement membership. Therefore, several of the words and expressions used in this lesson may well have fallen by the way by the time your class picks up EW in ±1990. This also applies to euphemism, circumlocution, clips, blends, hyperbole, acronyms, many loan words, and, of course, slang. Instructors are encouraged to update their examples in these areas as life goes on.

ASSIGNMENT

I. Discussion of Adjective-Forming Suffixes

-able* from OF *-able,* from L *-abilis,* an adjective suffix from verbs of the
1st conjugation (those ending in *-are*); *-ible* is from *-ibilis* from verbs
of the 2nd, 3rd and 4th conjugations. Variously defined in addition to
EW: suitable for (readable = suitable for reading); inclined to (peace-
able); fit to be, deserving of (enjoyable, washable, pitiable); given to,
liable to (perishable, knowledgeable).

-ile from the suffix *-ilis.* Also defined as capable of (contractile, expan-
sile), liable to (fragile).

-acious not generally listed in contemporary dictionaries. This is a compound suffix (*-aci-* + *-ous*), the *-aci-* being an adjective-forming particle from the genitive of certain nouns, as in *audax, audacis* daring,
bold, from *audēre* to be bold; or *vivax, vivacis* long-lived, from *vivere*
to live. Usually defined as given to, inclined to, abounding in.

II. Discussion of Bases

CRED- from the verb *credere* to trust, rely upon, believe (in), lend
(money). Also, credit, accredit (through F), incredible, credence,
Credo ("I believe" as first word of the Apostles' and Nicene creeds),
credo (= any formal or authorized statement of beliefs). Also, creed
(through OE), a doublet of credo.

DOC- from the verb *docēre* to teach, instruct; DOCT- is from the past
participle *doctus.* Doctor came from the derivative *doctor* a teacher.
Document came in through the noun *documentum* example, pattern.
Also, docile.

FA- from the deponent verb infinitive *fari* to say or speak; FAT- is from the
past participle *fatus.* Infant is from *in-* not + FA-. Also, infatuated,
fate. FAB- appears in fabulous (through *fabula* narrative, story), fable
(from OF *fable,* a contraction of the L *fabula*), affable (from *affabilis*
easy to speak to). FESS-, a past participle stem, is used only with
prefixes, as confess and profess (-or, -ion). FAM- is from *fama* rumor,
tradition, talk, report, a derivative of *fari,* and giving fame, famous,
infamy (*in-* without), defame. Compare fatuous and infatuate, from
fatuus foolish, idiotic, silly; fatigue and indefatigable, from *fatigare* to

---

*-ability, -ibility and *-bility* are recognized as suffixes in some dictionaries. It is a living suffix
much used today, attaching itself analogically to nouns. It is a bona fide suffix in those words
which have never had the *-able* or *-ible* adjective form. For example, we say that a car has
roadability, but we would not say the car is roadable.

weary, tire; efface (through F) and face (and its doublet facies), from *facies* form, shape.

FALL- from the verb *fallere* to deceive; FALS- from the past participle *falsus*. Also, fallacy, fallible, falsify (*-ify* to make). Compare fall, from OE *feallan*; fallow, from OE in both senses.

MOD- from *modus,* a measure, limit, boundary. Modest is from a derivative *modestus* in due measure, moderate; modern from *modo* (ablative of *modus* + *-ernus* adjective suffix of time). *Modo* assumed meanings on its own as an adverb: only, merely; (in terms of time) lately, soon, directly. Moderate (n., v., and adj.) from the verb stem *moder-* to regulate (derived from *modus*) + *-at-* verbal suffix.

MUT- from the verb *mutare* move, shift, change, alter. Mutate and mutation are from the past participle *mutatus.* Also, permutation. Compare mute, from *mutus* silent, unable to speak; mutiny, ultimately from *movēre* to move; also, mutton from ML *multo* a ram.

TANG- from the verb *tangere* to touch. TACT- is from the past participle *tactus.* TING- is in prefixed words as contingent (from the verb *contingere* to touch, from *com-* with + *tangere*), with the 'i' coming from vowel weakening. Also, tangent, tangible, tactile, tact, attain (through OF). Compare retain, through OF, from TAIN- to hold, of Lesson VIII.

TRACT- from *tractus,* past participle of *trahere* to draw, drag. Also, attract, tractable, distract, protract (-or), subtract (-ion).

III. Analysis and Definition of Words

1. *in-* not + *effabilis* (*ex-* out + FAB- to speak + *-able* able to be) easy to speak to: too great or intense to be expressed in words; indescribable.

2. from the derivative noun *creditum* a loan, from CRED- to believe + *-it-* verbal suffix: to have faith in; believe; trust.

3. *trans-* across + MUT- to change + *-ed* E past participial suffix: to change from one nature, form, or substance to another. (*Trans-* here carries more a sense of 'completely' or 'thoroughly,' reflected in the L *transmutare,* which means simply 'to change.')

4. from the derivative noun *fatum* (from the neuter past participle of *fari*) an utterance, a divine utterance, the expressed will of a god (so FAT- to speak): here, with a capital *F* and in plural, in Roman and Greek mythology the three goddesses (also called the Parcae) who controlled human life—Clotho, who spun the thread of life; Lachesis, who decided how long it should be; and Atropos, who cut it off. (Extra credit, and fond remembrance, should be extended to any student who offers all this.)

5. FALL- to deceive + -ible able to be: capable of being mistaken.

6. CRED- to believe + -ible able to be: believable; reliable; trustworthy.

7. in- not + TRACT- to drag, draw + -able tending to be, able to be: difficult to persuade, influence, or manage.

8. con- with + TING- to touch + -ent -ing: depending on something uncertain; conditional.

9. GEN- to produce + -it- verbal suffix + -al pertaining to + -ly E adverb suffix: by means of the sex organs; in a manner pertaining to the sex organs.

10. in- not + TANG- to touch + -ible able to be: not capable of being touched.

11. de- down + SPIC- to look + -able able to be, tending to be—these two definitions are not generally stro   enough for many dictionaries; more like provoking: despised; c. .temptible.

12. from assimil(ate) (ad- to + SIMIL- like) + -able able to be: here, figurative, capable of being absorbed into a nation and adapting to its customs and general lifestyle, said, for example, of immigrants.

13. in- not + contro- against + VERT- to turn + -ible able to be: not capable of being denied, opposed, or changed.

14. from diffamare to spread evil reports about, from dis- in different directions + FAM- to speak (rumor is better here): to speak evil of; attack or harm the reputation of; slander; libel.

15. EQU- even + -able tending to be: unvaried; even.

16. FALL- to deceive + -acious tending to, being apt or likely to: deceptive or misleading; or, logically unsound or erroneous.

17. im- not + MUT- to change + -able tending to: not tending to change; never changing.

18. DOC- to teach + -ile able to be: easy to manage or control.

19. TEN- to hold + -able able to be: capable of being defended.

20. from obsessum, past participle of obsidēre in the (transitive) sense of to beset, haunt, occupy, fill, from ob- by, against + SID- to sit, settle + -ed E past participial suffix: to keep one's attention to an unreasonable, illogical, or unhealthy extent.

IV. Original or Etymological Meanings

1. cancer—a crab, or tumor.
2. eradicate—to pull up by the roots, root out.
3. flourish—(of flowers) to bloom, grow luxuriantly.

4. focus—a hearth, a fireplace in a house.
5. gladiolus—from *gladiolus* iris, a diminutive of *gladius* a sword.
6. gland—an acorn.
7. insult—to leap, prance, or spring upon.
8. muscle—from *musculus* a little mouse, a diminutive of *mus* mouse.
9. pastor—a herdsman, a shepherd.
10. remorse—to bite again.
11. scruple—from *scrupulus* a sharp stone, from *scrupus* a sharp stone.
12. seminary—a plantation, a nursery.

LESSON XII

ASSIGNMENT

I. Discussion of Adjective-Forming Suffixes

-itious from *-itius* and *-icius,* originally *-icius,* the appearance of 't' arising from a confusion with 'c' in LL and ML manuscripts (OED), as in fictitious, from *ficticius.* Defined in some dictionaries as having the nature of, as fictitious (= having the nature of fiction). Called a combining form in some dictionaries.

-id from the adjective-forming suffix *-idus,* as *frigidus, rapidus,* and *humidus.* Frigid is really the stem of the adjective *frigidus*; as with rapid, humid, horrid, placid, rancid, torpid, torrid.

-ulous from the adjective-forming suffix *-ulus,* as *tremulus* and *garrulus*; also from the suffix *-ulosus* as *fabulosus* (= fabulous) and *nebulosus* (= nebulous). Not recorded in all dictionaries. The suffix *-ulose* is generally considered a variant, as granulose and heptulose.

II. Discussion of Bases

AC(U)-, ACR- from the adjective *acer* sharp, with ACR- coming in through the stem *acr-.* The root *ac-* in Latin whelped some twenty different words in that language. The noun *acetum,* meaning vinegar, provides the base ACET-; the combining form *acet(o)-* (= acetic acid or acetyl), itself has spawned, another twenty or so words into English. Also, acerbic, acetic (acid), acrimony, acuity, acumen, acupuncture.

CAD- from the verb *cadere* to fall; CAS- is from *casus*, its past participle. CID- is used in prefixed words, as accident (from the assimilated verb *accidere*, from *ad-* to + CAD-), incident, deciduous, and recidivism. Also, casualty, casual, case (= an example or instance), casuist (-ic, -ics, -ry).

CAP- from the verb *capere* to take, seize; CAPT- is from *captus*, the past participle. Both CIP- and CEPT- are used in prefixed words, as in recipient and except. CEIV- forms came in via French. Also, accept, conceive, deceive, perceive, preconceive, susceptible, perceptive. Compare captain, capital, decapitate, precipitate from CAPIT-, CIPIT- head.

FAC- from the verb *facere* to do, make; FACT- from *factus*, the past participle; FIC- and FECT- are used in prefixed words, as in efficient and perfect. Also, affect (*ad-* to + FECT-), confection, defect, disinfect, infect, prefect, artifice, artificial, artifact, suffice and sufficient (*sub-* + FIC-).

FLOR- from the noun *flos, floris* a flower, blossom. Also flower and flour (through OF *flour*), and the figurative deflower.

FLU- from the verb *fluere* to flow; FLUX- from *fluxus*, its past participle. Effluvium is a direct lift (with *-ia* and *-iums* plurals) from *effluvium* a flowing out; fluvial from *fluvius* river—both of which derive from *fluere*, whence FLUV-. FLUOR(O)- is from another derivative, *fluor, fluoris* a flowing. *Fluere* also provided the derivative *fluctus* a wave, or a wave of the sea, which in turn provided the verb *fluctuare* to be in a wave-like motion, to move up and down, which in turn provided the noun *fluctuatio* a moving backwards and forwards, and (in transfer) indecision—landing us finally at the E fluctuate (-ion). *Flumen* (from *fluere*) gives us flume; and the adjective *fluidus* (also from *fluere*) gives fluid. Also, affluent (-ce), effluent, superfluous, and the doublets influence and influenza.

FOLI- from the stem *foli-* of the noun *folium* leaf. Also, foliage, foliate, folic acid (= a constituent of vitamin B complex, found in green leaves and animal tissue).

NOC- from *nocēre* to hurt, injure, harm, a derivative of *necare* to kill, slay, whence NEC-. *Noxa* (from *nocēre*) harm, injury, damage gives the base NOX-. The base NIC- appears with prefixes, as pernicious (*per-* completely). Also, innocuous.

NOV- from *novus* new. Also nova (feminine of the adjective *novus*) with its two plurals novae (L) and novas (E), supernova, novocaine (*nov-* + *cocaine*) (Novocaine is the trademark for this compound), Nova Scotia (L for New Scotland), novella (through Italian).

III. Analysis and Definition of Words

1. *in-* + CRED- to believe + *-ulous* tending to: not willing (or not ready) to believe; skeptical; unbelieving. (It is suggested that the difference between this word and 'incredible' be pointed out here, as these two words are often confused.)

2. *de-* down, apart + CAD- to fall + *-ent* -ing: falling into an inferior condition; growing worse; declining; decaying; degenerating.

3. *dis-* away + TRACT- to drag + *-ing* E participial suffix: to turn (the mind or attention) away from a course or direction.

4. *e-* (*ex-*) + LEV- to lift + *-at-* verbal suffix: here, figurative, to raise in quality.

5. PEND- to hang + *-ulous* tending to: hanging downward.

6. FLOR- flower + *-id* tending to: here, figurative, excessively ornate or showy (i.e. flowery) in style.

7. *ef-* out, from + FLU- to flow + *-ent* -ing: here, substantive, sewage, waste water from industrial plants, or other waste liquid that is discharged into a river or lake. (Students should be challenged to justify any other response here in view of other words in the sentence, as tottery, invalid, skin of the teeth, ravages, slump.)

8. *per-* completely, thoroughly + NIC- to harm, kill + *-ious* full of: causing great damage or harm; that will destroy or ruin; injurious.

9. FACT- to do, make + *-itious* characterized by: not natural; forced.

10. *feas-* (= FAC-) to do, make + *-ible* able to be: capable of being done or accomplished.

11. *con-* together + FLU- to flow + *-ent* -ing: flowing into one.

12. *re-* again + NOV- new + *-at-* verbal suffix (here, to make): to make like new; restore to a good condition.

13. VERS- to turn + *-at-* verbal suffix + *-ile* able to be: able to do many things well.

14. *de-* away + FOLI- leaf + *-at-* verbal suffix + *-ed* E past participial suffix: to strip (land, jungle, forest, etc.) of all foliage, as with chemical sprays or bombs so as to deprive the enemy of places to hide.

15. *per-* thoroughly + CEIV- to grasp: to become aware of through the mind; understand; comprehend.

16. ACR- sharp + *-id* tending to: sharp, bitter, and stinging to the nose.

17. *ad-* to + VENT- to come + *-itious* tending to: added as something extra; incidental; nonessential.

18. CAP- to take, seize + *-acious* tending to: capable of holding a great quantity.

19. *ef-* out + FIC- to do, make + *-acious*: having, showing, or producing the desired result or effect; effective as a means, measure, or remedy.

20. *pre-* before + CEPT- to take: a rule of action or conduct; directive; teaching; guide.

LESSON XIII

FUNCTIONAL CHANGE

All languages have mechanisms to proliferate words of different function (part of speech) from a basic root. A prime example of this in Latin is the word *gigno, gignere* (originally *geno*) to beget, bear, produce, bring forth—which, directly or second- or third-hand, begot, produced, brought forth the following: 1) *gener* a son-in-law; 2) *generalis* belonging to a kind, generic; 3) *generatim* according to kinds or classes; 4) *generator* a begetter, producer; 5) *genero* to beget, bring to life; 6) *genetivus* inborn, innate; 7) *genetrix* one who brings forth; a mother; 8) *genialis* belonging to the 'genius' of a person; hence, genial, joyful; 9) *genitabilis* fruitful, productive; 10) *genitalis* belonging to birth; creative, fruitful; 11) *genius* the guardian spirit of a man, a genius; one's taste; spirit of enjoyment, inclination; 12) *gens* a clan; 13) *genticus* belonging to a nation, national; 14) *gentilis* belonging to a clan; (as a noun) a member of a clan; also, foreign (whence gentile, genteel, jaunty, and gentle—all quadruplets); 15) *gentilitas* the relationship between members of a clan; 16) *genuinus* natural, innate; 17) *genus* birth, descent, origin; class, kind, variety. From this splendid array it is easy to spot the several words together with their varying senses that have come into English, as well as the few which never made it. Similarly with many words in English, a simple suffix changes both the meaning and the part of speech of the base word. Consider rose/rosy, screw/screwy, ration/rational, chirp/chirpy, hard/hardly. All of these are involved in functional change via inflection as well as semantic change.

English is peculiar, however, in the fact that a vast number of words are used as several different parts of speech—a true functional change, that is, with no alteration to the base word although the base word can assume the inflections of the various parts of speech in which it can perform. Here consider the word cross: (noun) cross/es, (adjective, including participles) cross/ed/ing, (verb) cross/es/ed/ing; also, content: (noun) content/s, (adjective, including participle) content/ed, (verb) content/s/ed/ing; also consort: (noun) consort/s, (verb) consort/s/ed/ing. Not only can these words function as different parts of speech, they all have in common the fact that each has a meaning (or meanings) in one part of speech that is not found in its other part(s) of speech. This is not uncommon with many words, and although this area of semantic-function alteration goes beyond the mere functional alteration in this lesson, it is an expansion that could, depending upon time and level of instruction, be introduced here.

Functional change in English is, in large part, due to historical accident. In some instances in Old English two words of a similar form simply grew up together as OE *sar*, which as an adjective meant sore or grievous, and as a noun meant soreness or pain—in ModE to give us a sore, or something that is sore. Most other instances of functional change were not this simple. After the Norman invasion of the eleventh century, English speakers—from the inevitable pressure of the French invaders who could not be bothered to learn the English inflections—began, themselves, to drop the endings of words willy-nilly so that by the time Middle English (1150 – 1500) was in full swing, many nouns and verbs had a similar appearance and began slipping from one part of speech to another. Not only that, but case endings on nouns also dropped off. Whereas in Latin it was (and, of course, still is) possible to say *Puer* (nominative) *amat puellam* (accusative), or *Puellam amat puer,* or *Puer puellam amat,* or *Puellam puer amat,* and know that they all mean The boy loves the girl, with English inflections having disappeared during Middle English—at least the important ones, i.e., those that determined case—it became no longer possible to have such varied word order. In English, The boy loves the girl is one thing; The girl loves the boy is quite another. Word order in English therefore became increasingly important. The subject-verb-object word order came, incidentally, from Latin. EW's 'stone' (in Exercise IV of this lesson) was only a noun in OE, and first appeared as a verb around 1200 (during the Middle English period), and although it went through several guises over the years, both eventually landed at its present spelling. The only way we know whether stone(s) is a noun or a verb is by the syntax. Further, the only way we know whether stoned in the following sentences is a verb or an adjective is by sense: The man was stoned to death by thugs in the alley (verb); The man had been toking for an hour and was stoned out of his mind (adjective); The man was stoned in the alley (ambiguous).

Hundreds of other words underwent a similar process. For example, screen, race, monitor, stomach, and load were originally nouns which we use freely today as verbs. Likewise permit, shake, and sink were originally verbs which we also use today as nouns.

ASSIGNMENT

I. Discussion of Adjective-Forming Suffixes

-ive   directly from L -ivus (activus active), or through F -ive. Also defined as using or reason by (as in inductive), or having to do with (as in interrogative).

-uous   not generally listed in contemporary dictionaries. It derives through OF -uous, from LL adjectives ending in -osus, from nouns ending in -us, as OF vertuous from LL virtuosus virtuous, from virtus virtue; or from the past participial adjective, as ambiguus (= ambiguous), strenuus, continuus.

-ory   from -orius a compound suffix (-ori- + -us), from nouns ending in -or as accusatorius accusatory, from accusator; and, by analogy, as compulsory (that is, without there ever having been a compulsor). Also defined as containing or expressing (accusatory = containing or expressing accusation); involving (compulsory = involving compulsion; dispensatory = involving dispensation); serving to (compensatory = serving to compensate).

II. Discussion of Bases

CERN-   from the verb cernere to separate, sift; CRET- is from cretus, the past participle. The base CERT- (from certus, the original past participle of cernere) gives certain, ascertain, certify, certitude, certificate, and the informal British clip cert ("a dead cert" = something that is a certainty)—all from the (participial) adjective certus settled, resolved, decided. Also, discrete, discreet, secrete (verb, to hide), and the other secrete a back formation from secretion. Note also metathesis in cret- and cert-; metathesis is a topical section at Lesson XXIV.

DUR-   from durus hard to the touch, harsh to the senses; tough, strong, enduring; (in demeanor) rough, rude, uncouth; etc. Most E words came in through its derivative durare to make or become hard or dry; to endure, hold out; to be hard or callous; to remain, last, continue—some senses which still endure today in endurance, durable, duress, durain, durum wheat, unendurable (person, weather, love), duration, durative; although other dur- words have dropped out, such as durance (= endurance), dure (adjective = hard, severe), and dure (verb = to endure, last, which survives only in the present-participle form, during, now a preposition).

FUND-   from the verb fundere to pour (out), scatter, squander; FUS- from fusus, the past participle. The 'o' in FOUND- came in during ME or through AF. Also, to found (to melt [metal]), foundry, confound (= to pour together), confuse (= to pour together) and confusion, refuse (verb = to pour back; noun = waste), infuse (= to pour into), perfuse (= to pour through), suffuse (= to overspread with). Also, funnel (through F). Compare obfuscate from *fuscus* dark.

NASC- from the deponent verb infinitive *nasci* to be born; NAT- from the past participle *natus*. Nature came in through its derivative *natura* birth; nature, natural qualities; (of men) natural disposition, character; the nature of things in general, the laws of nature, etc., senses which survive today. Natural came in through *naturalis* produced by birth or nature, as natural childbirth or natural food (as opposed to artificial, or enduced or grown by some artificial method or material); also, one's own (father, child, as opposed to a stepfather, stepchild, adopted child, etc.)—senses which have also been handed down. Also, nativity, nation, naturism (British = nudism), naturopathy. If anyone asks if NATO (British, Nato) comes from this base, please tell them to go home.

PEL(L)- from verb *pellere* to strike, beat; PULS- from *pulsus*, the past participle. Also, compulsion, impel, expel, repel, dispel, impulsion, etc.

PON- from the verb *ponere* to place, lay, put; POSIT- from positus, the past participle. The variant (contracted) past participle *postus* could be included here as the base POST-, giving impostor (or imposter), compost, and post (as in trading post, army post; a job; a bugle call; to post a letter—the other post, as a fence post or to post notice on a wall, is from *por*- forth + ST- to stand). Also, dispose, compote, impose, interpose, propose, suppose, presuppose—all through F. Also, composite, impound (but not either pound). Compost, compote, and composite are triplets. As a further extension of this list, *ponere/positus* derive ultimately from the verb *sinere/situs* (infinitive and past participle) to place, put down; its derivative noun *situs* a layout, position, site, has produced the English site, situate, situation.

TORT- from the past participle *tortus* of the verb *torquere* to twist, wind, wrench—which produced the E torque (in mechanics) and torques (in zoology). Also, contort, contortion, retort. As verbs, the more commonly expected forms would have been contorque, from the L verb infinitive *contorquere*—as we have inquire as a verb, not inquest; or commit as a verb, not commiss. But contorque never made it into English, although retorque(d), distorque, and distorquement did, but all had short lives. There was also once an obtortion (= a twisting, a wresting), which also aborted early.

III. Analysis and Definition of Words

1. *de-* off, thoroughly + SULT- to leap + *-ory* tending to: jumping from one thing to another; unmethodical.

2. *intro-* within + SPECT- to look + *-ive* tending to + *ness** quality: the quality of tending to look inward and examine one's own thoughts and feelings.

3. *pre-* before + FAT- to speak + *-ory* serving as: serving as a forward; introductory.

4. *dis-* in different directions + CURS- to run + *-ive* tending to: wandering, or tending to wander, from one subject to another; rambling.

5. DUR- to last + -ing E participial suffix: throughout the time of.

6. *con-* with + SERV- to save (or preserve) + *-at-* verbal suffix + *-ive* tending to: here, with a capital *C*, a member of the Conservative Party of Great Britain or Canada (which generally favors keeping things as they are or were in the recent past).

7. TORT- to twist + *-uous* tending to: inclined to twist or wind; full of twists and turns.

8. *com-* very (an intensive) + PULS- to drive or push + *-ive* inclined to: having the power to drive or urge forcefully or irresistibly.

9. *dis-* apart + CERN- to distinguish + *-ible* able to be: able to be recognized or perceived clearly. (Also spelled with -able.)

10. assimilated from *ad-* to + SID- to sit, settle + *-uous* inclined to: showing diligence or careful attention.

11. SENS- to feel + *-uous* tending to: made aware of through the senses; having an affect upon the senses.

12. CURS- to run + *-ory* tending to: showing haste and superficiality.

13. *ef-* out + FUS- to pour + *-ive* tending to: showing or tending to show too much feeling or emotion.

14. *ex-* out + POSIT- to put, place + *-ory* serving to: characteristic of a speech or writing that explains an idea, a process, etc.

15. *ob-* against + DUR- hard (through *durare* to harden) + *-at-* verbal suffix (or *-ate* possessing, being, of Lesson X): unmoved by persuasion; stubbon; unyielding; obstinate.

16. NASC- to be born + *-ent* -ing: just beginning to exist or develop.

17. *im-* into, against + PULS- to drive, to push + *-ive* tending to: acting on or tending to act on a sudden influence, direct force, or idea.

---

*As with other predictable English suffixes, students will have to look under -ness in their dictionaries, find the best definition for the word at hand and piece it on. This suffix is defined as a quality or condition (darkness = the condition of being dark; hard-headedness = the quality of being hard-headed); also, action or behavior (carefulness = careful action; cautiousness = cautious action or behavior).

18. *per-* through + SPIC- to look + *-uous* tending to: (able to be) easily understood.

19. *de-* off, from + CID- to fall + *-uous* tending to: shedding leaves each year at the end of the growing season.

20. *re-* back + PULS- to drive + *-ive* inclined to: causing strong dislike, disgust, or aversion.

IV. Words That Change Function

1. stone—(originally) noun; (here) verb.
2. front—(originally) noun; (here) adjective.
3. down—(originally) adverb; (here) noun.
4. steel—(originally) noun; (here) verb.
5. out—(originally) adverb; (here) noun.
6. black—(originally) adjective; (here) verb.
7. find—(originally) verb; (here) noun.
8. oh—(originally) interjection; (here) noun.
9. off—(originally) adverb; (here) adjective.
10. mother—(originally) noun; (here) verb.

V. Students' Examples of Functional Change

In exercise IV above the original part of speech can be guessed at with reasonable accuracy, but this cannot be done so easily, of course, if we are just handed the word—out of context. How many of us would know if such as hit and stand were originally nouns? or verbs? As an academic exercise, students could be asked to trace the etymology for the original part of speech of the words they choose. For example, paint, stand, repair, ride, walk were originally verbs. Place, load, parole were originally nouns. Choice (n. and adj.) derived from a verb. Urge students to use as some of their examples common words like these as well as words like the oh's and ah's of the crowd, which, by syntactical patterning, we simply force into another generally unfamiliar part of speech. Function shift in dialect could also be mentioned here, as 'I don't like them boys over there," where them is an adjective; or 'these here books,' or 'that there dog' in which here and there are syntactically adjectives.

Attributive nouns, and their various types and functions, could also be discussed here. The word 'snow' would be a good example to use. Consider these attributive types: snowball, snowman, snowbank, snow storm (a ball, etc., consisting of or made up of snow); snowfall (uninflected genitive, i.e. a falling of the snow); snowshoe (for walking on); snow fence (to hold back);

snow goggles/spectacles (protection against); snow gauge (for measuring); snow-blown, snow-bound (instrumental); snow-clearing, snow-making (objective, with the combination used as an attributive); snow remover, snow gatherer (objective); snow-soft, snow-bright, snow-white (Snow White) (as or like, i.e. soft as snow). Snow is also used in many special collocations that name plants and animals, such as snow-apple, snow-bush, snow-pear, and snow-pigeon, snow-sparrow, snow-flea, snow-mouse.

LESSON XIV

ASSIGNMENT

I. Discussion of Noun-Forming Suffixes

-ity (-ety, -ty)   from the noun suffix *-itas*, as *gravitas* gravity, *sanitas* sanity, *societas* society, all of these being noun derivatives from *gravis* heavy, *sanus* healthy, *socius* sharing. The English suffix is also defined as the condition of, as in timidity (= the condition of being timid). The 'i' was originally part of the stem, as the stem *puri* (from the noun *purus* pure), giving purity; as with veloci + ty. At most levels it would seem unimportant whether verity (in sentence 9) was broken as ver + i + ty or ver + ity, although verisimilitude (sentence 7) must show an attached 'i', to appear as VER- true + *i* connecting vowel. The *-ety* form is used before 'i', as in society.

-(i)tude   from *-tudo*, as *longitudo* and *multitudo*, from *longus* long, and *multus* much. The 'i' came in through the derivatives.

-acy   from the noun suffix *-acia*, as *fallacia* fallacy; also from the noun suffix *-atia*, as *advocatia* advocacy and ?*atia* legacy (from the past participles *advocatus* and *legatus*); also derived from *-ate* adjectives in English, such as accurate and alternate. Some *-acy* words have come in through French. Not generally recognized as a suffix in contemporary dictionaries. This *-acy* is a variation of the *-cy* suffix, which also forms nouns denoting office, position, or rank, as in baronetcy, captaincy; the *-cy* suffix (not noted in EW) comes from various Gk endings as well as the above Latin ones (i.e., *-tia, -cia*).   .

II. Discussion of Bases

AM-   from the verb *amare* to love. Enamor (British enamour) came in through F *enamourer*, the F *amour* being an alteration of L *amor* love, a derivative of *amare*. The *-at-* (Lesson II) of amateur (F, one who loves) and amatory are from *amatus*, the past participle of *amare*.

DE-   from *deus* a god; DIV- from *divus*, a word used both as an adjective (= divine, deified) and a noun (= a god) and related to *deus*.

JOURN-   from *journal* daily (an adjective), with 'j' being an alteration of 'di' in LL *diurnalis* (giving the E diurnal, a doublet of journal), from L *diurnus* belonging to a day or lasting for a day, a derivative of *dies* day. *Dies* and E day are related through common Germanic stock.

OR-   from the stem *or-* of the noun *os* the mouth (not to be confused with the G base ORA- to see, as in panorama—Part Two, Lesson XIV; or the L *os* a bone, from the G base OST- bone, as in osteopath—Part Two, Lesson XX). *Os* also produced osculate (*os* mouth + *-cule* little—Lesson XVII + *-at-* verbal suffix), meaning to come in close contact with, and, humorously, to kiss. Oration, oratory, oratorio, etc., are from *oratus* (OR- + *-at-*) of the verb *orare* to speak, to speak formally (whence oracle), pray, beg, entreat.

PROB-   from the verb *probare* to make good, judge by an agreed standard, show, prove, as in probe, probable, improbably; from the past participle *probatus* come probation, probate, approbate (*ad-* to), reprobate. *Probare* comes from the adjective *probus* good, excellent, fine. Hence, EW's adjective 'good' and verb 'to test' here. Prove, approve, disprove, reprove, from EW's base PROV-, came in through French.

RAP-   from the verb *rapere* to seize, snatch, tear away; RAPT- from its past participle *raptus*. REPT-, before prefixes, is from the part participle of *-ripere*, as *surreptum*, giving surreptitious. Rap (= to talk informally) is a clip of rapport.

STRING-   from the verb *stringere* to draw tight together, bind, tie; STRICT- from the past participle *strictus*; STRAIN-, and its noun form *-straint*, came in through OF. Several strict/strain- pairs are, or have, doublets, such as strict/strait/stretto, constrain/constrict, etc.

VER-   from the adjective *verus* true. Veritable and verity arrived through the derivative *veritas* truth, reality: aver is prefixed with *ad-*. Average, with a questionable history, has no connection with this base. Compare, avert, aversion, revert, etc. from VERS-/VERT- of Lesson IV.

III. Analysis and Definition of Words

1. DE- a god + *-ity* state of: a god.

2. RECT- straight + -(i)tude quality: moral integrity; honesty.

3. STRING- to draw tight + -ent marked by: marked by strictness (concerning rules and standards).

4. LUC- light + -id inclined to + -ity quality of: clearness of thought or perception.

5. trans- across, through + LUC- to shine + -ent -ing: letting light through.

6. in- not + EQU- equal + -ity state (or instance): a state of being unfair or unjust. (This could also be defined as an instance of unfairness.)

7. VER- true + i connecting vowel + SIMIL- like + -itude quality of: an appearance of truth.

8. in- not + ex- out + OR- to plead -able able to be + -ly E adverb suffix: in a relentless and unyielding manner; implacably; unrelentingly; relentlessly.

9. VER- true + -ity an instance of: a truth or a true statement.

10. FORT- strong + -itude quality of: courage in the face of pain, danger, adversity, etc.

11. PRIM- first + -acy condition: the fact or condition of being first.

12. PROB- good + -ity quality of: the quality of being good; honesty, uprightness.

13. sub- under + REPT- to seize + -itious characterized by: secret and unauthorized; clandestine.

14. ACU- sharp + -ity quality: quality or fact of being perceptive; sharpness; acuteness.

15. from efficere (ex- + facere) to accomplish, from ex- completely + FIC- to do, make + -acy quality: the power to produce the desired effect.

16. a- (ad-) to + FA- to speak + -(a)ble tending to + -ity quality: courteous and considerate manners.

17. ANIM- feeling + -os(e) full of + -ity quality: strong and active dislike.

18. RAP- to seize + -acious tending to: given to plundering and seizing by force.

19. in- not + FIRM- strong + -ity state of: the state of being in bad health; weakness; debility. (It could be pointed out that an infirmary—from infirmaria quarters for the sick—cares not only for the infirm but also, by extension, the injured. This -ary is in Lesson XVIII.)

20. AM- to love + -ity state of: friendly relations.

IV. Degeneration of Meaning

Students will find that whereas most of these earlier, or etymological, meanings have long ago disappeared from current common vocabulary (some perhaps not so long ago as guessed, as with gossip, for which the OED has an entry in the original meaning as late as 1886), some dictionaries carry, together with the modern sense of some of these words, the original word with no time marker, as with grandiose and egregious. Students will, of course, have to understand the sequencing of entries in their dictionaries. WNCD, for example, has older meanings first, then graduates to modern meanings. Some dictionaries do the reverse—they list modern meaning(s) first and older meaning(s) last.

1. artificial: (once) displaying special art or skill; also, cunning or deceitful—(now) not natural; feigned; hollow; pretended.
2. boor: (once) a peasant; countryman—(now) a rude or ill-bred person.
3. churl: (once) a man; a countryman or peasant; (now) a rude or ill-bred person.
4. egregious: (once) distinguished; remarkable; excellent—(now) outrageous; flagrant.
5. gossip: (from OE *godsipp,* from *god* God + *sibb* a relative, i.e., a grandparent) (once) a godparent; a sponsor—(now) idle, often untrue, talk about others and their affairs.
6. grandiose: (once) characterized by grandness or greatness—(now) showy; pompous.
7. knave: (once) a boy—(now) a dishonest person; a rogue.
8. sensual: (once) pertaining to or perceptible by the senses (etymological: to know, perceive, feel—(now) indulging too much in the pleasures of the senses; lewd; lustful.
9. slave: (once) a Slav—(now) an enslaved person.

V. Elevation of Meaning

1. frank: (once) without restriction; free; also, liberal or generous; originally a Frank; a freeman—(now) free in expressing one's thoughts, feelings, etc.; also, clearly manifest or undisguised.
2. marshal: (once) a groom, a person in charge of horses—(now) an officer of various kinds, as a police officer or army officer; a chief of police; also, a person in charge of ceremonies, etc.
3. minister: (once) a servant—(now) a clergyman; a person in charge of a department of a government; a diplomat ranking below an ambassador.

4. nice: (once) foolish; stupid; simple-minded; lascivious; wanton; affectedly modest (etymologically, ignorant, from *ne-* not + SCI- to know)—(now) pleasing; agreeable, satisfactory; gratifying; enjoyable; very fine; minute; subtle; precise; exact.

5. shrewd: (once) mischievous; abusive; dangerous (etymologically, malignant, ill-disposed, originally *shrewed*, past participle of ME *shrew* to scold or curse)—(now) marked by clever discerning awareness and hard-headed acumen; having a sharp mind; showing a keen wit; given to wily or artful ways or dealing.

6. sturdy: (once, in Middle English) reckless; violent; stubborn; from OF *estourdir* to stun or daze—(now) hardy; substantial; firm; resolute.

LESSON XV

CHANGE FROM ABSTRACT TO CONCRETE, AND VICE VERSA

Many examples can be used here. Several -ion words function both as abstract and concrete, such as concession, possession, organization, imposition. Also, horror: fear or dread in the abstract; someone or something to be feared, as concrete (He is the horror of the neighborhood). Also, substantives from verbs, such as dread: He turned back in dread (abstract), and Sanctify the Lord of hosts ... and let him be your dread (Isaiah 8:13) (concrete). The word youth splits three ways: 1) the stamina of youth (abstract); the youth of America (collective); a youth standing on the corner (concrete). With love: Love turns the brain to mush (abstract); He was my first love (concrete). Other examples are practice, business.

ASSIGNMENT

I. Discussion of Noun-Forming Suffixes

-(i)mony from the suffixes *-monia* (as *acrimonia* acrimony) and *-monium* (as *matrimonium* matrimony). Not always listed in contemporary dictionaries. Also defined as result or condition and in this sense it often

equals -*ment* (see Lesson XVI), as in fragment (= the result of an action). Also, palimony.

-*acity*　a compound suffix, joining -*ity* (see Lesson XIV) onto the genitive stem -*ac*- of certain adjectives (as *audax, audacis; capax, capacis; rapax, rapacis*). Generally not recorded in contemporary dictionaries. Also defined as the quality of or abounding in, as in voracity (= the quality of being voracious).

-*y*　from the noun suffix -*ia* (as in *custodia* custody) and other origins. It is also a native English suffix: (a) used for pet names, as kitty and Billy; (b) meaning one having to do with, as towny and groupy; (c) meaning one of a (particular) kind of, as smarty. This English -*y* is often interchangeable with *ie*, as Billie (feminine of Billy), groupie, roadie, cutie. In some words, of course, the -*ie* is preferred; in other words the -*y* is preferred.

-*ate*　from the suffix -*atus, -us* of 4th declension nouns—either directly, through F, or by analogy. Examples are syndicate, professorate, caliphate, senate, consulate. Also, as a special use of -*ate* of Lesson II, -*ate* has a chemical sense, indicating a salt of an acid ending in -*ic*, as sulfate (sulfuric acid), phosphate (phosphoric acid).

II. Discussion of Bases

CID-　from *caedere* to strike, cut down, kill. The verb was combined with its object to give a series of words denoting 'the killer of _____ ,' as in *matricida,* the killer of (one's) mother. Another series was invented denoting 'the killing of _____ ,' as in *matricidium,* the killing of one's mother. The endings of both series are reduced in English to the combining form -cide, which carries both meanings: (a) killer, as in pesticide, insecticide; and (b) the act of killing, as in suicide (*sui* of oneself), homocide (*homo* man), fratricide (from the stem *fratri*- of the noun *frater* brother); etc. CIS- is from the past participle *caesus* of *caedere*, giving excise, incise. Also, concise, circumcision, decide, decisive. Compare the base CID- to fall, befall, in Latin Lesson XII.

MATR-　from the stem *matr*- of the noun *mater* mother; MATERN- from the derivative adjective *maternus* of a mother, maternal. Matron is from *matrona* a married woman.

PATR-　from the stem *patr*- of the noun *pater* father; PATERN- is from the derivative adjective *paternus* of a father, paternal. Patron is from *patronus* a protector, defender. Compare the Gk base PATR- father, which gives patriarch and other words that combine with Gk bases. The combining form PATR-, generally listed, is etymologized to both languages. For most classes it is probably unnecessary to separate most of the English words that derive from these two bases. To fill out the family, the instructor might wish to introduce FRATERN- and FRATR-, meaning brother, giving fraternity, fratricide, fraternal, fraternize, and the clip frat (n. and adj.); and SOROR-, meaning sister, and giving sorority, sororal, sororicide.

PATRI- from the noun *patria* fatherland, native land (ultimately from *pater*, just above). Also, expatriate. Compare the Gk base PATRI- family, clan, which gives patriot.

PATRON- from *patronus* a protector, defender, a derivative of *pater*.

SEQU- from the deponent verb infinitive *sequi* to follow, accompany, attend; SECUT- from the past participle *secutus*. Also, persecute, execute (*ex*- out + *sequi*), executive, executor, obsequies.

SOL- from the adjective *solus* alone, only, sole. Also solo, sole (= solitary). Compare SOLUT- to loosen and other sol- words, as solar (from *sol* sun), solace and console (from *solari* to console), sole (from *solea* a sandal), and others.

VIV- from the verb *vivere* to live; the past participle *victus* gives victual. Also, convivial, revival, vivify, vivisection.

III. Analysis and Definition of Words

1. from *perfidus* (*per*- through + FID- faith) unfaithful, from the phrase *per fidem decipere* to deceive by faith (i.e., to betray) + *-y* state or quality of: a state of being faithless, disloyal, or treacherous.

2. TEN- to hold + *-acity* quality of being inclined to: state or quality of holding firmly.

3. *suf*- under + FUS- to pour + *-ed* E past tense suffix: here, figurative, to spread over like a fluid or a light.

4. *ex*- from + PATRI- fatherland, country + *-at*- verbal suffix + *-ed* E past participial suffix: to force to lea   ne's country; banish; exile. (Point out that repatriate—from LL *reputriare*—means to send *back* to one's own country; it is a doublet of repair, meaning to go [to a specified place].)

5. FIDEL- faithful + *-ity* quality: the ability of a radio receiver or transmitter or other electronic device to receive or transmit signals and sound clearly and accurately. (High fidelity is usually entered as a head word, as the reproduction of such sound by radio, etc., with as little distortion as possible.)

6. *ob*- after + SEQU- to follow + *-ious* inclined to: inclined to be obedient from fear or hope of gain; servile; fawning; slavish.

7. *ob*- after + SEQU- to follow + *-y* act of: usually in plural, funeral rites.

8. POT- to have power + *-ent* -ing + *-ate* holder of an office: one having controlling power.

9. *a-* (*ad-*) toward + VER- true + *-ed* E past tense suffix: to say with confidence; to say to be true; affirm; declare; assert.

10. VIV- to live + *-acity* quality of being inclined to: the quality of being lively.

11. *in-* into + CIS- to cut + *-ive* tending to: penetrating or keen; or (if synonymous with caustic), biting, sharp, or cutting.

12. *re-* back + TORT- to twist: a harsh or witty reply, especially one that turns the first speaker's statement or argument against him; comeback; repartee (re- back, again + PART-); ripost(e) (through F and It, from L *respondēre*; a doublet of respond).

13. PLEN- full + *-ary* of, pertaining to: complete in every way; full; absolute.

14. *con-* together + FEDER- league + *-acy* quality of being: a union of states; confederation; federation; league; here, with a capital, specifically the group of eleven southern states that seceded from the United States in 1860 and 1861.

15. SANCT- holy + *-imony* quality of + *-ious* having the character of: pretending to be pious; making a show of being holy; putting on airs of godliness or saintliness.

16. ACR- sharp + *-imony* quality of: sharpness and bitterness in language.

17. MATR- mother + *i* connecting vowel + CID- (or *-cide*, the combining form): murder of one's mother.

18. PATR- father + *-imony* result: an estate inherited from one's father.

19. VER- true + *-acity* quality of being inclined to: truthfulness.

20. *re-* back + TENT- to hold + *-ive* tending to: able to remember easily.

IV. Abstract and Concrete Nouns in Students' Sentences

The sentences given here show examples of abstract and concrete use.

1. authority—(abstract) He had no authority to make such a decision. (concrete) The authorities clamped down on skateboarding on busy sidewalks.

2. scholarship—(abstract) Scholarship was highly respected in ancient Greece. (concrete) The high school's best swimmer was awarded a scholarship to the university.

3. impurity—(abstract) Impurity of the water made several people ill. (concrete) An impurity in the water made several people ill.

4. novelty—(abstract) After a few days the novelty of the toy wore off. (concrete) He bought a novelty for his sister at Niagara Falls.

5. justice—(abstract) The drab clothes he wore never did him justice. (abstract) There is little justice in a dictatorship. (concrete) The justice of the probate court died last week.

6. favor—(abstract) She was always showing favor toward her oldest child. (concrete) Favors were passed out at the birthday party.

7. divinity—(abstract) His brother went to a divinity college. (concrete) The divinities in their culture largely controlled their everyday lives.* (concrete) We didn't have enough sugar so couldn't make any divinity.

8. likeness—(abstract) There was very little likeness between the mother and her daughter. (concrete) The portrait of their grandfather was a perfect likeness.

9. brotherhood—(abstract) There was a strong feeling of brotherhood among the members of the Order. (concrete) The grey brotherhood Chaunted the solemn mass (OED).

10. inheritance—(abstract) Our goodness ... whether it comes to us by nature, or by inheritance from our parents (OED). (concrete) He came into a large inheritance from his great-uncle's will.

LESSON XVI

ASSIGNMENT

I. Discussion of Noun-Forming Suffixes

-ion   from nouns ending in *-ionis,* the stem of nouns ending in *-io,* as *conventio, convention(is),* convention. Some *-ion* words can also be a thing, as a connection (= a thing that connects), concoction (= something concocted); see more of these in the opening paragraph to Lesson XV in IM. Also carries the meaning of an assembly of persons, as in convention and congregation.

---

*Concrete here if construed as idols or other physical manifestations of worship; abstract if construed as concepts of the mind.

-*ment*   from the ending -*mentum* the result of, as *ligamentum* (originally) a bandage, the result of binding, from *ligare* to bind or tie.

-*men*   from nouns ending in -*men*, as *regimen* a directing, a guiding (now also a set of rules), from *regere* to rule. Not generally listed in contemporary dictionaries.

II. Discussion of Bases

CRE-, CRESC-   from the verb *crescere* to come into existence, arise, grow; CRET- from the past participle *cretus*. Also crescendo (a loan word from Italian), accretion (*ad-* to), accrue (through F; assimilated in L from *ad-* to), increase and decrease (the 'ea' came in through the F 'ei' alteration of the L). Compare discrete and discretion (from *discretus,* past participle of *discernere* to separate, distinguish), and secret, secrete, and secretion (from *secretus*, past participle of *secernere* to set apart)—all from *cernere* to separate. This CRE- base is connected with the verb *creare* to make, giving create, recreation, re-creation, etc.

I-   from the verb *ire* to go; IT- from the past participle *itus*. Also itinerant and itinerary (both through the deponent infinitive *itinerari* to travel), issue (through F, from L *exire* to go out, from *ex-* + *ire*).

JUG-   from the noun *iugum* a yoke or collar on the necks of work animals; (of men) a pair, a couple; bond, union; crossbar, the beam of a pair of scales, etc. This is the primitive base from which the verb *iungere* (to connect, join, unite) derived, whence JUNCT- its past participle. The 'n' in this verb is a verbal infix. JOIN- is from the OF *joindre*; JOINT- from its past participle *joint.* Also, join, conjoin, disjoint, disjunct (-ion, etc.), enjoin, injunction.

LEG-   from the verb *legere* to gather, pick, read, peruse; LECT- from the past participle *lectus*; LIG- is used only after prefixes as in eligible (from *eligere*, from *ex-* from + *legere*). Also, lecture, lectern, illegible, legion, legume. Compare legate and legation from *legare* to bequeath; and legal, etc., from *lex, legis* law.

MON-   from the verb *monēre* to remind, admonish, warn. Also, admonition, monition, monish. Compare money and monetary from *moneta* mint, money.

SOLV-   from the verb *solvere* to loosen, untie, free, solve, explain; SOLUT- from the past participle *solutus*. Also, solvent, dissolve, resolve, resolution, dissolution.

III. Analysis and Definition of Words

1. *pre-* before + *di-* apart + LECT- to choose + -*ion* act of: a tendency to think favorably of something; partiality; preference.

2. ACU- sharp + -*men* the state of: keenness of perception; superior mental discernment.

3. *con-* together + JUNCT- to join + -*ion* act of: the act of joining together.

4. ANIM- mind, spirit + *ad-* to + VERS- to turn + -*ion* act of: harsh, unfair, or ill-natured criticism.

5. *in-* not + PROB- good + -*ity* quality or state: lack of integrity or moral principles; dishonesty; wickedness.

6. *ac-* + CRET- to grow + -*ion* result: the product of growth or enlargement.

7. *sed-* apart + IT- to go + -*ion* act of: incitement or insurrection against lawful authority.

8. *trans-* across + I- to go + -*ent* -ing: passing soon; not lasting.

9. CAP- to hold + -*acity* the quality of being inclined to: the ability to do; mental ability; competency.

10. *re-* back + SOLUT- to loosen: characterized by firmness and determination; determined, firm; or, bold. (It could be pointed out here that clarion in this sentence is related to clear, through OF, and clarity, both from L *clarus* bright, clear.)

11. *ad-* to + MON- to warn + -*it-* verbal suffix + -*ion* act of: a warning against fault or oversight.

12. SOL- alone + *i* connecting vowel + LOQU- to speak + -*y* act of: the act of talking as if alone; or, an utterance or discourse by one who is disregardful or oblivious to others present.

13. *pro-* forth, forward + FUS- to pour + -*ion* result of: great abundance.

14. *in-* in + CRE- to grow + -*ment* result: an increase in money.

15. *co-* together + HER- to stick + -*ent* -ing: here, figurative, logically connected, united, or congruous. (It could be pointed out here that coHERent/-ence is usually used figuratively, and coHESive/-ion is generally used literally.)

16. from *firmamentum* a means of support, from FIRM- strong + *a* connecting vowel + -*ment* result of: here, figurative, sky. (The 'a' came in through the infinitive stem *firma(re)* to strengthen.)

17. *pre-* before + MON- to warn + -*it-* verbal suffix + -*ory* tending to: giving warning beforehand.

18. *ad-* to + JUNCT- to join: something, unnecessary but helpful, added to something else; an accessory.

19. *ambi-* around + IT- to go + -*ion* state of: a strong desire for success, fame, wealth, power, or other position or distinction.

20. from *complēre* to fill up (*com-* + PLE-) + *-ment* product of result of: the number required to provide something with all necessary parts, elements, steps, etc.

IV. Words Often Confused

1. **Adverse** means hostile or unfriendly—adverse criticism; also unfavorable, harmful, injurious—adverse circumstances. **Averse** means having a strong dislike, opposed, unwilling—Cowardice made him averse to fighting.

2. **Compulsive** means compelling or coercive; that compels (active)—a compulsive desire to eat. **Compulsory** means compelled or required (passive)—a compulsory attendance at school.

3. **Congenital** (literally, born with) means present at birth, inherent. **Congenial** (literally, together in spirit) means having similar tastes and interests.

4. **Discrete** means separate or distinct from others—a discrete hi-fi component. **Discreet** refers to the showing of good judgment in action or speech, prudent.

5. **Illicit** is an adjective and means unlawful or not permitted. **Elicit** is a verb and means to entice (information) from someone, to draw out in a skillful, perhaps manipulative, way (something that is being held back).

6. **Imminent** means likely to happen or occur soon—the imminent death of his old dog. **Immanent** means existing or remaining within, inherent—His religion is immanent in nature.

7. **Ingenious** means clever, skillful, good at making or inventing— Mozart was an ingenious boy wonder. **Ingenuous** means sincere, frank, or open—Very young children are innocent and ingenuous.

8. **Lurid** means glaring in brightness, especially in a red or fiery color; also, figuratively, ghastly or terrible—lurid crimes, lurid tales. **Livid** means having a dull grayish color, discolored by bruising, black and blue; also, figuratively, very angry or enraged.

9. **Presumptuous** means forward, bold and daring beyond normal limits, impudent, presuming (active)—a presumptuous remark. **Presumptive** means based on probability, presumed (passive)—a presumptive inheritance of an estate (i.e., an inheritance that is presumed or likely to come about).

10. Both words are connected with the senses. **Sensuous**, always positive and favorable, suggests a fine sensitivity to beauty, art, etc., as perceived through the senses and feelings—a sensuous delight in listening to

Bach. **Sensual** is especially concerned with the physical appetites and often carries a negative or perhaps uncomfortable implication of lewdness or lust—He had a sensual interest in his teacher.

11. **Tortuous** denotes twisting, turning, winding, or bending—a tortuous little mountain road. **Torturous** means full of, involving, or causing torture—He suffered torturous agony with his infected wisdom tooth.

12. **Turbid** (TURB- to disturb) means not clear, or clouded with mud—a turbid creek after a storm; also, figuratively, confused or not organized—a turbid examination paper. **Turgid** (from L *turgere* to swell) means swollen or puffed out, bloated, distended; also, figuratively, using long, unusual words and complex, embellished style; pompous; bombastic—a turgid diatribe of criticism.

LESSON XVII

CHANGE OF MEANING DUE TO CHANGING CONCEPTS

The prefatory section in EW at this lesson is concerned primarily with words that were originally associated with science but which now, with those scientific ideas discarded, have changed their meaning. In the 1970s and 1980s, a kind of reverse process took place, i.e., some common (non-technical) words never before associated with science have assumed an additional, scientific sense. In high-energy physics one speaks of flavor, strange, charm, beauty, up, down, bottom, top, color, red, white, and green; in biochemistry there is sentence, word, and synonym; a slingshot and time-line in aerospace; a plume in geology; and singularity and wormhole in astronomy. Other, open collocations include sticky ends (molecular biology); black hole, white hole, event horizon, blue shift, red shift, bow shock (astronomy); and a fuzzy set (mathematics).* Some of these words have, obviously, been plucked from the general vocabulary with an air of whimsy.

---

*A few of these examples are taken from *The Second Barnhart Dictionary of New English*, Barnhart/Harper & Row, 1980.

ASSIGNMENT

I. Discussion of Diminutive Suffixes

-cule   represented by the stem *-cul,* as in *minusculus* somewhat small; *particula* a small part, particle; and *avunculus* uncle, diminutive of *avus* grandfather. Not listed in all dictionaries. The *-cle* is a (frequently F) reduction.

-el   from various sources, as the L *-ell-* (*novellus* novel, *panellus* panel); the F *-ele* (*tonele* tunnel, *gravele* gravel); from L *-icul-* (*feniculum* fennel). Morsel is a direct lift from OF (from *mors* a bite). Also, runnel. Many *-el* words are not connected with this suffix, as brothel, drivel, funnel, carrel, barrel. Not listed in most dictionaries.

-il   ultimately from the diminutive suffix *-illus*, as *codicillus* a short writing, or *pupillus* an orphan, ward, or minor. Not listed in contemporary dictionaries as a suffix, although *-il* is occasionally found as a variant of *-ile* (Lesson IX).

-ole, -ule   from, respectively, the adjective stems *-ol-* (as *aureolus* golden, in reference to small objects, from *aureus* golden), and *-ul-* (as *capsula* a little chest, from *capsa* a box or case, as for books—now capsule). Vacuole came in through F. Formule, an older English word, competed for a while with the original L *formula* but lost out.

II. Discussion of Bases

FERV-   from the verb *fervere* to boil, seethe. Derived from this is the L noun *febris* (a contracted alteration of *ferbris*), meaning 'fever' and which came into OE as *fefer*, ended up in ModE as fever.

FRANG-   from the verb *frangere* to break, shatter; FRACT- is from *fractus,* its past participle. Also, fragile (through *fragilis*), infrangible, infract, infraction, refract (-ile, -ion, -ive, -ometer, -ory), fragment, fracture. FRING- only after prefixes, as infringe. Compare fringe, from the plural noun *fimbriae* fringe, border.

GRAN-   from the noun *granum* grain, seed. Also, granule, granulate, and the combining form granul- (= concerned with granules or granulation).

MINOR-   from *minor,* which is the comparative degree of the adjective *parvus* small; MINUS- from *minus,* which is the neuter form of *minor*; MINUT- comes in through *minutus*, the past participle of the verb *minuere* to diminish or make smaller. MINIM- (from *minimus*, superlative degree of *parvus*) might also be included here, giving minim, minimize, minimal.

PATI- from the deponent verb infinitive *pati* to suffer, experience, undergo; PASS- is from the past participle *pass(us sum)*. Also, compassion, dispassionate, compatible.

QUIR- from the verb *quaerere* to seek, demand, require, ask, etc.; QUISIT- and QUEST- are from the past participle *quaesitus* ('ae' is reduced to 'e'), with QUISIT- being used after prefixes. QUIR- is also used only after prefixes, as inquire, require, acquire. Also, query, request, inquisitive, acquisition, quest.

SEC- from the verb *secare* to cut; SECT- from the past participle *sectum*. SEG- is a variant form of SEC-, with the voiceless /k/ going to the voiced /g/. Also, transsect, resect.

III. Analysis and Definition of Words

1. MINUS- small + *-cule* little: very small. (Students should be cautioned against the erroneous analogical miniscule, which is built on the popular combining form mini-, a clip of miniature.)

2. *ex-* out + QUISIT- to seek: of rare and highest excellence.

3. *trans-* across + SECT- to cut + *-ion* act or process of: the act or process of cutting across; a cross section.

4. *in-* not + *cor-* very (intensive) + RIG- to rule + *-ible* able to be: bad beyond punishment; impervious to punishment. (Impervious: *im-* + *per-* + *VI-* way.)

5. *re-* back + FRACT- to break + *-ion* result of, or (preferably) process of: the process of bending a ray of (here) light when it passes at an angle from one medium into another of different density.

6. *re-* back, again + QUISIT- to ask + *-ion*: an authoritative or formal request for something to be supplied.

7. *com-* with + MOD- measure + *-ious* full of: having plenty of room; spacious; roomy; large. (Here, a pun.)

8. *pro-* forth + GEN- to produce + *-y* result of: here, figurative, something that is produced as the result of something else.

9. *re-* back + VENU- to come: a source of income.

10. *com-* with + PASS- to suffer + *-ion* state of + *-ate* possessing: showing or having pity for the distress or suffering of another, usually including a desire to help.

11. AC- sharp + *-id* tending to + *-ulous* tending to (from *acidulus* sourish): here, figurative, harsh or caustic.

12. CANT- to sing + *-icle*: here, a short song.

13. *ap-* (*ad-*) to + PROB- to prove + *-at-* verbal suffix + *-ion* act of: approval; praise; commendation.

14. *di-* (a variant of *de-*) thoroughly (intensive) + MINUT- smaller + *-ion* act of: a lessening; reduction; decrease.

15. from *iugulum* collarbone, throat, neck; from JUG- a yoke + *-ul(e)* little + *-ar* pertaining to: of (or pertaining to) the neck or throat.

16. *ad-* to + JOURN- day: to postpone (suspend, put off) until a later time.

17. CUR- care + *-ette* little: a small, scoop-shaped surgical instrument used for scraping away and removing tissue from the wall of a body cavity.

18. *in-* not + *com-* with + PATI- to suffer + *-ible* able to be: not capable of being used together without special modification or adaptation. (Few dictionaries in 1985 had a machine sense, even of 'compatible'; allowance should be made for this in students' answers.)

19. *di-* apart + SECT- to cut: to cut apart so as to examine the structure, parts, etc.

20. *-in* not + FRANG- to break + *-ible* able to be: here, figurative, not able to be interrupted (i.e., broken).

IV. Words Often Confused

1. **Choler** is the state of being irritable or angry. **Cholera** is a gastrointestinal disease.

2. **Jovial** means good-natured. **Jovian** means pertaining to the god Jove.

3. Both mean containing mercury, which is an exclusive definition of **mercuric. Mercurial** has the added figurative sense of being either sprightly and agile, or fickle and changeable.

4. **Sanguine** means hopeful, confident, cheerful; also, having a healthy red color, as of the cheeks. **Sanguinary** means bloody or bloodthirsty.

5. **Saturnine** means gloomy, glum, morose (the planet Saturn was supposed to make those born under its sign morose). A **saturnalia** is any time of revelry or unrestrained celebration.

LESSON XVIII

EUPHEMISM AND SLANG

Taboo deformation has remained fairly steady over the years without much change. Circumlocution appears as an effort, generally, toward exclusivity, and writers of circumlocutory jargon of, for example, the fields of psychology and linguistics are well aware that a lot of their language is by and large unintelligible to the man on the street—as it is meant to be.

Slang

As an opposite to euphemism, slang could also be introduced in this section. Both of these share three characteristics, two of them antithetical:
1. Both a euphemism and a slang word have to be a synonym for another word. If the euphemism or slang word is the only lexeme for a person, thing, activity, etc., then the word is not a euphemism or a slang word.
2. A euphemism attempts to *raise* the standard of the person, thing, etc., and make it more dignified. Slang attempts to *lower* the standard or dignity of the activity, etc.
3. Euphemism has an element of complimentariness and sometimes evasiveness. Slang has an element of the offensive and is often very direct.

For example:

Euphemisms (of varying degree): reformatory, correctional institution, community home (British)
Common words: prison, jail, penitentiary, reform school
Slang words: can, cooler, pen, pokey, stir, big house, slammer, up the river (i.e., to or in prison).

The following list contains additional examples of euphemisms/common words/slang which could be discussed or made into an exercise. Perhaps both instructor and students could add to these examples.

1. senior citizen, oldster, old-timer, golden-ager, geri.
2. sanitation engineer, garbage man/collector, trash man.
3. roommate, housemate, cohabitee, live-in lover.

94

4. correctional officer, prison guard, screw (prison slang). Also, in some prisons, inmates and prisoners are referred to as residents.
5. adult bookshop/store, pornographic bookstore, smut shop.
6. lover, boyfriend, paramour, sugar daddy, beau, flame, steady, sweetheart, mistress, girlfriend, main squeeze.

Slang is generally restricted to things and activities that are illegal (as drugs and crime), private (sex, toilet), and to people, things and activities that, in varying degrees, we feel hostility toward or superior (and even inferior) to. Anything, for example, can be (from top to bottom, more or less) unpleasant, disagreeable, worthless, rotten, baloney, claptrap, stinking, a drag, gross, a piece of junk, crap, bull, on down into the depths of the illustrious quadriliterals—where an old, abandoned car being called a piece of junk is one thing, and a fellow-student's science project being called a piece of junk is quite another. But not all derogatory words are slang. Worthless is derogatory in many contexts (Our governor is worthless), but is not slang. Drag (My date last night was a drag) is both derogatory and slang. Weed, pot, joint, roach, toke, and reefer (all associated with marijuana smoking) are all slang but are not derogatory.

Negative slang reaches its full flower in our derogatory names for people who are sexually deviant or are otherwise considered socially unacceptable or unconventional, and for minority groups and foreigners. The degree of derogation depends, in many instances, upon context, attitude, tone of voice, and such; for example, the otherwise harmless appelative Taffy (= Welshman) can be colored when a swear word is attached and the speaker is yelling in anger. Some words can be derogatory without being offensive; for example, many non-Chicano speakers and writers consider the word Chicano to be derogatory, but the word is not considered offensive by Mexican Americans, who apply the name to themselves. Conversely, the innocuous (even generic) Miss is considered offensive by some lesbians when applied to them, and even to some heterosexual women when the term exudes condescension. Dimwit, an example of the majority type, is both derogatory and offensive.

A discussion of derogatory/offensive slang can, when well moderated, prompt candid and honest opinions and feelings. One approach would be to request a showing of hands (with a brief discussion if one gets started) for two questions on each word from the following list: 1) Do you consider this word to be derogatory? (from the point of view of the speaker); 2) Do you consider this word offensive? (from the point of view of the person spoken to). It is recognized that many students may not be able to answer the second question from their own experience, in which case at most levels students could shop around. Another approach would be to give the students a selected number of words, have them record the label (if any) applied to each word as found in their dictionaries, and comment, in writing or orally, as to whether they concur or disagree with their findings. For the first approach, the instructor should be selective in terms of what he/she considers to be the students' general familiarity with the words—Jap, Jerry, Kraut, yid (= Yiddish), Yank, Nip (= Nipponese, i.e. Japanese), Nazi, commie, Chink (= Chinese), sheila (Australian, = a young woman), blockhead, dunce, jerk, egghead, loser, Jesus freak, penpusher, frog (= Frenchman), camel jockey (= Arab), mick (= Irishman), spic/spick (= a Spanish-speaking person), spade (= a Black), whitey (= a white person; used esp. by Blacks), gringo (= a foreigner, esp. one from the U.S.; used esp. by Mexicans), fag/faggot, wop (= Italian), hippie, nigger, dyke and lezzy (= lesbian), longhair, kike (= Jew), greaser (= Mexican or Latin American; also, any tough and aggressive young white male), queer, fairy, pansy, goy, greaseball (= Spaniard, Italian, Greek, or Portuguese), jungle bunny (New Zealand, = a Black), Snopes, cracker, redneck, Jewboy, fruit, spook, four-eyes, gook (= an Oriental; or, a North Vietnamese soldier or guerrilla in the Vietnam War), Polack, dago (= Italian, Spaniard, or Portuguese), bohunk, coon, white trash, codger, geri (= geriatric, i.e. an old person), schlemiel, sheeny (= a Jew), schmo/schmoe, schmuck.

This list, of course, hardly scratches the sur..ce. No doubt both instructor and students can come with other examples.

ASSIGNMENT

I. Discussion of Noun-Forming Suffixes

-ance, -ancy; -ence, -ency   ultimately fom the suffixes *-antia, -entia*. These suffixes, together with *-ant* and *-ent,* have a complicated and muddy history. Some words with these English suffixes came in through F *-ance,* as provenance and contrivance. Others are built on analogy, as abidance and furtherance (abide and further are English). Also defined as an act or a fact, as avoidance (= the act or fact of avoiding); also following EW, it can be the quality or state of being _____ant, as importance (= the quality or state of being important). It also means an instance of an action, as in reference. The suffixes *-ant* and *-ent* might be reintroduced here as noun suffixes in modern English, covering words such as agent and servant, words which began as adjectives but are now considered only nouns.

-or (British *-our*)   comes from various sources: (1) from the suffix *-or* as *horror* horror, from the base horr-, as with error and pallor; (2) through French, as donor, from *doneur*; (3) from Latin nouns ending

in -*tor* as creator, from *creat-*, the past participle stem of the verb *creare* to create; (4) from other sources, as sailor, an alteration of sailer. Compare -*or* in the following lesson.

-*ary*, -*arium*   came usually either from the suffix -*arium*, as library (from *librarium*) and granary (from *granarium*); or from the suffix -*arius*, as adversary (from *adversarius*) and February (from *febrarius*). A few words came in from the suffix -*aris*, as military (from *militaris*). Usually recorded in dictionaries.

-*ory*   came in mostly through the noun suffix -*orium*, as *dormitorium* dormitory; some derived from the adjective suffix -*orius*, as directory (from LL *directorius* directorial). In some cases this suffix is -*or* + -*y*, as in oratory, from orator. The suffix -*orial* (-*ory* + -*al*) might also be introduced here, used in such words as dictatorial, pictorial, professorial, equatorial, where there is no longer (or never was) a dictatory, pictory, etc.

II. Discussion of Bases

AG-   from the verb *agere* to set in motion, drive, do, perform; ACT- from the past participle *actus*. IG- is used with prefixes, as exigency. Also, agitate (much used figuratively), act, react, retroactive, exact, agenda (on loan).

CLAM-   from the verb *clamare* to call, shout. Also, clamor, claimant, acclaim, reclaim, acclamation, etc.

COG-   from the verb *cogere* (to bring together, collect; restrict, confine; compel), from *co-* (*cum*) + *agere* (AG-) to drive. Cogitate is from *cogitare*, from *co-* (here, intensive) + *agitare*, a frequentative of *agere*. *Co-* and AG- also came together normally in the L *coagulum* a means of curding, rennet—producing the E coagulate.

DIC-   from the verb *dicere* to indicate, appoint, say, speak, tell; DICT- from *dictus*, the past participle. Also, addict, addiction, dictaphone, predict, indict, indictment, condition (from *condicio* condition, from *condicere* to agree), indicate. Compare sedition (*sed-* away + IT- to go).

GER-   from the verb *gerere* to carry, bear, give birth to; GEST- from the past participle *gestus*. Also, predigested, egest, gestate, indigestion, gesticulate, suggest (*sub-* under, next to). The adjective combining form -*gerous*, often listed, as in dentigerous, might also be introduced here. Compare geriatric (Gk *geras* old age + -*iatric* an adjective combining form meaning relating to a [specified] medical treatment).

MIT(T)-   from the verb *mittere* to send, let go; MIS(S)- from the past participle *missus*. Also, admission, commission, commit, remit, remission, dismiss, emit, emission, permit, permission, readmit, submit, submission.

SCI- from the verb *scire* to know, understand. Also, prescience, nice (*ne-not* + *scire* "not to know," i.e. to be ignorant).

SON- from the noun *sonus* sound, noise. Since sonor has never been an English word, EW's base could be expanded to include SONOR- (the base of the adjective *sonorus* resonant, loud, which derived ultimately from *sonus*), as in sonority. Also, sound (which picked up a 'u' in Middle English), resound, re-sound. Sound (= healthy) is from OE *gesund.* Compare the acronym sonar.

VAL- from the verb *valēre* to be strong, to be worth. Also, valence (chemistry) and its combining form -valent (with two chemical definitions), evaluate, devalue, invaluable, validate, and prevail (through F).

III. Analysis and Definition of Words

1. *ex-* out, from + CRESC- to grow + *-ence* here, an instance of an action (from the obsolete verb to excresce): an abnormal outgrowth or enlargement.

2. *pre-* before + *di-* apart + GEST- to carry + *-ed* E past participial suffix: to subject (food) to partial digestion through an artificial process in order to facilitate digestion by the body.

3. *en-* in + DUR- hard + *-ance* quality of: the power or ability to endure or tolerate something.

4. *com-* with + MOD- measure + *-ity* quality of: an article of trade or commerce, especially a product as distinguished from a service. (There is really no reason to insist upon 'quality of,' or 'state of' or anything else for *-ity* here since all abstract senses of commodity are now labeled obsolete, and dictionaries do not generally offer any concrete definition for *-ity.*)

5. FERV- to boil + *-or* quality or state of: strong emotional feeling; intense emotion.

6. *re-* again + NASC- to be born + *-ence* state of: a revival; rebirth.

7. *re-* back + POSIT- to put + *-ory* place for: a place where something is kept or stored.

8. *con-* with + SCI- to know + *-ence* quality: the sense of right and wrong in one's motives and conduct, generally impelling one toward right action; the ethical and moral principles (or the ideas and feelings) that control one's actions or thoughts.

9. SON- sound + *-or* state of (or SONOR-) + *-ous* full of + *-ly* E adverb suffix: in an imposing or impressive (or full or loud) style or manner.

10. *dis-* out + PENS- to weight + *-ary* place for: a place where medical aid is given (out).

11. *con-* together + FLU- to flow + *-ence* state of: here, figurative, a coming together.

12. CLAM- to cry out + *-or* state of + *-ous* full of: full of noise; loud and noisy.

13. *inter-* between + DICT- to say + *-ed* E past participial suffix: to prevent from doing something; prohibit; forbid; restrain.

14. *dis-* apart + SON- sound + *-ance* quality of being: a harshness of sound; a sound that is not harmonious or consonant.

15. VAL- to be strong + *-or* quality + *-ous* full of: full of bravery or strength of mind.

16. *in-* not + *trans-* through + IG- to do + *-ence* state of: a state of refusing to compromise; uncompromising hostility.

17. MALE- bad, evil + DICT- to say + *-ion* act of: an act of cursing.

18. CRED- to believe + *-ence* state of: an acceptance that something is true; belief.

19. *as-* (*ad-*) to + SON- sound + *-ance* quality: resemblance in sound, especially as a substitute for rhyme in which vowels are alike in the substituted words but the consonants are different.

20. CAD- to fall + *-ence* quality: rhythmic sequence or beat.

LESSON XIX

FOLK ETYMOLOGY

Folk etymology also blends over into the often humorous area of false homonyms and paronomasia (or punning). Some additional examples of folk etymology (the first four) and examples of false homonyms or paronomasia are the following*:

1. Welsh rarebit, from Welsh rabbit.
2. sparrowgrass, from asparagus.
3. hairbrained, from harebrained.
4. chaise lounge, from chaise longue.

---

*A few of these examples are adapted in part from William Safire's *On Language* (Times Books, New York, 1980).

5. harden-fast rules, from hard 'n' fast (i.e., hard and fast).

6. kitten caboodle, from kit 'n' caboodle (i.e., kit and caboodle).

7. spitting (or spitten) image, from spit 'n' image (spit = likeness).

8. from Macbeth, "...Double, double, toilet trouble."

Or, as one wit put it, a nuff is a nuff.

ASSIGNMENT

I. Discussion of Noun-Forming Suffixes

-ure   through F *-ure* from L *-ura* (as F *fracture* from L *fractura* fracture), or directly from L (as *punctura* puncture). Also, a body that performs a particular function, as legislature; also, a thing that has been ____ed, as disclosure (= a thing that has been disclosed). Other words have special meanings, as denture.

-(u)lence, -(o)lence   Not listed as a suffix in contemporary dictionaries. This is an augmentation of the suffix *-ence* (Lesson XVIII). These words came in through *-ent*, as in violent, from the genitive *violentis* of the noun *violens.*

-or   from a variety of suffixes from Latin (*-or*, as actor; *-ator,* as curator) and French (*-eur*, as donor; *-urre*, as in succor; *-eor*, as in visitor— some of these originated from Latin).

-rix   The recognized suffix here is *-trix,* from the L suffix, corresponding to the L masculine suffix *-tor.*

-and(um), -(i)end(um)   is the suffix of the neuter gerundive of verbs, with the *-a* (agenda, memoranda) being the plural; as with addendum ("that which must be added"). All -um forms are your actual Latin and take the L -a plural; but the Englished clips take the E -s plural, as in addend, subtrahend (from *subtrahere*), multiplicand (from *multiplicare* to increase many times—MULT- + PLEX-), dividend. Also, hacienda, from Old Spanish *facienda,* a direct lift from L, from FAC- to do + *-ienda.*

II. Discussion of Bases

ERR-   from the verb *errare* to wander, stray. Erratic is from the past participle *errat(us)*—ERR- + -at-. Also, err, errant, errata (neuter plural of the L past participle). Compare errand, from OE *aerende* message, which has a complicated history and obscure origin.

JAC-   from the verb *iacere* (older dictionaries and classical texts printed a 'j' when 'i' was used as a consonant) to throw, cast, hurl; JECT- from the past participle *iactus.* Also, with prefixes, inject, from *iniectus (in-* + *iactus*), as with eject, abject, deject, object, project, subject.

NOMEN- from the noun *nomen* name, noun; NOMIN- is its stem *nomin-.* The English word 'noun' (which came in through AF, where it picked up the 'u') is a contracted doublet of nomen. Also appears in the F loan nom de guerre, and the analogical nom de plume. Compare nomad (from the stem *nomad-* of the noun *Nomas* a wandering tribe, from Gk *nomas* pasturing flocks), and the (Gk) combining form nomo- custom, law, as in nomocracy, nomogram, nomography, nomology.

SCRIB- from the verb *scribere* to write; SCRIPT- from the past participle *scriptus.* Also, scribe, scribble (through the verb *scribillare*), pre- scribe, proscribe, subscribe, transcribe, script, prescription, transcrip- tion, etc.

ST(A)- from the verb *stare* to stand; STAT- from the past participle *status.* Also, instant, instance, instate, reinstate, rest (= remainder—*re-* back + ST-), stanza and its doublet stance, statistics, statue, statute, and the three doublets state, estate, and status. The verb *sistere* to cause to stand, to place, to be placed, whence SIST-, is connected with *stare*, giving assist, consist, exist (*ex-* forth + SIST-), insist, persist, resist, subsist. *Stare* also whelped *statuere* to cause to stand, etc., whose past participle *statut(us)* gives statute and the various prefixed words with the weakened form STIT(ut)-, as constitute, destitute, institute, pros- titute, restitution, substitute.

VOLV- from the verb *volvere* to roll, wind, turn around. VOLUT- from the past participle *volutus.* Also, convolve, convolute, devolve, devolution, evolve.

III. Analysis and Definition of Words

1. *re-* back + FER- to take, bring + *-endum* that which must be: the principle or practice of submitting a bill already passed by a leg- islative body to a direct vote of the citizens for approval or rejection.

2. *con-* together + JECT- to throw + *-ure* act of + *-al* pertaining to: involving or depending on a guess.

3. *re-* back + ST- to stand + *-ive* characterized by: restless; uneasy.

4. *circum-* around + SCRIB- to write: restrict; hold in by bounds or limits.

5. BENE- good + FACT- to do + *-or* one who (does): here (as opposite to destroyer), one who preserves, protects, saves, es- pecially through kindly help or financial assistance.

6. *ex-* out + ST- to stand + *-ant* -ing: still in existence.

7. *con-* together + VOLUT- to roll + *-ion* instance of: a coiling; winding.

8. PRIM(o)- (from *primo* at first) + GENIT- to give birth to + *-ure* condition of being: inheritance by the first-born son.

9. STAT- to stand + *-ure* act of: here, figurative, distinguished development and achievement.

10. NOMIN- name + *-al* pertaining to: being something in name only; not real.

11. from *superstitiosus* superstitious, from *superstitio* unreasonable ideas, superstition, fanaticism, from *superstes* standing over; living beyond—from *super-* over + STIT- to stand + *-ious* having the character of: characterized by an unreasonable fear of what is unknown, mysterious, or imaginary

12. TEN- to hold + *-ure* condition: condition or terms under which something is held.

13. *pre-* before + *re-* back, again + QUISIT- to ask, seek: something required as a prior condition to something else.

14. ERR- to wander: here, figurative, to do wrong or to sin.

15. *in-* in + FER- to bring, carry + *-ence* act or instance: that which is concluded or found out by reasoning.

16. TERR- land + *-arium* place for: a glass or plastic container in which small (miniature) plants are grown in a soil mixture; a plant vivarium. (Not all dictionaries include plants in their definition.)

17. *in-* in + FLU- flow + *-ence* quality of: the capacity or power to produce effects on others by tangible or indirect means.

18. *ex-* out + IG- to drive + *-ency* here, an instance of an action: a situation (instance) which demands immediate action or attention.

19. *per-* completely (intensive) + QUISIT- to seek: anything, such as fringe benefits or a bonus, received for work above the regular salary. (Perk, originally British, is the informal clip.)

20. *con-* together + SIST- to stand + *-ency* quality of: the condition of holding together and retaining form; firmness; stiffness.

IV. Words Influenced by Folk Etymology

1. belfry—from ME *belfrey,* an alteration of berfrey from MF *berfrei* (the 'l' appearing through dissimilation). The word originally meant a moveable tower of war. Later on it passed on to mean a watchtower, later to be the present bell tower.

2. crayfish—from OF *crevice*. When it came into ME the second syllable was confused with -*vish*, meaning fish. Its meaning is a fresh-water crustacean.

3. curtail—an alteration of the obsolete adjective curtal, from OF *curtald* cut off short, from L *curtus* short. Curtal, referring to an animal with a docked tail, has always had the stress (at least in English) on the first syllable, but the second syllable became associated, quite naturally, with 'tail' very early.

4. cutlass—originally from F *coutelas,* an augmentation of *coutel* (= *couteau* knife). The current 'cut' was but one of several perversions of the first syllable, in that the blade of this knife is curved, making it more usable for cutting than any other motion. It is a sword used by sailors on warships.

5. hangnail—from OE *angnaegl* corn (on the toe), from *ang* tight, painful + *naegl* nail; later *agnail*. The modern sense of hangnail developed in the 17th century and with it the 'h,' by association with a 'hanging' piece of flesh near a toenail or fingernail.

6. headlong—originally ME *headling,* meaning with the head first. Headlong appeared in the 15th century out of erroneous association with 'long.'

7. penthouse—from ME *pentis,* through OF, ultimately from L *appendere* to weigh, hence to hang (compare the modern 'appendage'). It meant a small building or structure attached to a larger building; hence a small house, or penthouse.

8. shamefaced—a 16th-century corruption of the OE *shamefast* meaning modest or bashful (in both positive and negative senses). The association of aspect, or facial expression, undoubtedly led to this shift of misinterpretation to shamefaced.

9. sovereign—from OF *soverain,* this word went through some 50 different spellings before landing at the present sovereign, ultimately from L *super* "above," and meaning one who has authority over another, together with the sense of ruler, monarch; hence, to reign.

10. surround—from ME *surrounden* to overflow, ultimately from L *super* + *und(are)* of waves, to rise up or surge. Syllabification no doubt contributed to its association with round.

LESSON XX

CLIPS

The British also contribute their fair share of clips, many of which are unintelligible on this side of the Atlantic—which contributes toward making a certain amount of the humor in such as *The Benny Hill Show* and *Monty Python's Flying Circus* fall flat in the States. A few examples of British clips are panto (= pantomime), budgie (= budgerigar), aggro (= aggravation), char (= charwoman, i.e. cleaning lady), caff (= cafe), brolly (= umbrella), gen (= general information, as in We've got the gen on that place), lav/lavie/lavvy (= lavatory), lolly (= lollipop), maths (= mathematics), lino (= linoleum), pud (rhymes with 'hood' = pudding), pee (= pence, as in 1 pee, 50 pee), mo (= moment), pram (= perambulator, British for U.S. baby carriage), prep (= preparation, i.e. homework—school jargon), pub (= public bar, i.e. a bar or saloon), tele/telly (= television), sod (= sodomite, derogatory and offensive slang; also, a swear word, as in Sod it! = Damn it!, and Sod off! = Scram! Beat it!), and many others.

From Australia there is the colorful bikie (= biker), Aussie (= Australian), muso (= musician), journo (= journalist), garbo (= garbage collector), Abo/abo (= Aboriginal, often derogatory), arvo (= afternoon), Commo (= Communist), speedo (= speedometer), smoko (= stoppage of work for a rest and a smoke; U.S. coffee break).

ASSIGNMENT

I. Discussion of Verb-Forming Suffix

-esce not generally listed in contemporary dictionaries. It is equivalent to the Latin infinitive inflection *-escere*, which is inceptive in Latin, and often so in English where it has become stretched to include the meaning 'continue' (over a period of time)—as in coalesce (grow), effervesce (give off), phosphoresce (produce), luminesce (exhibit), obsolesce (fall into disuse), affloresce (burst into). The word acquiesce contains more a sense of stativity than continuity of an activity. Some *-esce* possibilities, such as adolesce, curiously never caught on in English, although the equivalent verb *adolescere* (= to grow up), was popular enough in Latin.

104

II. Discussion of Bases

CAPIT-, CIPIT- (the latter, with vowel weakening, being used with prefixes) from the noun *caput* the head. Also, capitulate, recapitulate, capitate, capitation, and the two doublets of capital (itself from L), which are chattel (from OF), and cattle (from Old North F).

GNO- from the verb *gnoscere* to learn, become acquainted with, investigate, get to know, the old form of *noscere* and cognate with the OE *cnawan,* in ModE to know, and with the Gk reduplicative *gignoskein.* NO- and NOT- are from *noscere* and its past participle *notum.* The verb *(g)noscere* is inceptive in Latin. Compare the Gk base GNO- (Lesson VI), which gives gnosis, agnostic, gnotobiote, etc.

LOC- from the verb *locare* to place, lay, put, set. Also, allocate, delocalize, relocate, locale, locative, location. For some classes, LIEU- (from OF from L *locus* a place) could be introduced here, as in milieu (*medius* middle + LIEU-), lieu, lieutenant (LIEU- + TEN- to hold).

PUT- from the verb *putare* to cleanse, prune, settle, reckon; to consider, hold, believe, think. With the -*at*- verbal suffix there is imputation, reputation, computation, putative, etc., where there is no imputate, etc. Also, amputate (in which *am*- is a reduction of *ambi*- about + PUT- to prune), computer, repute, count (reduced in OF to *conter,* from L *com*- an intensive + PUT-). Compare putrefy, putrescent, putrid, putresce, from the verb *putēre* to stink.

RADIC- from the stem *radic*- of the noun *radix* root, foundation, basis origin. Also, radicle, radicate, eradicate (*ex*- out).

ROG- from the verb *rogare* to ask, inquire. Also, interrogate (-ive, -ion), derogate (-ion, -ive, -or, -ory), prerogative.

SPIR- from the verb *spirare*. Also, respire, aspirate, respirate, aspire, perspire, suspire, transpire. Students could be referred back to Lesson II for a discussion of this base and some additional words from it.

III. Analysis and Definition of Words

1. *de*- away from + ROG- to ask + -*at*- verbal suffix + -*ion* state of: a lessening or impairment of status.

2. *at*- (*ad*-) to + TENU- stretched, thin + -*ate* verbal suffix + -*d* E past participial suffix: to weaken in force.

3. *ef*- out + FLOR- flower + -*esce* to begin + -*ence* state of: here, figurative, the state of bursting into bloom; the state of growth and development.

4. *in*- not + *dis*- apart, separately + PUT- to reckon (calculate) + -*able* able to be + -*ly* E adverb suffix: in a manner that is not meant to be questioned; unquestionably.

5. *re-* back, again + SPIR- to breathe + *-at-* verbal suffix + *-ory* serving for: having to do with breathing.

6. *circum-* around + ST- to stand + *-ance* state of: existing situation or state of affairs..

7. UND- wave + *-ul(e)* little + *-ate* to make + *-d* past tense suffix: to rise and fall, or form or move like waves.

8. *pre-* before + ROG- to ask + *-ate* verbal suffix + *-ive* tending to: here, a substantive use of the adjective, an exclusive or special right or privilege.

9. *e-* out + RADIC- root + *-ate* verbal suffix: to get rid of completely.

10. *im-* in + PUT- reckon, think + *-at-* verbal suffix + *-ion* act of: an insinuation, accusation, or charge.

11. *counter-* against + VAIL- to be strong, be worthy + *-ing* E participial suffix: to have force or an affect against; oppose with equal power or force; counteract.

12. *-ab* away + ERR- to wander + *-ent* -ing: deviating (straying, turning aside) from what is right.

13. LUMIN- light + *-esce* to become + *-ence* quality of: an emission of light (including both phosphorescence and florescence) that occurs at temperatures below incandescence.

14. *e-* out + LUC- light + *-id* full of + *-ate* verbal suffix: now only figurative, shed light on, make clear or explain.

15. PUT- to think + *-at-* verbal suffix + *-ive* having to do with + *-ly* E adverb suffix: supposedly; reputedly.

16. *ig-* (*in-*) not + NOMIN- name + ·*-ious* full of: shameful; disgraceful; dishonorable; humiliating.

17. *con-* together + SON- sound + *-ance* quality of: agreement; accord; accordance.

18. *ex-* out + COG- to think + *-it-* verbal suffix + *-at-* verbal suffix + *-ion* result of: the result of devising or contriving; contrivance.

19. *ig-* not + (G)NO- to know + *-able* able to be: of humble birth (as opposed to noble birth). (L *nobilis*—NO- + *-ble* means noble.)

20. SEN- old + *-esce* to become + *-ent* -ing: growing old; beginning to show age.

IV. Derivation of Clipped Words

1. bus—omnibus, from F (*voiture*) *omnibus* common (conveyance), from L *omnibus* for all, the dative plural of the noun *omnis* all, whole.

2. cab—cabriolet, a French borrowing, where it meant a carriage for hire, from the It *capriolare* to capriole, leap, caper, ultimately from L *caper* goat. Taxicab is a clip-blend from the F *taximeter cabriolet* a taxicab.

3. cad—caddie or cadet, from Scottish, an unskilled worker, hence supposedly unmannered in niceties.

4. narc—narcotics agent, from Gk *narcotikos* numbing, ultimately from *narke* numbness.

5. gin—(a, the drink) geneva, an alteration of the Du *genever* liquor, ultimately from L *juniperus* juniper (whose berries originally flavored the drink); (b, the machine) engine, from OF *engin* engine (through ME *ginne* a contrivance; skill, cleverness), from L *ingenium* inborn qualities, talent, from *in-* in + GEN- produce.

6. pep—pepper, ultimately from Gk *piperi*.

7. prop—property, ultimately from the base PROPRI- one's own.

8. van—(a, forefront) vanguard (a doublet of avant-garde), from F *avant* before + *garde* guard, ultimately from L *ab-* from + *ante* before + *garde* guard; (b, the vehicle) caravan, from OF *caravane*, from Persian *karwan* caravan. Also found in ML as *carvana*.

9. varsity—university, penultimately from LL *universitas* corporation, society, from L *universus* combined in one, whole, entire; also (n.) the universe (itself a derivative of *unus* one + VERS- to turn).

10. wayward—awayward, from ME *weiward*, short for *aweiward*, from *awei* + *-ward* in the direction of.

11. wig—periwig, earlier perwyke, alteration of peruck, from MF *perruque* peruke, periwig, ultimately from L *pilus* hair.

V. Clips on Campus

College students, who often come from all over the country, will no doubt come up with colorful and varied lists here. Prof and exam are standard fare, but some schools and colleges undoubtedly have clips that are peculiar to a certain school or, perhaps, geographical area. This list is a sampling: ag (= agriculture), aggie (= an agricultural student), anthro (= anthropology), biochem (= biochemistry), chem, dorm, econ (= economics), exam, frat, (= a fraternity; a male student in a fraternity), freshman comp (= composition), grad (= graduate), math, poly sci (= political science), psych (= psychology), ed psych (= educational psychology), phys ed, primary ed, secondary ed, special ed, prof, soc (= sociology), stat (= statistics), tech (as in Georgia Tech), the U (= University), undergrad, western civ (= civilization).

LESSON XXI

ASSIGNMENT

I. Discussion of Verb-Forming Suffix

-(i)fy, -(e)fy   through the F suffix *-fier,* ultima y from L FAC- to do, make.
The *-ify* is considered by contemporary dictionaries to be a variant of
the suffix *-fy.* Also carries the sense to become, make, or cause to be
(for both v.t and v.i.), as liquify, solidify, gasify, magnify; also, to
make or cause to be (as v.t. only), as simplify; also, to make similar to,
as dandify; also, to have the attributes or characteristics of, as in
countrified. As with other similar situations, the 'i' and 'e' were introduced through derivatives.

-(i)fic   is a suffixal derivative from the above. Also to be included here is
the suffix *-fication* (usually recorded in dictionaries), meaning the act
of, which is generally attached to verbs ending in *-fy,* as in rectifica-
tion, from rectify (i.e., where there is no rectificate), verification.

II. Discussion of Bases

AL-   from the verb *alere* to nourish, support. ALT- is from the past participle *altus,* which, when used as an attribute, meant grown, great, high,
lofty. Compare alter, alteration, alternate, alternative, altercation,
from *alter* one of two, the one, the other.

MEDI-   from the adjective *medius* middle, in the middle of. Also, medi-
eval, mediocre, Mediterranean, meditate, medisect. Compare the stem
medic-, as in medical, from the deponent infinitive *medicari* to heal,
cure; and *medit-,* as in meditate, from the deponent infinitive *meditari*
to think over, consider, meditate, intend.

MIGR-   to move (intransitive) or take (transitive) from one place to another; migrate; transport. Also, emigrate (*ex-* out), remigrate, remi-
gration, and the F émigré.

MORT-   from the stem *mort-* of the noun *mors* death, from the deponent
infinitive *mori* to die. Also, mortify, immortal, mortgage, mortician.
Compare mortar and mortise, from other sources.

PET-   from the verb *petere* make for, go to, ask for, request, seek, attack.
Also, impetuous, impetus, repeat (the 'ea' was picked up in English
around the sixteenth century).

PUG-   from *pugil* a boxer, connected with *pugnus* a fist, and *pugna* a fight,
a battle—whence (from the latter) the base PUGN-. Also, pugnacious.

III. Analysis and Definition of Words

1. MIGR- to move from one place to another + -*ant* -ing: here, substantive tive, a person who goes from one region to another in accordance with the demand for seasonal work of an agricultural nature.

2. *prod*- (variant of *pro*-) forth + IG- to do, drive + -*ious* full of + -*ly* E adverb suffix: in a manner that is great in extent; in great numbers.

3. DE- god + -*ific* making (or -*ify* + -*ic*) + -*at*- verbal suffix + -*ion* act of: a being made into a god; the state of being exalted to the rank of a god. (Cheers to those who see that the verb here must be passive.)

4. *inter*- between + MEDI- middle + -*ary* pertaining to (anyone who calls -*ary* a "place for" should go stand in the corner): here, substantive, a person who acts for one person with another, for bringing about an agreement or understanding; a go-between.

5. PUGN- to fight + -*acious* tending to + -*ly* E adverb suffix: in a manner showing a tendency to fight; combatively (from *battuere* to beat).

6. PET- to seek, aim at + -*ul*- little + -*ant* -ing: showing sudden, impatient irritation over trifles; likely to have little fits of bad temper; ill-humored; fretful; peevish.

7. *re*- again + VIV- to live + -*ify* to make + -*ed* E past participial suffix: give new life to; revive.

8. *ad*- to + JUDIC- judgment + -*at*- verbal suffix (to make) + -*ion* act of: judgment in a law court.

9. *in*- not + *ex*- out + PUGN- to fight, assault + -*able* able to be: incapable of being taken by force; unconquerable; impregnable.

10. *di*- apart, in different directions + SPIR- to breathe + -*it*- verbal suffix + -*ed* E past tense suffix: to lower the spirits, enthusiasm, hope, etc., of; discourage; dishearten, depress.

11. (a) *in*- in + GRESS- to go: the act of going in or entering an enclosed place; (b) *e*- out + GRESS- to go: the act of going out or leaving an enclosed place. (If students have "a means or place for going in . . .; an entrance," etc., this should be acceptable.)

12. *in*- not + VAL- to be worth + -*id* tending to + -*ate* verbal suffix: to make not (legally) binding.

13. *re*- back + PUGN- to fight + -*ance* quality of: a strong dislike or distaste; aversion (*a*- from + VERT- to turn).

14. from *perpetuatus* (*perpetuare*), from *perpetuus* continuous, uninterrupted, from *petere*—*per-* through + PET- to seek + *-ate* verbal suffix: preserve from extinction.

15. *e-* from, out + MIGR- to move from one place to another + *-ate* verbal suffix + *-d* E past tense suffix: to leave one's own country to settle in another.

16. *-ob* across + VI- away + *-ate* verbal suffix: to prevent or eliminate.

17. *con-* together + STRAIN- to draw tight + *-ed* E past participial suffix: to force; compel; oblige.

18. *dis-* apart + QUISIT- to ask + *-ion* result of: a long speech.

19. *in-* in + PET- to assail, attack + *-uous* full of: characterized by rash or sudden action, energy, etc.; impulsive (PULS- to drive, push).

20. *ab-* away + ROG- to ask + *-at-* verbal suffix + *-ion* act of: a doing away with; a putting aside or putting an end to.

IV. Blended Words

1. Amerind—American Indian. The word sometimes means Eskimo.

2. dumfound—dumb + confound.

3. electrocute—electricity (which has the combining form electro-) + execute.

4. agitprop—(imported from Russia) *agitatsiya* (= agitation) + *propaganda* (= propaganda).

5. Gestapo—G*e*heime + Sta*at*spolizei (German, secret State police).

6. motel—motor + hotel.

7. quasar—quasi + stellar.

8. moped—motor + pedal.

9. telecast—television + broadcast.

10. transistor—transfer + resistor.

LESSON XXII

DOUBLETS

Additional Exercise on Doublets

In the following list, the second word is the one to offer the students since this is the one that will point to the doublet, as in No. 8, respite points to *respectus,* whence respect. All of them, however, are not this easy to track down, such as No. 4.

1. tempo (from L *tempus*)—tense (= the form of the verb that shows the time of the action or state) (from OF *tens* time, from L *tempus*).
2. complement (from L *complementum,* from *complēre* to fill up)— compliment (from F *compliment,* from It *complimento,* from Sp *cumplimiento,* from *cumplir* to fulfill or accomplish, from L *complēre*).
3. penicillin (from L *penicillus* a painter's brush, pencil, a diminutive of *peniculus* a brush, a diminutive of *penis* a tail)—pencil (from OF *pincel,* ultimately from *penicillus* from *penis*)—penis (originally) a tail.
4. spatula (from LL *spatula* a spoon, a diminutive of L *spatha* a broad flat blade, from Gk *spathe*)—spade (from It *spade,* from L *spatha*). The similarity between the sounds /t/, /th/, and /d/ could be pointed out here. Also doublets of these two words are the less familiar épée and spathe.
5. terrene (from L *terrenus* worldly, earthly, from *terra* of Lesson X)— terrain (from F *terrain,* from OF *terain,* ultimately from *terra*).
6. vassal (from OF *vassal,* from ML *vassallus* retainer)—varlet (from OF *varlet,* variant of *vaslet* squire, young man, from *vassal*).
7. tinge (from L *tingere* to dye, color)—*taint* (from OF *teint* past participle of *teindre* to dye, from L *tingere*)—tint (alteration of tinct, an archaic E word meaning tinged, flavored, a clip of the L *tinctus* a dyeing, from the past participle *tinctus* of *tingere*).
8. respect (from L *respectus* a looking back, from the past participle *respicere* to look back, have regard for)—respite (from OF *respit,* ultimately from L *respectus*).

Other doublets are omelet/lamella, crone/carrion, rage/rabies, ravish/rape, tinsel/scintella/stencil.

ASSIGNMENT

I. Discussion of Bases

GRAT-   from the adjective *gratus* pleasing, agreeable. Also, grateful, gratify, ingratitude, ingratiate, congratulate.

MISC-   from the verb *miscēre* to mix, mingle; MIXT- from its past participle *mixtus.* Also, miscible, miscellaneous, mixture, admixture, and mix (a back formation from MF *mixte,* from L *mixtus*); also, mestizo, on loan from Sp, from LL *mixticius,* from L *mixtus.* Mixt was the original, now obsolete, past participial adjective until mixed took over.

MOV- from the verb *movēre* to move, set in motion, move away, remove, influence, stir; MOT- from the past participle *motus.* Also, commotion, demote, emote, emotion, immovable, promote, motor, motive, movie.

NEG- from the verb *negare* to say no, deny, refuse. (*Negare* is from *ne* not + the defective verb *aio* to say yes, affirm.) Also, abnegate, negate.

PURG- from the verb *purgare* to clean, cleanse, purge (from *purus* clean, pure + AG- to make). Also, expurgate, purgative, purgatory. PUR- as a base (from *purus*) could be added in passing, covering pure, purify, impurity, purist, etc.

VULG- from *vulgus* the common people, with the *vulgat-* of E derivatives, as vulgate, coming from the past participle *vulgatus* of the verb *vulgare* to make common, spread, publish—which sense shows in the E divulge.

II. Analysis and Definition of Words

1. *di-* in different directions + VULG- common: to make public; reveal.

2. *pre-* in front of + TENT- to strive + *-ious* full of: making claims to importance or doing something for show.

3. MISC- to mix + *-e-* connecting vowel (from the stem *misce-*) + GEN- race + *-at-* verbal suffix + *-ion* act of: of mixing of races by intermarriage or interbreeding.

4. *ambi-* on both sides + VAL- to be strong + *-ence* instance of: an instance of having conflicting attitudes about something.

5. *in-* not + CRED- to believe + *-ul(ous)* tending to + *-ity* quality of: a lack of belief; doubt; disbelief.

6. *in-* not + *co-* together + HER- to stick + *-ent* exhibiting + *-ly* E adverb suffix: in a manner not showing logical connection or consistency.

7. *e-* out + MOT- to move + *-ion* state + *-al* belonging to: showing strong feeling of any kind.

8. *pro-* forth + MISC- to mix + *-uous* inclined to: mixed; not in order.

9. *dis-* not + SIMUL- like + *-at-* verbal suffix + *-ion* act of: the act of disguising or hiding under a pretense; a feigning; hypocrisy.

10. PURG- to clean, cleanse + *-at-* verbal suffix + *-ory* place for: in the Roman Catholic religion, a condition or place in which those who have died remorseful about their sins or wrongdoing are purified from sin by punishment.

11. *ex-* out + TENU- thin + *-at-* verbal suffix + *-ion* act of: the act of making (here, guilt) seem less serious.

12. *pre-* before + VAIL- to be strong + *-ing* E participial suffix: to be the most usual or strongest; have the most influence.

13. *inter-* between + VEN- to come + *-ing* E participial suffix: entering or occurring incidentally or extraneously.

14. SPEC- to look + *-ious* full of: having deceptive attraction or a false appearance of truth or goodness.

15. *ex-* out + PURG- to clean + *-at-* verbal suffix + *-ed* E past participle inflection: to cleanse of something considered to be morally harmful, offensive, or erroneous, as material in a book, play, film, etc.

16. from *dilatus*, past participle of *differre* to put off, from *dis-* not + LAT- to carry + *-ory* tending to: tending to delay.

17. *im-* (*in-*) not + POT- power + *-ence* state of: the state of having no power; helplessness.

18. *ab-* away + NEG- to deny + *-at-* verbal suffix + *-ion* act of: the act of denying (luxuries, etc.). (Abnegate is a back formation of abnegation.)

19. *con-* with + VIV- to live + *-ial* pertaining to: fond of feasting and joviality; sociable.

20. from the prepositional phrase *in gratiam* into favor, from *in-* into + GRAT(i)- favor (or *-i-* connecting vowel) + *-ate* verbal suffix: to gain favor or acceptance through deliberate effort. (The stem of *gratiam* is *grati.*)

III. Doublets

Ultimate etymologies are not necessarily shown here.

1. overture (from OF *overture,* an alteration of L *apertura* opening)—aperture (from L *apertura*).

2. ancestor (from OF *ancestre*, from L *antecessor—ante-* before + CED- to go)—antecessor (= predecessor; from L *antecessor*). Ante- + CED- also produced antecedent, antecede, etc.

3. attitude (from F *attitude,* through It, from LL *aptitudo, -inis*)—aptitude (from LL *aptitudo,* from L *aptus* joined, fitted—whence E apt).

4. hostel (from OF *hostel,* from ML *hospitale* an inn, ultimately from L *hospes* guest, host = one who receives a guest). Several words are related to this: a) the doublet hospital (from ML *hospitale*); b) spital (apheretic variant of hospital); c) the doublet hotel (from F *hôtel,* from OF *hostel*), whence hotelier; d) host (= one who receives a

guest; from OF *hoste*, from *hospes*), also hostess (from OF *hostesse*, feminine of *hoste*); e) hospice (from ⸗ *hospice*, ultimately from L *hospes*); f) hospitable (from MF *hos, able*, from the deponent L verb *hospitari* to stay as a guest, from *hospes*); g) hospitium (=hospice, of which it is a doublet; from L *hospitium* guest house, from *hospes*).

5. slander (from AF *esclandre* scandal, from L *scandalum*)—scandal (from L *scandalum*).

6. balm (from OF *basme, baume*, from L *balsamum*)—balsam (from L *balsamum*).

7. chase (from OF *chacier*, ultimately from L *captare* to hunt, seize— Lesson XII)—catch (from Old North French *cachier*, ultimately from L *captare*). Captive, captor, and capture are also related to these.

8. fashion (from OF *façon*, from L *factio* a doing or making, from past participle *factum* of *facere*)—faction (from L *facio*).

9. grace (from OF *grace*, from L *gratia* thanks, favor, from *gratus* pleasing)—gratitude (from LL *gratitudo*, from *gratis*).

10. comprise (from OF *compris*, past participle of *comprendre*, from L *comprehendere*)—comprehend (from L *comprehendere*).

11. comply (from It *complire*, from Sp *complir*, from L *complēre*)— complete (from *completus*, past participle of *complēre*—com- + PLE-).

12. treasure (from OF *tresor*, from L *thesaurus*)—thesaurus (from L *thesaurus*).

LESSON XXIII

LATINISMS IN SHAKESPEARE

Additional Exercise

Other examples* that could be discussed with the students are the following:

---

*From Edith F. Claflin, "The Latinisms in Shakespeare's Diction," *Classical Journal*, 16 (1920 – 21), pp. 346 – 59.

1. nervy (in *Coriolanus*) meaning sinewy: "... nervy arm," from L *nervus* sinew.

2. generosity (in *Coriolanus*), meaning noble birth: "... to break the heart of generosity," from L *generosus* of noble birth, from GENER- race, kind.

3. clamor (in *Coriolanus*), meaning shouting: "... the applause and clamor of the host," from CLAM- to cry out.

4. vulgar (in *Hamlet*), meaning common: "... is as common as the most vulgar thing to sense," from VULG- common.

5. comfortable (in *Romeo and Juliet*), meaning strengthening: "... O comfortable friar! Where is my lord?", from FORT- strong.

ASSIGNMENT

I. Analysis and Definition of Words

1. crescent—from CRESC- to grow + -*ent* -ing: growing; increasing.

2. digested—from *dis*- apart + GEST- to carry, produce + -*ed* E past participial suffix: to combine; set in order.

3. extravagant—from *extra*- outside + VAG- to wander + -*ant* -ing: wandering out of bounds; straying.

4. continents—from *con*- together + TIN- to hold + -*ent* that which: a thing that holds or contains; a container.

5. fortitude—from FORT- strong + -*itude* quality of: strength.

6. investments—from *in*- in + VEST- garment + -*ment* result of (a thing that invests, from an obsolete verb meaning to put on): outer clothing.

7. probation—from PROB- to test + -*ate* verbal suffix + -*ion* act of or result: proof.

8. reduce—from *re*- again + DUC- to lead: bring back.

9. tenable—from TEN- to hold + -*able* tending to: held close.

II. Analysis and Definition of Obsolete or Archaic Words

It should be noted that not all dictionaries label all of these words as being obsolete or archaic.

1. cadent—from CAD- to fall + -*ent* -ing: falling.

2. credent—from CRED- to believe + -*ent* -ing: believing; credulous.

3. disanimates—from *dis*- not + ANIM- feeling, spirit + -*ate* verbal suffix (to make): to dispirit; discourage.

4. expulsed—from *ex*- from + PULS- to drive: expel; drive out.

5. propugnation—from *propugnare* to defend, from *pro*- before + PUGN- to fight + -*ate* verbal suffix + -*ion* act of: defense.

6. repugn—from *re*- back + PUGN- to fight: to reject.

7. sequent—from SEQU- to follow + -*ent* that which: that follows or comes after.

8. simular—from SIMUL- like: false.

9. tortive—from TORT- to twist + -*ive* inclined to be: twisted.

III. Discussion of Bases

CORD-   from *cord*-, the stem of the noun *cor* heart. Also, cordiform, concord, concordance, cordate. Compare cord, cordage, cordite, cordon, cordillera, from OF *corde* cord, ultimately from Gk *chorde* gut; cordoba, from Francisco Córdoba; and cordovan, from Córdoba, Spain.

FLECT-   from the verb *flectere* to bend, twist, curve; FLEX- from the past participle *flexus*. Also, inflect, inflection, circumflect, circumflex, circumflexion, deflect, deflex, deflection, flex, flection, flexion. Other -ect- words often retain the older -ex- in England, as connexion, inflexion, deflexion.

MAN(U)-   from the noun *manus* hand. Manicure is from MAN- + CUR- care; manipulate, a back formation of manipulation, from *manipulus* a handful, from MAN- + PLE- to fill; manuscript (SCRIPT- to write). Also, manufacture (FACT- to make); manuduction (DUCT- to lead); manumit (MIT- to send); maneuver, through F from MAN- + *oper*- to work (not in EW) and its doublet manure, a contraction from OF *manouvrer* to work with the hands (= maneuver); manage, through It *maneggiare* to handle or train (horses); manacle, penultimately from *manicae* sleeves, manacles, from MANU-. Compare man- in mansion, manse, manor, ménage, menagerie, ultimately from the verb *manēre* to remain, stay; and manic, mania, maniac, from Gk *mania* madness.

PORT-   from the verb *portare* carry. Also, comport, comportment, disport, disportment, import (n. and v.) important, support (*sub*- [up from] under), transport, portative.

STRU-   from the verb *struere* to put together, put in order, build, erect. STRUCT- is from the past participle *structus*. Also, construct, destruct, infrastructure, superstructure, obstruct, substructure.

TERMIN-   from the noun *terminus* end, boundary line. Also, exterminate, interminable, predetermine, terminate, terminology, and the (loan) terminus. Term picks up from the OF clip *terme*, from *terminus*.

VINC- from the verb *vincere* to overcome, conquer; VICT- from the past participle *victus*. Also, invincible, evict (*ex-*). Compare vinculum, from L *vincire* to bind; and victim, from L *victima* an animal to be sacrificed, victim.

IV. Analysis and Definition of Words

1. from the deponent verb *vociferari* to cry aloud, shout, from VOC- to call + *i* connecting vowel + FER- to bear + *-at-* verbal suffix + *-ion* act of: (an instance of) a noisy outcry; shout.

2. from *artificium* the work of a craftsman, from ART- skill, art + *i* connecting vowel + FIC- to make: a trick or clever stratagem. (Artifice is a back formation of artificer.)

3. *circum-* around + SPECT- to look + *-ion* act of: the act of looking around; watchfulness.

4. *in-* not + FLEX- to bend + *-ible* tending to be: not yielding; firm.

5. *con-* with + STRU- to build, erect: to interpret; explain.

6. *dis-* apart + CORD- heart + *-ant* -ing: disagreeing; differing; not in agreement.

7. *in-* into + NAT- to be born: born in a person; inherent.

8. *in-* not + VINC- to conquer + *-ible* able to be: incapable of being overcome.

9. *de-* from + TERMIN- boundary, end + *-ant* -ing (here, substantive, "that which"): a thing that is a deciding fact in reaching a certain (specified, particular) result; a determining factor or agent.

10. *ef-* out + FERV- to boil, bubble + *-esce* to begin + *-ent* -ing: giving off bubbles of gas. (To accommodate the second half of the sentence: here, figurative, lively; showing high spirits.)

11. *pro-* before + SCRIB- to write: to prohibit as wrong; forbid; or, to condemn (presuming the family could not prohibit those things).

12. *ac-* to, toward + CLAM- to cry out + *-at-* verbal suffix + *-ion* act of: an act (instance) of showing approval.

13. *-ap* (*ad-*) toward, near + POS- to put, place + *-ite* being (or POSIT-): suitable, appropriate.

14. *trans-* across + IT- to go + *-ory* tending to: tending to be brief or temporary; lasting only a short time; brief; short-lived.

15. *in-* not + TERMIN- boundary, end + *-able* tending to: having no end or limit; never stopping; unceasing; endless.

16. DICT- to say + *-ion* state of, act of + *-ary* place for: a book that explains the words of language.

17. *e-* away + MAN- hand + CIP- to take + *-at-* verbal suffix + *-ion* state of: the act of setting one free of something (here, of want).

18. *ab-* from + JECT- to throw: showing absolute hopelessness; wretched.

19. *extro-* outside, beyond + VERT- to turn: a person who is primarily more interested in what is going on around him than in his own thoughts and feelings—hence, here, a sociable person; one who makes friends easily.

20. MAN- hand + *u* connecting vowel, or inflection (*manu* = by hand; ablative of *manus*) + MISS- to let go + *-ion* act of: the act of letting go (i.e. freeing) of slaves; emancipation (cf. sentence 17 above).

LESSON XXIV

ASSIGNMENT

I. Analysis and Definition of Words with Uncommon Meanings

1. aggravated—from *aggravatus,* past participle of *aggravare* to make heavy, from *ad-* to + GRAV- heavy + *-ate* verbal suffix: to load.

2. comfortable—*com-* very (intensive) + FORT- strong + *-able* able to be: strengthening or supporting (morally or spiritually).

3. convenience—*con-* together + VEN(i)- to come (from the verb stem *veni-*) + *-ence* quality of: agreement; accordance.

4. conversion—*con-* altogether + VERS- to turn + *-ion* action: the action of turning around or revolving.

5. convinced—*con-* altogether, wholly + VINC- to conquer: here, figurative, to overcome.

6. decimating—DECIM- tenth + *-ate* to make: to tax to the amount of one-tenth.

7. deducted—*de-* away + DUCT- to lead: to conduct (a colony).

8. dejected—*de-* down + JECT- to throw: to throw or cast down; overthrow.

9. depends —*de-* down + PEND- to hang: to hand down; be suspended.

10. excursion—*ex-* out + CURS- to run + *-ion* act of: something that runs out or projects; a projection (as of land).

11. fact—from *factum* the thing done, from FACT- to do: an evil deed; a crime.

12. object—*ob-* against + JECT- to throw: to expose (to danger or evil).

13. pretended—*pre-* before + TEND- to stretch: to bring forward; offer for acceptance.

14. prevalent—*pre-* before + VAL- to be strong + *-ent* -ing: having great power; powerful.

15. prevented + *pre-* before + VENT- to come: act before; anticipate.

16. produced—*pro-* in front of, forward + DUC- to lead: to lengthen (something) out; extend; enlarge.

17. punctuated—PUNCT(u)- to prick (from the verb stem *punctu-*) + *-ate* to make: to point out; note.

18. translated—*trans-* across + LAT- to carry: to transfer (a bishop) from one see to another.

II. Discussion of Bases

AUD-   from the verb *audire* to hear. Also audible, inaudible, audiometer, audimeter, audition, and some twenty words, including the clip audio, from the combining form audio-, meaning hearing or sound. Compare audacious, audacity from *audēre* to dare.

CARN-   from the stem *carn-* of the noun *caro* flesh. Also, carnal, carnation (originally the flesh tints in a painting, and the color of human skin), carnelian (or cornelian), carnify, carnitine, carnival (from It *carnevale*, a shortening of Old It *carnelevare* a leaving off of eating meat, referring to fasting during Lent), and carnivore.

NUNCI-   from the infinitive *nunciare* to announce, a derivative of *nuntius* messenger, an announcing. Latin forms with -nunci(at)- took a parallel course into English with the F -nounc- forms, streaming doublets in their wake. Thus we have renunciate (-ion, etc.) and renounce (-ment, etc.); annunciate and announce; pronunciate (which had a meager existence, although pronunciation has lived on) and pronounce, which has taken over all senses, although pronunciation and pronouncement have kept their separate senses; denunciate and denounce; and enunciate and enounce.

PRESS-   from the past participle *pressus* of the verb *premere* to press, squeeze. Also, depress, depression, compress (n. and v.), express (n. and v.), impress, repress, suppress.

PROPRI- from the adjective *proprius* one's own, special, particular. Also proper (an alteration of OF *propre*) and property (an alteration of OF *propriete*), the latter a doublet of propriety.

SAT(IS)- from *satis* or *sat* enough (an indeclinable word used as an adjective, noun, and adverb). Also, insatiable, satire, saturate (through *satuare* to glut).

III. Analysis and Definition of Words

1. *pre-* in front of + CIPIT- head + *-ate* being (or verbal suffix): here, figurative, with great haste.

2. *ex-* from, out of + PATRI- country + *-ate* being (or verbal suffix): here, noun use of the participial adjective 'expatriated,' one who has left his native country or renounced his citizenship; an exile; an expatriated person.

3. *re-* back + NUNCI- to announce + *-at-* verbal suffix + *-ion* act of: the act of giving up something.

4. *in-* not + AUD- to hear + *-ible* able: not able to be heard.

5. *pre-* before + SCI- to know + *-ent* -ing: having foresight; knowing beforehand.

6. ART- art, skill + *i* connecting vowel (from the stem *arti-*) + FACT- to make: any man-made object, such as a tool or ornament, that shows skill or workmanship.

7. *re-* again + PLET- to fill: filled; abundantly provided.

8. *in-* in + VID- to see + *-ious* inclined to: inclined to cause ill will, resentment, or envy.

9. *e-* out + NUNCI- to announce + *-ate* verbal suffix: to state; utter.

10. SAT- enough + *-iety* state: state or condition of being overly gratified; the feeling of having had too much.

11. SENT- to feel, think + *-ent* -ing + *-ious* consisting of + *-ly* E adverb suffix: in a manner inclined to moralize or utter sayings, like a judge settling a dispute.

12. CARN- flesh + *-al* pertaining to: pertaining to the passions of the body; sensual.

13. *com-* together + PORT- to carry + *-ed* E past tense suffix: to conduct (oneself) in a right and proper manner; behave properly.

14. *op-* against + PRESS- to press + *-ion* act of: the act (or fact) of governing harshly, unjustly, or cruelly.

15. *ex-* from, away from + PROPRI- one's own + *-ate* verbal suffix + *-d* E past participial suffix: to take (here, property) away from an owner.

16. *con-* very (intensive) + TENT- to stretch, strive + *-ious* inclined to: inclined to perverse quarreling; quarrelsome.

17. *re-* back + PRESS- to press + *-ive* tending to: tending to curb or check.

18. *in-* not + *con-* very (intensive) + SEQU- to follow (through) + *-ent* -ing + *-ial* having: having an unimportant effect or outcome; irrelevant.

19. AUD- to hear + *-it-* verbal suffix + *-ory* pertaining to: pertaining to hearing. (Some dictionaries list auditory nerve as a main entry.)

20. *in-* in + CARN- flesh + *-ate* being: embodied in the flesh, often (as here) in human form.

LESSON XXV

ASSIGNMENT

I. Definition and Bases of Latin Loan Words

1. a list of things to be done or considered: AG- to do.

2. malevolent ill will; violent hatred: ANIM- mind, feeling.

3. a collection: *con-* with + GER- to carry. Although there is a singular form, congery, of this word, this -ies form is used both as singular (as here) and plural.

4. agreement in opinion: *con-* with + SENS- to think.

5. a list of errors in a book collected together with their corrections: *cor-* an intensive + RIG- to guide, direct. This is the L plural of the noun *corrigendum,* which in English means an error (as in a book) to be corrected.

6. a creed or statement of belief: CRED- to believe. *Credo* (= I believe) is the 1st person, present indicative of the verb *creer.* Credo is a doublet of creed.

7. the central or most important point or issue: the L noun *crux* (nominative singular), of EW's base CRUC- (Lesson IV).

8. a maxim; a saying: DICT- to say.

9. an offensive odor: *ef-* out + FLUV- to flow.

10. impromptu; offhand; unplanned: *ex-* out + TEMPOR- time.

11. free of charge: GRAT- grateful. *Gratis* is a contracted form of the ablative plural *gratiis* out of favor or kindness; free.

12. provisional; for the time being: *inter-* between. The *-im* is an adverb inflection in Latin.

13. minor or trifling details: MINUT- small. *Minutiae* is the plural of *minutia* smallness.

14. including many items at the same time: OMN- all. *Omnibus*, meaning 'for all,' is the dative plural (inflection *-ibus*) of the adjective *omnis* all, every.

15. a printed statement which describes and advertises: *pro-* forward + SPECT- to look. *Prospectus, -us* is a 4th declension noun.

II. Plurals of Latin Loan Words

All of the words in this exercise are in the nominative singular. Where the Latin plural is used, the form is the nominative plural. The general trend in recent years has been in favor of the English plural, which will indiscriminately be given first here. There is a fuller discussion of loan words at Greek Lesson VII, in both EW and IM.

1. apex—apexes, apices.
2. apparatus—apparatuses, apparatus.
3. arena—arenas (E only).
4. cactus—cactuses, cacti.
5. campus—campuses (E only).
6. crux—cruxes, cruces.
7. curriculum—curriculums, curricula.
8. focus—focuses, foci.
9. formula—formulas, formulae.
10. genus—genuses, genera.
11. index—indexes, indices.
12. memorandum—memorandums, memoranda.
13. species—species.
14. stadium—stadiums, stadia

Others are: cerebellum (-s, -a), cerebrum (-s, -a), codex (codices, L only), copula (-s, -ae), helix (-es, -ices), optimum (-s, -a), opus (opera,* L only), radius (-es, -dii), syllabus (-es, -bi), tabula rasa (tabulae rasae, L only), virus (-es, E only), viscus (viscera, L only), vortex (-es, -ices). Also datum and its popular plural data which in informal English is treated as a collective noun, like audience, and takes a singular verb. Formal usage still demands a plural verb with data. Helix and syllabus came into L from Gk. They both admit L and E plurals.

---

*The E opera (literally 'works') is also a loan word, with its own E plural operas.

III. Definitions of Latin Phrases Used in English

1. concerned with a particular purpose; special.
2. appealing to a person's prejudice, emotions, or some special interest rather than to intellect or reason.
3. to a sickening degree.
4. levied in proportion to the stated value of the goods.
5. a person's school, college, or university that he/she has attended.
6. a second self, especially a close, trusted friend or associate.
7. in fact or reality; actual.
8. by right; according to law.
9. and others; and the rest; and so forth.
10. from the seat of office or authority.
11. because of one's office. (Also appears as *ex officiis,* the *-is* being the ablative plural of *officium,* the *-o* being the ablative singular.)
12. having retroactive force.
13. an order requiring that a person be brought before a judge or court in order to decide if he/she is being lawfully confined, used as a protection against illegal imprisonment.
14. in the entirety; completely.
15. by the fact itself.
16. a method of operating or working.
17. a working arrangement or practical compromise, especially as designed to avoid difficulties.
18. the highest point of excellence obtainable.
19. an inference or conclusion that does not follow from the premise.
20. for each person.
21. for each day.
22. in or of himself; intrinsically.
23. a person unacceptable or unwelcome.
24. prior to investigation.
25. (a) part; halfway; (b) partly; almost.
26. one thing in return for another; compensation.
27. the number of members, usually a majority, of any assembly that must be present if the business at hand is to be done legally.
28. the share of a total amount due; a proportional part of a fixed total amount. In another sense a quota is the number of persons, or persons of a specified kind, permitted to immigrate to a country, join a club, enroll in a university, etc.

29. a method of disproving a proposition by showing the absurdity of its inevitable consequences.
30. thus; so. Sic is used to show that something has been copied just as it is in the original.
31. essential element.
32. the way things are; the existing state or condition.

INDEX OF WORDS APPEARING IN CONTEXT (LATIN)

The Roman numerals appearing after the word indicate the lesson in which the word is to be found.

PREFIXES (LATIN)

The Roman numerals in parentheses following the meanings indicate the lesson in which each prefix is to be found.

ab-, *a-*, *abs-*, away, from (III)
ad-, *ac-*, etc., to, toward (III)
ambi-, both, around (III)
ante-, before, in front of (III)
circum-, around (III)
con-, *com-*, *co-*, etc., with, together, very (III)
contra-, *contro-*, *counter-*, against (III)
de-, down, off, thoroughly (III)
dis-, *di-*, *dif-*, apart, in different directions, not (III)
en-, *em-*, in, into, against (IV)
ex-, *e-*, *ef-*, out, from, completely (IV)
extra-, *extro-*, outside, beyond (IV)
in-, *im-*, etc., in, into, against; not (IV)
infra-, below, beneath (IV)

inter-, between, among (IV)
intra-, *intro-*, within (IV)
non-, not (IV)
ob-, etc., toward, against, completely (IV)
per-, through, wrongly, completely (IV)
post-, after, behind (V)
pre-, before, in front of (V)
pro-, forward, in front of, for (V)
re-, *red-*, back, again (V)
retro-, backward, behind (V)
se-, *sed-*, aside, away (V)
sub-, *sus-*, *suc-*, etc., under, up from under, secretly (V)
super-, above, over (V)
trans-, *tran-*, *tra-*, across, through (V)
ultra-, beyond, exceedingly (V)

SUFFIXES (LATIN)

The Roman numerals in parentheses following the meanings indicate the lesson in which each suffix is to be found.

-able, able to be, etc. (XI)
-acious, tending to, etc. (XI)
-acity, quality of being inclined to (XV)
-acy, quality of being or having (XIV)
-ain, pertaining to, etc. (VIII)
-al (*-ial*, *-eal*), pertaining to, etc. (VIII)

-an (*-ian*), pertaining to, etc. (VIII)
-ance, *-ancy*, quality of ____ing, etc. (XVIII)
-and(um), *-(i)end(um)*, that which must be ____-ed (XIX)
-ane, pertaining to, etc. (VIII)
-ant, present participle ending -ing (X)

-ar, pertaining to, etc. (VIII)
-ary, pertaining to, etc. (IX)
-ary (-arium), place for (XVIII)
-at(e), verbal suffix (II)
-ate, possessing, etc. (X)
-ate, office of, etc. (XV)
-cle (-icle), little (XVII)
-cule (-icule), little (XVII)
-el, little (XVII)
-ence, -ency, quality of ___ing, etc. (XVIII)
-ent (-ient) present participle ending -ing (X)
-esce, to begin, etc. (XX)
-et, ette, little (XVII, footnote)
-(i)fic, making, etc. (XXI)
-(i)fy, -(e)fy, to make (XXI)
-ible, able to be, etc. (XI)
-ic, pertaining to, etc. (IX)
-id, tending to, etc. (XII)
-il, little (XVII)
-il, pertaining to, etc. (IX)
-ile, pertaining to, etc. (IX)
-ile, able to be, etc. (XI)
-ine, pertaining to, etc. (X)
-ion, act of, etc. (XVI)
-it(e), possessing, etc. (X)

-it(e), verbal suffix (II)
-itude, quality of, etc. (XIV)
-itious, tending to, etc. (XII)
-ity (-ety, -ty), quality of, etc. (XIV)
-ive, tending to, etc. (XIII)
-le, little (XVII)
-(u)lence, -(o)lence, state or quality of being full of (XIX)
-(u)lent, -(o)lent, full of, etc. (IX)
-men, result of, etc. (XVI)
-ment, result of, etc. (XVI)
-(i)mony, quality of (XV)
-ole, little (XVII)
-or, one who does, etc. (XIX)
-or (-our), state of, etc. (XVIII)
-ory, tending to, etc. (XIII)
-ory (-orium), place for (XVIII)
-ose (-iose), full of (VIII)
-ous (-ious, -eous), full of, etc. (VIII)
-rix, she who does (XIX)
-tic, pertaining to, etc. (IX)
-ule, little (XVII)
-ulous, tending to, etc. (XII)
-uous, tending to, etc. (XIII)
-ure, act of, etc. (XIX)
-y, quality of, etc. (XV)

BASES (LATIN)

The Roman numerals in parentheses following the meaning(s) indicate the lesson in which each base is to be found.

A

AB-, to have, hold as customary (IV)
AC(U), ACR-, ACET-, sharp, bitter (XII)
ACT-, AG-, to do, drive (XVIII)
AL-, ALT-, to nourish, grow tall (XXI)

ALIEN-, of another (II)
AM-, to love (XIV)
ANIM-, mind, feeling, life (VII)
ANN(U)-, year (VII)
AQU(A)-, water (VIII)
ART-, art, skill (II)
AUD-, to hear (XXIV)

B

BENE-, well; good (VII)
BI-, BIN-, two; twice (VI)
BON-, well; good (VII)

C

CAD-, to fall, befall (XII)
CANT-, to sing (VII)
CAP-, CAPT-, to take, seize (XII)
CAPIT-, head (XX)
CARN-, flesh (XXIV)
CAS-, to fall, befall (XII)
CED-, to go, yield (III)
CEIV-, to take, seize (XII)
CENT-, hundred (VI)
CENT-, to sing (VII)
CEPT-, to take, seize (XII)
CERN-, CERT-, to separate, distinguish (XIII)
CESS-, to go, yield (III)
CHANT-, to sing (VII)
CID-, to fall, befall (XII)
CID-, to kill, cut (XV)
CIP-, to take, seize (XII)
CIPIT-, head (XX)
CIS-, to kill, cut (XV)
CLAIM-, CLAM-, to cry out (XVIII)
CLOS-, CLUD-, CLUS-, to shut (V)
COG-, to think, reflect, consider (XVIII)
COR(S)-, to run, go (V)
CORD-, heart (XXIII)
CORPOR-, CORP(US)-, body (VIII)
COURS-, to run, go (V)
CRE-, to grow (XVI)
CRED-, to believe, trust (XI)
CRESC-, CRET-, to grow (XVI)
CRET-, to separate, distinguish (XIII)
CRUC-, cross (IV)

CUB-, CUMB-, to lie down (X)
CUR-, cure, care (VII)
CUR(R)-, CURS-, to run, go (V)

D

DE-, god (XIV)
DECI(M)-, tenth (VI)
DIC-, DICT-, to say (XVIII)
DIV-, god (XIV)
DOC-, DOCT-, to teach (XI)
DOM(IN)-, house, master (IX)
DU-, two (VI)
DUC-, DUCT-, to lead (III)
DUR-, hard; to last (XIII)

E

ENNI-, year (VII)
EQU-, equal, even (VII)
ERR-, to wander (XIX)

F

FA(B)-, to speak (XI)
FAC-, FACT-, to do, make (XII)
FAIL-, FALL-, FALS-, to deceive (XI)
FAM-, FAT-, to speak (XI)
FAULT-, to deceive (XI)
FEAS-, FEAT-, FECT-, to do, make (XII)
FEDER-, treaty, league (X)
FER-, to bear, carry (VII)
FERV-, to boil, bubble (XVII)
FESS-, to speak (XI)
FIC-, to do, make (XII)
FID-, faith (X)
FIDEL-, faithful (X)
FIN-, end, limit (II)
FIRM-, firm, strong (II)
FLAG(R)-, FLAM(M)-, to burn; flame (IX)
FLAT-, to blow (IX)
FLECT-, FLEX-, to bend (XXIII)
FLOR-, flower (XII)

FLU-, FLUX-, FLUV-,
 FLUOR(O)-, to flow (XII)
FOLI-, FOIL-, leaf (XII)
FORT-, strong (II)
FOUND-, to pour, melt (XIII)
FRANG-, FRING-, FRACT-, to
 break (XVII)
FUND-, FUS-, to pour, melt (XIII)

G

GEN-, to give birth to, produce (IX)
GEN-, GENER-, race, kind, origin
 (IX)
GER-, GEST-, to carry, produce
 (XVIII)
GNO-, to know (XX)
GRAD-, to step, go (V)
GRAN-, grain (XVII)
GRAND-, great (II)
GRAT-, pleasing, grateful (XXII)
GRAV-, heavy (II)
GREG-, flock, herd (IV)
GRESS-, to step, go (V)
GRIEV, heavy (II)

H

HAB-, to have, hold as customary
 (IV)
HER-, HES-, to stick (X)
HIB-, to have, hold as customary
 (IV)

I

I-, to go (XVI)
IG-, to do, drive (XVIII)
IQU-, equal, even (VII)
IT-, to go (XVI)

J

JAC-, JECT-, to throw (XIX)
JOIN-, JOINT-, a yoke; to join
 (XVI)
JOURN-, day (XIV)
JUDIC-, judgment (III)

JUG-, JUNCT-, a yoke; to joint
 (XVI)
JUR-, JUST-, right, law; to take an
 oath, form an opinion (III)

L

LAT-, to bear, carry (VII)
LATER-, side (IX)
LECT-, LEG-, to choose, pick out,
 read (XVI)
LEV-, light (in weight); to lift (III)
LIG-, to choose, pick out, read
 (XVI)
LIGN-, LINE-, line (II)
LOC-, place (XX)
LOCUT-, LOQU-, to speak (III)
LUC-, to shine; light (IX)
LUD-, to play, mock (III)
LUMIN-, to shine; light (IX)
LUS-, to play, mock (III)

M

MAGN-, great (VII)
MAL(E)-, bad (VII)
MAN(U)-, hand (XXIII)
MATR-, MATERN-, mother (XV)
MEDI-, middle (XXI)
MIGR-, to move from one place to
 another (XXI)
MILL-, thousand (VI)
MINOR-, MINUS-, MINUT-,
 small, smaller (XVII)
MISC-, to mix (XXII)
MIS(S)-, MIT(T)-, to send, let go
 (XVIII)
MIXT-, to mix (XXII)
MOD-, measure (XI)
MON-, to warn, advise (XVI)
MORT-, death (XXI)
MOT-, MOV-, to move (XXII)
MULT-, many (VII)
MUT-, to change (XI)

N

NASC-, NAT-, to be born (XIII)
NEC-, to harm, kill (XII)
NEG-, to deny (XXII)
NIC-, to harm, kill (XII)
NIHIL-, nothing (II)
NO-, to know (XX)
NOC-, to harm, kill (XII)
NOMEN-, NOMIN-, name, noun (XIX)
NOT-, to know (XX)
NOUNC-, to announce (XXIV)
NOV-, new (XII)
NOX-, to harm, kill (XII)
NUL(L)-, nothing (II)
NUNCI-, to announce (XXIV)

O

OCT-, eight (VI)
OCTAV-, eighth (VI)
OMN-, all (VIII)
OPTIM-, best (VII)
OR-, to speak formally, plead (XIV)
ORD(IN)-, to put in order, arrange (X)
OUND-, wave (V)

P

PAR-, to ready, bring forth, provide (IX)
PART-, part (II)
PASS-, PATI-, to endure, suffer (XVII)
PATR-, PATERN-, father (XV)
PATRI-, fatherland, country (XV)
PATRON-, protector (XV)
PED-, foot (IV)
PEL(L)-, to drive, push (XIII)
PEND-, PENS-, to hand, weigh, pay (V)
PET-, to seek, assail (XXI)

PLE-, PLET-, PLEN-, to fill; full (V)
PLEX-, PLIC-, PLY-, to fold, tangle, interweave (VII)
PON-, to place, put (XIII)
PORT-, to carry (XXIII)
POSE-, POSIT-, to place, put (XIII)
POSS-, POT-, to be able, have power (X)
POUND-, to place, put (XIII)
PREC-, to request, beg; prayer (III)
PRESS-, to press (XXIV)
PRIM-, first (VI)
PROB-, good; to test (XIV)
PROPRI-, one's own, fitting (XXIV)
PROV-, good; to test (XIV)
PUG(N)-, to fight, fist (XXI)
PULS-, to drive, push (XIII)
PUNCT-, PUNG-, to prick; point (IV)
PURG-, to clean (XXII)
PUT-, to prune, reckon, think (XX)

Q

QUADR(U)-, four (VI)
QUART-, fourth (VI)
QUEST-, to ask, seek (XVII)
QUINT-, fifth (VI)
QUIR-, QUISIT-, to ask, seek (XVII)

R

RADIC-, root (XX)
RAP-, RAPT-, to seize (XIV)
RECT-, REG-, right, straight; to rule, straighten, stiffen (VIII)
REPT-, to seize (XIV)
RIG-, right, straight; to rule, straighten, stiffen (VIII)
ROG-, to ask (XX)

S

SACR-, sacred (IV)
SAL-, SALT-, to leap (X)
SANCT-, holy (IV)
SAT(IS)-, enough (XXIV)
SCI-, to know (XIII)
SCRIB-, SCRIPT-, to write (XIX)
SEC-, to cut (XVII)
SECR-, sacred (IV)
SECT-, to cut (XVII)
SECUT-, to follow (XV)
SED-, to sit, settle (X)
SEG-, to cut (XVII)
SEMI-, half, partly (VI)
SEN-, old (IX)
SENS-, SENT-, to feel, think (IV)
SEPT(EM)-, seven (VI)
SEQU-, to follow (XV)
SERV-, to serve, save (IX)
SESS-, to sit, settle (X)
SEXT-, six; sixth (VI)
SID-, to sit, settle (X)
SIL-, to leap (X)
SIMIL-, SIMUL-, like, similar (VIII)
SIST-, to stand (XIX)
SOL-, alone (XV)
SOLUT-, SOLV-, to free, loosen (XVI)
SON-, sound (XVIII)
SPEC-, SPIC-, SPECT-, to look (V)
SPIR-, to breathe (XX)
ST(A)-, STIT-, to stand (XIX)
STRAIN-, STRICT-, STRING-, to draw tight (XIV)
STRU-, STRUCT-, to build (XXIII)
SULT-, to leap (X)

T

TACT-, to touch (XI)
TAIN-, to hold (VIII)
TANG-, to touch (XI)

TEMPER-, TEMPOR-, time, due season; to set bounds (VIII)
TEN-, to hold (VIII)
TEND-, TENS-, to stretch, strive (VIII)
TENT-, to hold (VIII)
TENT-, to stretch, strive (VIII)
TENU-, stretched, thin (VIII)
TERMIN-, boundary, end (XXIII)
TERR-, land, earth (X)
TIN-, to hold (VIII)
TING-, to touch (XI)
TRI-, three (VI)
TRACT-, to drag, draw (XI)
TORT-, to twist (XIII)
TRUD-, TRUS-, to push, thrust (III)
TURB-, to disturb (IV)

U

UN-, one (VI)
UND-, wave (V)

V

VAIL-, VAL-, to be strong, be worthy (XVIII)
VEN-, VENT-, VENU-, to come (III)
VER-, true (XIV)
VERB-, word, verb (II)
VERS-, VERT-, to turn (IV)
VEST-, garment (II)
VI(A)-, way, road (IV)
VID-, VIEW-, to see (V)
VINC-, VINCT-, to conquer (XXIII)
VIS-, to see (V)
VIV-, to live (XV)
VOC-, VOK-, voice; to call (V)
VOLUT-, VOLV-, to roll (XIX)
VULG-, common, ordinary (XXII)

PART II
Word elements
from Greek

INTRODUCTION TO THE GREEK SECTION

The accidence of Greek nouns is much like that of Latin. The are declined into five cases, the genitive singular being the one we use to determine the base. The verb has six principal parts, and English may derive words from several of them as well as from related nouns. EW will not as a rule give particular information about these technical facts. For example, the multiple base BALL-, BOL-, BLE-, to throw, to put, comes from two principal parts and a related noun *bolos* something caught, a throw, a cast (as of a net).

Greek phonetics is complicated, particularly in the manner in which neighboring sounds affect each other and result in variant spellings of the same base forms. Moreover, the transliteration of Greek words and names into English has a long history through Latin and French (as well as Italian) so that letter forms and spellings are often confusing; for example, phantom (and their doublets phantasm and phantasma), phantasy/fantasy (and its contracted fancy and doublet fantasia) all came into English ultimately from the base PHA(N)-, to show, appear. All of them—except phantasma, from L *phantasma*; and fantasia, from It *fantasia*, from L *phantasia*—came in through French, which supplied the 'f' from L 'ph.' Some even made it into ME with an 'f,' such as phantasm and phantom, later to get stuck with 'ph' again. Fantasy ends up with both an 'f' and 'ph.' Some changes took place over the centuries within Latin itself, such as fantastic, from ML *fantasticus*, a variant of the LL *phantasticus*. Not surprisingly, some desk dictionaries do better than others in tracking all this down; all of them short-cut what is often a maze of facts. As always, the OED is the best source.

Teachers and advanced students will be interested in learning the Greek alphabet because the best reference tool, the OED, does not transliterate Greek letters. Transliteration is used in all contemporary dictionaries, in W3, and in IM. Diacritics are not used in IM. Greek letter upsilon transliterates as both a *y* and a *u*, as in myriad, which in etymologies comes out *myrias* in some dictionaries and *murias* in others.

ASSIGNMENT

I. English Derivatives and Original Greek Words

1. bishop, from *episkopos* overseer—episcopal. Four changes: apheretic 'e'; voicing, from /p/, to /b/; /sk/ to the more English /sh/; clipping at the end.

2. blame, from *blasphemein* to blaspheme—blaspheme. Contracted as it passed through the Romance languages. Lost the 's' in OF *blamer*.

3. chair, from *kathedra* seat—cathedra. Originally three syllables *cha-ir-re* in OF (for L *cath-ed-ra*), in time it got chewed away to two syllables, finally to one. Chaise is also a doublet, through French.

4. desk, from *diskos* tray, collection plate, disc, disk, discus—discus, disk, disc. Vowel change and clipping. Dish and dais are also doublets, through OE and OF respectively.

5. devil, from *diabolos* slanderer—diabolic. Vowel reduction and clipping. The internal consonant appeared in other languages variously as 'b,' 'v,' and 'f,' and it was even absent at times when the word was contracted to one syllable.

6. glamour (or glamor), according to the OED, originally Scottish, "introduced into the literary language by Scott. A corrupt form of 'grammar' ..." from *grammatike* (*techne*) (art) of letters—grammar. The 'r' dissimilated. The word is related to gram, a unit of weight.

7. palsy, from *paralysis* paralysis, palsy, laxity—paralysis. Reduction of the Gk prefix *para-*.

8. parole, from *parabole* comparison, parable—parabola, parabole. Parable and palaver are also doublets. Reduction of the Gk prefix *para-*.

9. priest, from *presbyteros* and elder, a priest (comparative of *presbys* old man)—presbyter (-ial, -y, -ian). Vowel change and clipping.

10. story, from L *historia,* from Gk *istoria* history, inquiry—history. Apheretic 'hi.'

II. From Greek to Modern English

Students' answers may vary here since some dictionaries are more complete than others in giving the routes of words. If no definition is given for a foreign word, its meaning is carried over from the last English meaning offered.

1. alms—from ME *almes,* from OE *aelmysse,* from VL *alemosyna,* from LL *eleemosyna* from Gk *eleemosyne,* from *eleemon* charitable, merciful, from *eleos* mercy, pity, charity. A doublet of the E eleemosynary.

2. box—from ME *box,* from OE *box,* from LL *buxis,* from Gk *pyxis* little box, from *pyxos* box-tree.

3. chimney—from ME *chimenee* (or *chymenay,* and other forms), from MF *cheminee* fireplace, from LL *caminata,* from L *caminus* furnace, oven, from Gk *kaminos* kiln, furnace.

4. church—from ME *chirche*, from OE *circe* (or *cirice*), from VL *cyriaca* (WBD), from Gk *kyriakon* of the Lord, from *kyrios* master, lord, from *kyros* power.

5. elixir—from ME *elixir*, from ML *elixir*, from Arabic *al-iksir*, "probably" (OED, WBD, AHD, WNCD) from Gk *xerion* a powder for drying wounds, from *xeros* dry.

6. pew—from ME *puwe*, from MF *puye, puie* (etc.) balustrade, balcony, from L *podia*, neuter plural of *podium* elevated place, parapet, balcony, from Gk *podion* (diminutive of *pod-*, the stem of *pous* foot) little foot, base, pedestal.

7. prow—from MF *proue*, "probably" (WNCD) from dialectal It *prua*, "probably" (OED) from L *prora*, from Gk *prora*, earlier *proira*.

III. Original Greek Meanings

1. almond—from Gk *amygdale* almond tree. *Amygdalon* is almond.

2. cherry—from Gk *kerasos* cherry tree. *Kerasion* is cherry.

3. date—from Gk *daktylos* finger, date. This is the general word for finger. Greek has a distinct word for each finger. Dactyl (from the GK base DACTYL- finger) is a doublet.

4. fancy—from Gk *phantasia* appearance, imagination, ultimately from *phainein* to show. A contraction of fantasy, a doublet of fantasia.

5. frantic—from Gk *phrenitikos* frantic, furious, maniac, from *phrenitis* inflammation of the brain, frenzy, from *phren* mind, brain, reason. Note the Gk base PHREN- mind.

6. guitar—from Gk *kithara* cithara or lyre. Zither and cithara are doublets. (Sitar is a Hindi word, from Persian *si* three + *tar* string.)

7. lantern—from Gk *lampter* lamp, from *lampein* to shine. The E lamp also derives from this Gk verb.

8. licorice—from Gk *gylkyrrhiza* (or *gylkorriza*), from *glykys* sweet + *rhiza* (or *riza*) root. Glycerin is a doublet.

9. place—from Gk *plateia* (*hodos,*) a broad (way or street), from *platys* wide, broad, large. Plaza and piazza are both doublets of place.

10. surgeon—from OF *cirurgien*, from *cirurgie* surgery; penultimately derives through L from Gk *cheirourgos* surgeon, ultimately from *cheir* hand + *ergon* work (Gk bases CHEIR- and ERG-).

11. truck—from (dictionaries say variously "probably" or "apparently") Gk *trochos* wheel, from *trechein* to run.

LESSON I

ASSIGNMENT

I. Choosing the Correct Sound

1. **ae** of *aegis* = (3) the **e** in equal.
2. **g** of *aegis* = (2) the **g** in gem.
3. **ch** of *chimera* = (2) the **c** in can.
4. **i** of *chimera* = (2) the **i** in sanity; or, as second choice, (1) the **i** in bite.
5. **c** of *halcyon* = (1) the **c** in certain.
6. **a** of *labyrinth* = (4) the **a** in land.
7. **y** of *labyrinth* = (2) the **i** in sanity.
8. **i** of *Midas* = (1) the **i** in bite.
9. **oe** of *Oedipus* = (3) the **e** in tent; or, as second choice, (1) the **e** in equal.
10. **u** of *Oedipus* = (2) the **u** in put.
11. **ae** of *paean* = (3) the **e** in equal.
12. **e** of *siren* = (2) the **e** in agent—this sound is closest for most definitions; most dictionaries call this sound a schwa; the **e** in equal (1) is also used for an ambulance siren.
13. **y** of Stygian = (3) the **i** in tin.

II. Marking the Primary Accent

Primary accents are in italics.

1. ae*o*lian
2. chi*me*ra
3. her*cu*lean (also hercu*le*an)
4. *lab*yrinth
5. *nar*cissism
6. *nem*esis
7. Pro*crus*tean
8. sten*to*rian

LESSON II

WORDS FROM PROPER NOUNS

When we speak of words coming from proper nouns, we are covering a great deal of territory. Hundreds of words in English come from the names of cities (as brummagem, meaning cheap and tawdry in reference to jewelry, from Birmingham, England, where this kind of jewelry was sold; a contraction, which later produced the clip Brum, for Birmingham), counties, countries, and people of science, literature, history, and mythology. Some of these are direct lifts, as Samson (meaning strength), Philistine (anyone who is indifferent to or contemptuous of the fine arts), Solomon (wisdom), Shylock (avariciousness), Don Juan (rake, libertine). Others are modified, such as mausoleum and pander (in the exercise below).

Another class of words that can be mentioned here are those that are extended from trade names, some of which have become such common household words that they have, in many people's minds, become generic. A few examples are: Vaseline (meaning any petroleum jelly), Scotch tape (any cellulose tape), Band-Aid (literally, any small adhesive plaster; figuratively, and often in lower case, meaning any quick or temporary corrective measure), Coke (any cola drink), Realtor (any real-estate agent), Jello (any gelatin dessert or salad), Kleenex (any such tissue), Q-Tip (any such swab), and Xerox (noun and verb; any such dry-printing process; from Gk *xeros* dry). In the first half of the twentieth century when the majority of cameras were made by Kodak, the word Kodak meant camera, and did so for several years after that until the appearance on the market of other brand names. The same was true with the Hoover carpet sweeper, which is still used generically in England as both a noun and a verb (Mother hoovered the carpet yesterday). England also uses generically its Sellotape (= Scotch tape), Biro (any ballpoint pen), and Sylko (any mercerized thread). The house brand of bleach is probably cheaper, but Clorox is still frequently used as a common noun. Some of these companies, such as Kodak and Realtor (i.e. the National Association of Real Estate Boards, who coined the term), have jealously guarded their trade names, but others, such as aspirin, mimeograph, and linoleum, have lost the battle to overwhelming usage. After the U.S. Supreme Court denied the Miller Brewing Company of any exclusive use of the words Lite or Light, the door was open for anyone to walk through: at last count, eight different brands of beer, as well as peaches, pears, mixed fruit, syrup, cigarettes, soda, cheese, peanuts, potato chips, and frozen dinners, most of which came out in the calorie-conscious 1980s. The cigarettes, we were told, had lower tar.

Additional Exercise on Proper Names

The following list consists of other common nouns that derive from proper names. Derivations follow the dashes.

1. ampere—from Andre Maria Ampere (1775 – 1836), who contributed to the science of electromagnestism.
2. Fahrenheit—from Gabriel David Fahrenheit (1686 – 1736), who invented this temperature scale.
3. macadam—from John MacAdam (1756 – 1836), who suggested using broken stone for bad Scottish roads since a combination of the weather and normal traffic would beat them down to reasonable smoothness.
4. sadism—from the Count or Marquis Donatien de Sade (1740 – 1814), who wrote about the condition.
5. masochism—from Leopold von Sacher-Masoch (1836 – 1895), who first described the condition in his stories.
6. mausoleum—from Mausolus (d. 353 B.C), a king of Caria whose wife erected a large and splendid tomb to keep his memory alive.
7. pander—from Pandarus, a respectable Greek hero until literary figures like Boccaccio, Chaucer, and Shakespeare ruined his name in their writings by having him be a procurer for seeking out girlfriends.
8. saxophone—from Antoine Joseph Sax (1814 – 94), who invented the instrument in the 1840s.
9. braille—from Louis Braille (1809 – 52), a French teacher of the blind who developed a dot system which he published in 1829.
10. chauvinism—from Nicholas Chauvin, a soldier and admirer of Napoleon I.
11. mentor—from Mentor, a faithful friend of Odysseus; when Odysseus warred against the Trojans, he left his son with Mentor to be taught and advised.
12. vandal—from the Vandals, who invaded and ravaged parts of western Europe and northern Africa in the 4th and 5th centuries A.D.

ASSIGNMENT

I. Words Derived from Proper Nouns

1. bedlam—after the Hospital (for the insane) of St. Mary of Bethlehem in London: a place or state of noisy confusion or uproar. A contraction of Bethlehem, with /th/ slipping to /d/. Also, bedlamite.
2. boycott—after Charles Cunningham Boycott (1813 – 97), a land agent for Irish estates who raised rents, thus causing tenants to turn

on him; local shops would not sell him supplies, and his mail and food supplies were blocked: (as a verb) to refuse to have anything to do with (their shops) by not buying from them.

3. dunce—from John Duns Scotus, a brilliant thirteenth-century thinker and theologian whose reputation became curiously sabotaged after his death: a stupid or dull-witted person, a dolt.

4. Frankenstein—after Baron Frankenstein, who created a destructive monster from the parts of corpses in Mary Wollstonecraft Shelley's novel of 1818: anything that causes the ruin or downfall of its creator.

5. jeremiad—from Jeremiah (ca626 – 586 B.C), supposed author of the *Lamentations of Jeremiah* in the Bible, whose message was a summons to moral reform, personal and social, backed by threats of doom: a prolonged lamentation or complaint.

6. maudlin—from Mary Magdalene (a name which over the years took on the pronunciation of maudlin), who, in Biblical times, was supposedly freed of evil spirits by Christ; often depicted as weeping in paintings by classical artists: foolishly sentimental or tearful. A phonetic spelling of the contracted pronunciation of Magdelene.

7. quixotic—from Don Quixote of Cervantes' novel (1605, 1615) of the same name, a book which satirizes chivalry by making its hero, Quixote, sally forth into extravagant escapades of knight errantry: romantic, chivalrous, or idealistic to an impractical degree.

8. simony—from Simon Magnus, 1st century A.D. Samaritan sorcerer (Acts 8:9 – 24) who tried to buy the power of conferring the Holy Spirit: the act, generally considered now to be a sin, of buying or selling benefits of the church, such as positions, pardons, relics, preferments, etc.

9. tawdry—short for tawdry lace, from Saint Audrey (the 't' from saint), after whom a vanity scarf was named and sold in fairs each year on her birthday after her death; supposedly of good workmanship originally, the scarves deteriorated in quality as time went on: showy and cheap, gaudy, of poor quality.

10. utopia—from *Utopia* (1551), the title of a political romance by the English philosopher Sir Thomas More, which depicts the ideal society in which all things are perfect: any society, place, or state considered to be perfect or ideal. More coined the word from the Gk *ou* not + *topos* (TOP- place).

II. Choosing the Correct Sound

In instances where two answers are given, some dictionaries prefer the first, some the second.

1. **oe** of *Croesus* = (4) the **e** in equal.
2. first **a** of *Draconian* = (2) the **a** in gate; or as second choice in some dictionaries but first in others, (4) the **a** in about.
3. **o** of *Draconian* = (2) the **o** in tone.
4. **a** of *laconia* = (2) the **a** in about.
5. **o** of *laconic* = (1) the **o** in pot.
6. **e** of *mausoleum* = (4) the **e** in equal.
7. **y** of *Pyrrhic* = (3) the **i** in tin.
8. **o** of *solecism* = (2) the **o** in tone.
9. **c** of *solecism* = (3) the **c** in certain.
10. **y** of *sybarite* = (3) the **i** in tin.
11. **ei** of *Frankenstein* = (2) the **i** in bite.
12. **i** of *simony* = (1) the **i** in bite; or as second choice, (3) the **i** in tin.
13. **o** of *simony* = (3) the **o** in wisdom.

III. Marking the Primary Accent

The syllable with primary accent is in italics.

1. *Dam*ocles
2. Dra*con*ian
3. jere*mi*ad
4. la*con*ic
5. mauso*le*um
6. me*an*der
7. phi*lip*pic
8. quix*ot*ic
9. *si*mony
10. *sol*ecism
11. *soph*istry
12. *syb*arite

LESSON III

GREEK BASES

Unlike most Latin bases, the overwhelming majority of Greek bases are combining forms. A combining form is the root, also called stem, of a foreign word onto which affixes and other combining forms are attached. Some of these were combining forms in Greek and were carried over into living combining forms in English as new compounds were formed by analogy. Those that are not so used in English are often not recorded in desk dictionaries. Where a base in EW is found in contemporary dictionaries to be a combining form, this will be noted in IM, together with any variations. Some Greek bases have become free-standing words in English, as organ (a clip of L *organum*, from Gk *organon* instrument, body organ), angel (through OF from L *angelus*, from Gk *angelos* originally a messenger), graph (short for 'graphic formula,' from L *graphicus*, from Gk *graphikos*). The combining form is discussed fully at Lesson XII, where it is first introduced in EW.

An 'o' is attached to many Greek bases in creating many English combining forms—as bio- (which combines with -logy to form biology), chrono- (chronometer), geo- (geology), logo- (logotype), theo- (theology)—because 'o' is either in the original Greek word, as in *bios, chronos,* and *logos*, or in a Greek derivative, as *geographia* (from *ge* earth + -*graphy* writing) which produced geography, and *geodaisia* (from *ge* + *daiein* to divide) which produced geodesy. The attached 'o' form generally appears before consonants—as in geography, logopedics, chiropractor, cosmography, heterosexual, neologism, orthodox—while the EW form (the base without 'o') is used before vowels, as in thearchy (THE- god + -*archy* rule by) and podiatry (POD- foot + IATR- physician). Occasionally EW accommodates this alteration, in function a connecting vowel, as in PSYCH(o)-, THERM(o)-, and AUT(o)- in the examples used in the discussion of Combinations of Bases opening Lesson IV, and occasionally elsewhere, as with the PSYCH-chart at the opening of this lesson in EW. In its analysis of words, IM will follow EW in the formatting of this 'o'; however, since it is a connecting vowel (see Part I, Lesson VI), there is no reason students should not format it as such: + *o* connecting vowel + etc.

Incidentally, in Greek words that passed through Latin, where according to Latin an 'i' would ordinarily be used, the Gk 'o' was often picked up instead, as in the combining form historico-, from L *historicus*, from Gk *historikos*; as with politico-. The 'o' has become the standard connecting letter even in words that do not derive from Gk, as in the combining forms concavo-, convexo-, sado- (sadomasochism). It is also freely used in showing a relationship between two words, as Anglo-Saxon, Franco-American, Indo-European, Sino-Japanese.

ASSIGNMENT

I. Discussion of Bases

In this exercise additional English derivat. s are not offered since they are requested in Exercise II following.

BIBLI- from *biblion* book, a diminutive of *biblos* papyrus. The recognized combining form here is biblio-.

CANON-   from *kanon* a rule, a straight rod for measuring.

CRYPT-   from *kryptos* hidden; CRYPH- appears with a prefix. Crypt-(before vowels, as in cryptanalysis) and crypto- are usually found as the combining form.

CYCL-   from *kyklos* wheel, circle, ring. Both cycl- (before vowels, as in cyclic and cyclist) and cyclo- (as in cyclotron) are usually found as the combining form. This combining form also has a special chemistry sense, meaning ring, although this sense does not always figure very strongly. For example, whereas cyclohexane (C_6H_{12}) is considered as a ring of six bivalent radicals, in cyclonite and cycloserine the sense of a ring is not obvious.

GLOSS-   from *glossa* tongue; GLOT(T)- is from *glotta*, the Attic variant form of the Ionic *glossa*. (In ancient times Attica was a region of Greece, with Athens as its most important city; Ionia was a region on the west coast of Asia Minor.) Gloss- (before vowels), glosso-, and glotto- are often found as combining forms, together with -glot in final position, as in polyglot.

ICON-   from *eikon* image. Variously spelled ikon and eikon. Also, eikonogen.

MIM-   Both *mimos* a mime, which came in through L, and the later direct borrowing *mimeisthai* to imitate (whence mimeograph) have given MIM-. The mi- is a reduplication (compare GEN- in Lesson VII, GNO- of Lesson VI, and MNE- of Lesson IV).

OD-   from *oide* song, ode, from *aeiden* to sing. Compare other orthographic similarities, as odious (from L *odium* hate); OD- and HOD- in Lesson V; ODONT- in Lesson IX; and -*ode*, a combining form from Gk *odes*, from *eidos* shape, form, as in nematode.

PYR-   from *pyr* fire. Both pyr- (before h as in pyrheliometer, and before some vowels as in pyretic) and pyro- (before consonants, and some vowels as in pyroelectric) are usually listed as the combining form. Compare pyramid (from Gk *pyramis* pyramid), pyrene (from Gk *pyren* stone of a fruit), and pyriform (from ML *pyrum*, from L *pirum* a pear). Also has special chemical and mineralogical senses.

TOM-   from *tomos* a section, a piece cut off, from *temnein* to cut, used frequently in the two combining forms -tome (indicating an instrument for cutting), as in osteotome, and -tomy (indicating the surgical cutting of a [specified] tissue or part), as in lobotomy. See also -ectomy and -tomy, in Lesson XXI.

II. Additional Derivatives

Not all derivational suffixes are included here, nor are these lists otherwise meant to be complete.

BIBLI- Bible, bible, bibliography, bibliographical, biblioatry, bibliology, bibliomania, bibliopegy, bibliophile, bibliotheca, bibliothecary, bibliotherapy, bibliotics.

CANON- canon, canoness, canonic, canonical, canonicals, canonicity, canonist, canonize, canonization.

CRYPT- crypt, cryptanalysis, cryptanalyze, cryptic, cryptogram, cryptogenic, cryptograph, cryptology, cryptonym; hyphenated terms, such as crypto-Communist and crypto-Fascist; also, various words from medicine and botany. The doublet grotto (from Old It *grotta*, from LL *crypta*, ultimately from Gk *kryptos*) gives grotto, grotesque, grotty.

CYCL- cycle, cyclic, cyclist, cyclize, cyclometry, cyclone, cyclonology, cyclopedia, cyclopia, Cyclops, cyclops, cyclorama, cyclotron, bicycle, encyclical, encyclopedia, encyclopedize, recycle, tricycle, unicycle, and the trade name Exercycle.

GLOSS- gloss, glossa, glossary, glossectomy, glossematics, glosseme, glossitis, glossography, glossolalia, glossology, glossotomy; from GLOT(T)- comes glottal, glottalize, glottis, glottochronology, glottology, polyglot.

ICON- icon, iconize, iconoclasm, iconoclast, inconograph, iconography, iconolatry, iconology, iconophile, iconophobia, iconoscope, iconostasis.

MIM- mime, mimesis, mimic, mimosa, mimeograph, mimetite.

OD- monody, ode, odeon, odeum, thernody.

PYR- empyrean, empyreuma, pyracantha, pyralid, pyran, pyre, pyretic, pyrexia, pyrgeometer, pyrheliometer, pyrite, pryoacid, pyrochemical, pyroelectric, pyrogallic, pyrography, pyrolatry, pyromania, pyrometallurgy, pyrosis, pyrophosphoric acid, pyroxylin (XYL- wood), pyrotechnic, pyrrhic. There are also several other words in scientific senses.

TOM- tome, tomogram, tomograph, anatomy, dichotomy, entomology, osteotome, epitome.

III. Analysis and Definition of Words

A complete analysis of the words is given here.

1. BIBLI(o)- book + *-graphy* writing + *-ic* pertaining to + *-al* pertaining to: of or pertaining to a list of books or other written materials on a particular subject.

2. CANON- rule, standard + *-ical* pertaining to: belonging to or included in the official list of sacred books accepted by the Christian church as being genuine and inspired.

3. CRYPT(o)- hidden + *-graph* writing + *-ic* pertaining to: pertaining to the process of using or deciphering secret codes or ciphers.

4. from LL *epiglottis,* from Gk, from *epi-* on + GLOTTis: a valvelike cartilege structure that covers the entrance to the windpipe to prevent food and drink from entering the lungs during swallowing.

5. *en-* in + CYCL(o)- circle + -PEDIA to educate + *-ic* pertaining to: possessing wide and varied information.

6. *en-* in + TOM(o)- to cut + *-logy* science of + *-ist* specialist in: a person skilled in the branch of zoology that deals specifically with insects. (The Gk *entoma* means insect; its combining form is entom(o)-.)

7. ICON(o)- image + *-graphy* writing: the representing of persons, ideas, etc., by pictures, images, and the like.

8. MIM- to imitate + *-ic* pertaining to + *-ry* (a variant of *-ery*) the actions of: the act or practice of imitating.

9. from *paroidia* a satirical poem, from *par-* beyond + OD- poem + *-y* act of: a composition (here, literary) that mimics the style of another author in a humorous or satirical way.

10. POLY- more than one, many + GLOT- language: composed of many linguistic groups.

IV. Definition of Greek Loan Words

The source is given here for words not previously used in this lesson.

1. austere—from *austeros* strict, severe, austere: self-disciplined; ascetic; grave; serious.

2. canon: accepted principle or rule.

3. crypt: vault or chamber.

4. despot—from *despotes* despot, ruler, master: an absolute or tyrannical ruler.

5. icon: a religious image, usually painted: here, a representation of the Virgin Mary, probably painted in oil on a wooden panel, depicted in the traditional Byzantine style.

6. myriads—from *murias* (or *myrias*) ten thousand (the original, now archaic, sense): a large indefinite number.

7. nomad—from the stem *nomad-* of the noun *nomas* nomad: here, an attributive noun, a person who moves from place to place; a wanderer.

8. orgies—from the noun *orgia* orgies, revels, secret rites: a wild gathering of immoderate or frenzied indulgence.

9. tomes: a large and very heavy book.

10. zephyr—from *zephyros* zephyr, west wind, light breeze: a soft or gentle breeze.

LESSON IV

ASSIGNMENT

I. Discussion of Prefixes

a- is the Greek letter alpha, and when it is used as a prefix with the meaning 'without' or 'not,' it is known as alpha privative.

amphi- from *amphi* both, around. Considered a combining form by some dictionaries and a prefix by others. Amphoteric comes from *ampho*, which also means both. Most *amphi-* words are not part of the general vocabulary but are specialized words used in biology and other sciences.

ana- from *ana* up, through, over, about, back.

anti- from *anti* instead of, for, against. Always has a hyphen with proper nouns, as in anti-American, and before some vowels, as anti-intellectual; otherwise spelled solid. Compare other words beginning with anti-, as antimony (from ML *antimonium*) and antique (from L *antiquus*).

apo- from *apo* off, away. Considered a combining form by some dictionaries and a prefix by others. Also, apostrophe, apocalypse, apostate, apothecary, apothegm, apotheosis, aphorism, aphesis and apheresis (topical section of Latin Lesson V).

cata- from *kata* against, during, in, on, according to, after. Also appears rarely as *cath-*, as in cathexis (*kata-* + *echein* to hold). Also appears as *kata-* in the loan word katabasis, and the near loan katabatic (wind). Also, catheter, cathexis, catholic.

dia- from *dia* through, throughout, apart. Also, diabetes, diabolic, devil (ultimately from Gk *diabolos* a slanderer, from *diabellein* to slander, from *dia-* + BALL- to throw), deacon (from *diakonos* a servant, messenger, from *dia-* + *konis* dust—that is, one who is dusty from running), diagonal, diagram, dialect, and many others. Compare the Greek base DI- twice.

Additional Exercise Using the Prefix *a-*

Some of the following words are prefixed with *a-* (*an-*) not, without; others derive from Greek words that simply begin with the first letter of the alphabet. An exercise that would help familiarize students with this prefix would be to have them check these words in their dictionaries and then define them. Answers follow the dash.

1. anacanth—*an-* + *akantha* thorn.
2. asbestos—*a-* + *sbennynai* quench.
3. ascetic—*askein* to exercise (ASCE- Lesson XVIII).
4. asparagas—*asparagos.*
5. asphyxia—*a-* + *sphyxis* pulse.
6. astygmatism—*a-* + *stigma* point.
7. astronomy—*astron* star (ASTR- Lesson VII) + *-nomy* science of (Lesson XII).
8. asylum—*a-* + *syle* right of seizure.
9. atheist—*a-* + *theos* god (THE- Lesson IV).
10. athlete—*athlon* prize.

Additional Exercise Using the Prefixes *a*- and *ana*-

Some of the following words are prefixed with *ana*- up; others are prefixed with *an*- not, without. An exercise to help familiarize students with these two prefixes would be to have them check these words in their dictionaries and then define them. Answers follow the dash.

1. Anabaptist—*ana-* again + *baptismos* baptism.
2. anachronism—*ana-* back + *chronos* time (CHRON- Lesson IV).
3. anacoluthon—*an-* not + *akolouthos* following.
4. anacrusis—*ana-* up + *krouein* to strike.
5. anemia—*an-* without + *haima* blood (HEM- Lesson V).
6. anagram—*ana-* up or back + *gramma* letter (*-gram* Lesson XIV).
7. analgesia—*an-* without + *algein* to feel pain (ALG- Lesson IV).
8. anarchy—*an-* without + *archos* ruler (*-arch* Lesson XIII).
9. anathema—*ana-* up + *tithenai* to set (THE- Lesson X).

II. Discussion of Bases

ALG- from *algos* pain. Alg- (before vowels) and algo- are sometimes listed as a combining form. Also, in final position is the combining form -algia (with variant -algy), as in neuralgia. Also, algolagnia, algometer, algophilia, algophobia, arthralgia.

BI- from *bios* life. Some dictionaries recognize bi- as a variant of the combining form bio-, which is usually listed. Some dictionaries do not record this bi-. Nearly all English words prefixed with bi- carry the meaning of two or twice, from the Latin base BI-. There are some 175 words in English that begin with bio- meaning life.

CHRON- from *chronos* time. Chron- (before vowels, as in chronicle) and chrono- are generally found as the combining form. Also, anachronism, dyschronous (*dys-* disordered), chronology, chronometer, chronoscope, chronophotography. Not to be confused with the Gk base CHROM- color (Lesson VIII).

DEMON- from *daimon* divinity, spirit. DAEMON- is a variant spelling (*daemon* was the LL spelling). Also, demoniac, demonism, demonocracy, demonolatry. Compare such as demonstrate (*de-* thoroughly + *monstratus*, the past participle of *monstrare* to show) and demonetize (*de-* + *moneta* coin), both from Latin.

GE- from *ge* earth. Not many dictionaries main-entry ge-, but geo- is unanimously entered as the combining form for this base. There are some 150 words in English that begin with geo- meaning earth. Also, apogee, perigee, diageotropism, epigeous, hypogeum.

LOG- from *logos* speech, sermon, word, reason, account. Dictionaries vary in the treatment of -logue and -log as a combining form. Some have them and some do not. American dictionaries prefer -logue over -log, entering monologue, dialogue, prologue, etc., in favor of monolog, etc. Catalog, however, is preferred in the U.S. (except for AHD, which prefers catalogue), over the preferred British catalogue. British dictionaries as a rule do not recognize -log but, when they do, they call it U.S. The combining form -logy, also to be introduced here as coming from *logos*, carries two distinct meanings: (1) a doctrine, study, theory, or science of, as in biology, paleontology, ecology; (2) speech, discussion, oral or written expression, as in martyrology, culogy. The Gk noun *logos* derives from the verb *legein* to speak, to gather. This sense of gathering is found in a few words like anthology, analogous, analogy. Also, analogue, analog, apologize, apologue, antilogue, ecology, entomology, and monologue. The combining form -logy is treated by EW in Lesson XII. See also LECT- in Lesson VIII and IM's notes to accompany.

LY- from *lyein* to loosen. Lys-, lyso- (as in lysocline, lysogenic, lysogeny, lysosome, lysozyme—where lyso- ca⸱ ⸱s the sense of dissolve or destroy) and -lysis (as in analysis, ca⸱ ⸱sis, dialysis, paralysis) are occasionally recorded as combining forms. Lysimeter comes from *lysis* a loosening. Also, lysin, lysine, the English word lysis and its adjective lytic, and the back-formed verb lyse.

MNE- from *mnes-* (some dictionaries use *mimnes[kesthai]*) remember, recall. Not many dictionaries record -mnesia, a combining form denoting a certain type of memory, as amnesia (*a-* without) or paramnesia (*para-* disordered). Also, mnenomic (adjective and noun). A reduced form without the *mi-* reduplication was used in all English words borrowed from this base.

PAN- from *pan* (the neuter form of *pas* all). PANT- is the stem of this noun. The 'o' is retained in pantomime and its British clip panto, Pantocrator (=Christ), pantograph, pantography, pantology. Almost all dictionaries enter pan- as a combining form, but not as many recognize pant-, panto-. Also, panacea (*pan-* + *akos* cure; hence, a cure-all), Pan American, Pan-Arab, panchromatic, pancreas (*kreas* flesh), pandemic, Pandora (*dora* gifts—because of all the gifts the gods gave her at her creation), panjandrum, panoply, pansexualism, pansophy, pantheism, Pantheon, pantisocracy. Compare pan (from OE *panne*), panache (from L *penna* feather), pane (from *pannus* a piece of cloth—which in early times hung over the hole in the wall that served as a window), panel (also from *pannus*), and pantry (from L *panis* bread).

POD- from the stem *pod-* of the noun *pous* foot. Pod- (as in podiatry) and podo- (as in podocarpus, podophyllum) are sometimes found as a combining form. Also occasionally listed is -pod, as in cephalopod, arthropod, pleopod, tripod. Compare the English word pod (origin unknown).

THE- from *theos* god. Most dictionaries record both the- (as in thearchy, theism) and theo- as a combining form. Also occasionally listed are -theism and -theist, as in atheism (*a-* without), pantheism, monotheism, atheist, etc. Also, apotheosis, theobromine ("the food of the gods"), theocentrism, theocracy, theogony, theology, theonomy, theopathy, theophobia.

TROPH- from *trophe* nourishment, from the verb *trephein* to nourish, feed. In initial position, troph- (as in trophic) and tropho- (as in trophoblast, trophoplasm) are usually found as a combining form. In final position is -trophy, referring to nourishment or growth, as in hypertrophy, hypotrophy. Also, trophology, trophopathy (=a derangement of nourishment). Compare trophy and the combining form -tropy, from TROP- to turn.

III. Definition of Words Showing the Force of the Prefix

1. anonymous: (*an-* without) without a name.
2. antarctic: (*ant-* opposite + *arktos* bear [the constellation Bear]) opposite the north or arctic.
3. apostle: (*apo-* off) one who is sent off to preach the gospel.
4. catastrophe: (*cata-* against) an overturning or turning against.
5. aseptic: (*a-* without) without infection or disease-causing bacteria.
6. antiseptic: (*anti-* against) protecting against infection (as an adjective); a substance that protects against infection (as a noun).

7. amphitheater: (*amphi-* all around) a circular or oval construction with rows of seats (usually graduated) around a central open space (the arena).

8. anesthetic: (*an-* without) a substance that causes a person, or, if local, a body part, to be without the sensation of heat, pain, etc.

9. diameter: (*dia-* through, across) a straight line, or the length or measurement of that line, that passes from one side of a circle to the other through the center (or across from one side to the other).

10. amoral: (*a-* not) not moral, without morality. Amoral is not a Greek word but is built on analogy; moral is Latin. Compare immoral, meaning lewd, morally wrong.

11. catapult: (*cata-* against) a weapon that works like a slingshot, which hurls a missile against someone or something.

12. anarchy: (*an-* without) a political situation that is without any form of government or law.

IV. Analysis and Definition of Words

1. *apo-* away + CRYPH- hidden: of doubtful authenticity; false; spurious.

2. ana- up + LY- to loosen: skilled in thinking or reasoning.

3. *a-* without + TROPH- to grow: not to grow; to waste away.

4. from *amphibios* living a double life, from *amphi* both + BI- life: able to live both in the water and on land.

5. from *mnemonikos* memory, from MNE- to remember: relating to the memory. (Freak here is presumably a figurative use of the literal meaning, as a person that has developed in an abnormal way.)

6. PAN- all + THE- god: the entire group of gods (or perhaps exalted persons).

7. *ana-* back + CHRON- time: a person chronologically misplaced; a person occurring out of his proper time.

8. PANT(o)- all + MIM- to imitate: here, a figurative transfer of a play without words in which the person expresses herself by gesture (here, facial expression).

9. *a-* without + THE- god: a person who believes that there is no God.

10. *anti-* opposite + POD- foot: directly opposed (=opposite) or contrary.

11. *an-* without + ALG- pain: causing an insensitivity to pain without loss of consciousness.

12. *ana-* up, back + LOG- reasoning: a likeness or similarity in a certain limited number of details.

13. *anti-* against + BI(o)- life: a substance produced by a micro-organism that destroys or inhibits germs.

14. *ana-* up + TOM- to cut: the science of the structure of plants and animals that is based on dissection and certain observations.

15. *apo-* from + THE- god: to exalt to the rank of a god; glorify.

16. *cata-* completely + LY- to loosen: here, figurative, causing change.

17. *dia-* between + -LOGUE speech: a conversation.

18. from Pandemonium (coined by John Milton in *Paradise Lost*), from PAN- all + DEMON- evil spirit: wild uproar or disorder.

19. from *amnestia* forgetfulness, from *a-* not + MNE- to remember: a pardon granted to groups of individuals for past offenses against the government; a forgetting or an intentional overlooking.

20. *apo-* from + GE- earth: (a) the point farthest from the earth in the orbit of the moon or some other earth satellite; (b) here, figurative, the apex, highest point or peak.

LESSON V

ASSIGNMENT

I. Discussion of Prefixes

dys- from the Gk prefix *dys-*, with the notion of hard, bad, unlucky, etc., which destroys the good sense of a word or increases its bad sense. Used often in medical terminology carrying the sense of malformation, inability, degeneration, abnormality, etc., as dysentery (ENTER-intestine).

ec- from the preposition *ek* out of, from out of. *Ex-* appears before vowels, as in exegesis, and rarely before a consonant, as in extrophy (TROPH-to turn); otherwise ec-, as in ecclesiastic and ecstasy. *Ex-* is generally recorded in dictionaries but *ec-* is not always. Compare ec-, eco- (as in ecology, economy, ecumenical) from the noun *oikos* house, dwelling. Compare also *exo-* (below).

en- from the preposition *en* in. *Em-* appears before b, m, p, and ph, as in emblem (BLE- to throw), emmenagogue (= a drug that brings on menstruation), empathy, emphasis (PHA- to show). Both en- and em- are generally listed, but *el-* (rarely used) is not. Compare the other *en-* prefix (from L *in-* in), as in enslave, endear, enact; this prefix also appears as *em-*, as in embalm and employ.

endo-, ento- (*end-, ent-* before vowels or h)   from *endon* and *entos*, respectively, both of which are adverbs and prepositions meaning in, within, inside. Generally called combining forms. Not all dictionaries record all of these forms.

epi- (*ep-* before vowels or h)   from the preposition *epi* on. Some dictionaries also record the variant *eph-*, as in ephemeral, where the 'i' is deleted before h (*epi- + hemera* day).

eu- (*ev-* before vowels)   from the adverb *eu* well, the neuter form of the adjective *eus* good. Variously listed as a combining form and a prefix. Also defined as easily, as in euplastic (= that can be easily adapted to the formation of tissue). Sometimes defined as true, as in euchromosome (= any chromosome other than a sex chromosome) and euglobin (= any true globulin that does not dissolve in pure water). EW's *ev-*, rarely used, is not generally recorded. Also, eucalyptus (*calypt* to cover—from the covering on the bud), eulogy (LOG-speech, word), euphoria (PHOR- to bear).

exo-   from the preposition and adverb *exo* outside. Variously listed as a combining form and a prefix. The *ecto-*, generally called a combining form, is from the preposition and adverb *ektos* without, outside, beyond, etc. *Ect-* appears before vowels, as in ectostosis (OST- bone).

II. Discussion of Bases

AGON-   from *agonia* a struggle, from *agon* a contest, strife, conflict, from the verb *agein* to do. Protagonist is from PROT- first + AGON- struggle. Also, agonist, agonize, antagonist, and the free-standing agon.

ANGEL-   from *angelos* messenger.

CENTR-   from *kentron* center, sting, a sharp point. Centr- (before vowels), centri-, and centro- are usually listed as combining forms, as in centroid, centrist, centrifugal, centrosphere, and centrosome. In final position is -centric, variously listed as a suffix and combining form, as in concentric (formed when -centric passed into Latin), polycentric, heliocentric, eccentric. Also, epicenter, apocenter, metacenter.

DEM-   from *demos* people. Some dictionaries offer demo- as the combining form, as in demography. Also, epidemic and endemic. Compare the several English words beginning with dem- but not connected with this base, many of which are from the L prefix *de-* down, off, as in demolish and demonstrate (with its clip demo, meaning demonstration). Also compare the L *demi-* half, as in demigod.

GAM-   from *gamos* marriage. Dictionaries vary in etymologizing the bi- in bigamy. Some say it is from the L BI- two, twice; some derive it from the Gk base DI- twice. Usually listed as combining forms are the adjective-forming -gamous and noun-forming -gamy, both meaning concerned with marriage. Examples are monogamy, exogamy, monogamous, exogamous; -gamy is also used in biological terms where it means propagation or reproduction, as autogamy and allogamy. Another combining form, gam- (before vowels) and gamo-, is also generally recorded, as in gamete. Gamete has its own combining-form spin-off, gameto-, not generally listed; examples of this are gametocyte, gametogenesis, gametophore, and gametophyte. These and most gamo-words (as gamogenesis and gamophyllous) are concerned with biology, carrying the meaning united, joined, or sexual.

HEM-   all of these forms come from *haima* blood, with HEMAT- being the stem. Hem-, haem-, and hemat- are combining forms used before vowels, as in hemangioma (= birthmark) and hematemesis. The 'ae' forms, which appeared as the words passed through L, are still preferred in England, and the 'e' forms are preferred in the U.S. Hema-, etymologically "erroneous" according to the OED, appears generally as a variant of hemo-, in such as hemacytometer. These words are connected with science and medicine. Hemic (= having to do with blood) is not to be confused with the Gk base HEMI- half. Another combining form -emia (or -aemia), hemia (or -haemia) appears in leukemia and uremia, with the 'h' form being used after p, t, or k, as in leucocythemia (CYT- cell). At Lesson XXIII -*emia* is presented as a combining form.

HEMER-   from *hemera* day. The title of Boccaccio's *Decameron* is from DEC- ten + (H)EMER- because ten tales were told on each day. See footnote on ephemeral at the prefix *epi-* above. Also, hemeralopia (= day blindness)

OD-, HOD-   from *hodos* street, road, way, route. Anode, cathode, electrode, are covered under the combining form -ode, recorded in most dictionaries, to be distinguished from -ode (from the Gk suffix -*odes*, a contraction of -*oeides* -oid of Lesson VII), meaning 'like,' or 'resembling,' as in nematode and phyllode. Compare also ODONT(o)- tooth, as in odontology and orthodontist. Also compare OD- song, as in ode, parody.

STOL-, STAL-, -STLE   from *stellein* to make ready, set out, start, send on a mission, compress, bind, send. Epistle came in through OF. Also, apostle (*apo-* from, away), diastole and diastolic, systole and systolic (diastole and systole constitute the cardiac cycle). Compare stolon (from *stolo* a shoot or a sucker of a plant); and stalactite and stalagmite, both ultimately from Gk *stalassein* to trickle.

TAPH-   from *taphos* grave, tomb, grave. Cenotaph is from *kenos* empty + TAPH-.

THANAT-   from *thanatos* death. Its combining form thanat- and thanato- (seldom listed) is used chiefly in scientific words, as thanatometer, thanatology. Both THANAT- and THANAS- are extended roots from the stem *than-*.

III. Definition of Words Showing the Force of the Prefix

1. exoskeleton: (*exo-* external) any external covering or structure that supports or protects the body, as that of a turtle or a lobster.
2. dysentery: (*dys-* disordered) a disordered condition of the intestines causing diarrhea.
3. embryo: (*em-* in) an animal in its early developmental stage when it is still in the shell, womb, etc.
4. dysfunction: (*dys-* disordered) a functional abnormality or impairment, as of a bodily organ; also a verb, meaning to cease to function properly.
5. enthusiasm: (*en-* in) interest in (something).
6. exotic: (*exo-* outside) from outside one's country. Other definitions will not fit this literal mold: such as, fascinating because strange; or new, experimental, or high-energy, as rockets propelled by controlled nuclear explosions; or very unstable and hard to capture, as exotic nuclear particles; or in referring to a stripteaser, as exotic dancing.
7. ectoparasite: (*ecto-* outside) a parasite, as a flea, tick, or louse, living on the outside of its host.
8. epidermis: (*epi-* upon) of vertebrate animals, the outer layer of skin that is lying upon and covering the true skin or dermis.
9. eugenics: (*eu-* well, good) the science of making the human race better.
10. endocrine: (*endo-* within) that secretes within; secreting internally, as into the bloodstream for distributio⁻

IV. Analysis and Definition of Words

1. *epi-* into + TOM- to cut: (a) here, figurative (of the literal meaning of a condensed account, a summary), a thing that is typical of something; (b) here, the above literal meaning, a summary. 'In epitome' is also a set expression meaning in a brief or miniature form.
2. from *ekkentros* (*ex-* + *kentros* "out of center," i.e., not having the earth as center, eccentric), from *ec-* out of + CENTR- center: the condition of being odd, peculiar, or out of the ordinary.
3. *en-* in + DEM- people: peculiar to or found among a particular people.
4. *ant-* against, opposite + AGON- struggle: mutually opposed; conflicting.
5. GLOSS- language (also means a foreign word that needs explaining): a list of special words with explanations or comment.

6. *eu-* good + THANAS- death: a painless killing; mercy killing.

7. *ex-* out + OD- way: a departure, said of a large group.

8. *epi-* upon + DEM- people: an outbreak of disease that affects or tends to affect many people within a population.

9. PAN- all + DEM- people: a disease occurring over a vast geographic area, such as an entire country (here, throughout the world).

10. *exo-* outside + GAM- marriage: marriage outside of one's own group, tribe, clan, etc.

11. *epi-* on, at + TAPH- tomb: a brief statement put on a grave or headstone in memory of the person buried there.

12. *an-* without + EM- blood: here, figurative, lacking strength, power, vigor.

13. *en-* in + CYCL- circle: here, a substantive adjective, a papal letter to bishops, stating the position of the church on important issues.

14. *dys-* bad, disordered + TROPH- to nourish: defective nutrition. (By the 1980s muscular dystrophy was a main entry in almost all dictionaries, defined as an hereditary disease characterized by progressive wasting of muscles.)

15. *ep-* upon, on + HEMER- day: lasting only a short time.

16. *apo-* off + STOL- to send: coming from or originating from the Apostles.

17. *epi-* to + STOL- to send: that is found in letters.

18. *eu-* good + LOG- word: a speech in praise of someone or something.

19. *ev-* good + ANGEL- messenger: having to do with the Protestant churches that stress Christ's atonement and man's salvation by faith as the most important issues of Christianity.

20. *epi-* in addition + -LOGUE speech, word: a concluding part added to (here) a book.

V. Homonyms

1. cashier—(a) from the L adjective *cassus* empty; (b) from the L noun *capsa* box.

2. junk—(a) from Javanese *jong* (variants *jon* and *djong*) ship; (b) from ME *jonke* old cable or rope (of obscure origin).

3. policy—(a) from Gk *polis* city-state (with doublets police, through MF and ML, and polity, through MF and LL); (b) through MF *police*, ultimately from Gk *apodeixis* evidence, proof.

4. quarry—(a) from L *corium* hide, skin; (b) from the L noun *quadrum* a square.

5. school—(a) from OE *scol*, from L *scola*, from Gk *schole* leisure; (later) study, learning; (b) from Du *school* a multitude.

6. tatoo—(a) from Polynesian *tatau* (Marquesan *tatu*); (b) Du *taptoe*, from *tap* the tap (of a barrel) + *toe* to shut, turn off.

LESSON VI

ASSIGNMENT

I. Discussion of Prefixes

hyper- from *yper* (*hyper*) over, above, excessive. A living English prefix attached to many modern words. The free-standing informal adjective hyper was not generally recorded in the mid 1980s. There are currently some 150 words with hyper- as a prefix.

hypo- (*hyp-* before vowels or h) from *hypo* under, below. A living English prefix attached to many modern words having mainly to do with science. Hypo is also a free-standing clip with four meanings: a hypodermic ("under the skin"); sodium thiosulfate (used in photography); in a figurative sense meaning any stimulus; and a hypochondriac, a person affected with hypochondria, from *hypo-* under + *chondros* the cartilage in the breastbone in the region of the upper abdomen, this being where melancholy, earlier considered a disease, was supposed to be seated.

meta- (*met-* before vowels or h) from the preposition *meta* with, after, among (akin to OE *mid* with). Occurs with various meanings: among or between, as in metatarsus (= the bones between the ankle and the toes); change of place or condition, as in metathesis (topical essay at Latin Lesson XXIV is on metathesis); behind or after, as in metathorax; beyond, as in metalaw (= any system of law beyond the present human frame of reference); and other, scientific, senses.

para- (*par-* before vowels or h) from the preposition *para* by, near, against, beside. This has picked up new meanings in English, such as: (a) related to or as a supplement to, as in paramedic, paralegal, paramilitary; (b) beyond (suggesting alteration), as in parapsychology; (c) faulty or abnormal, as in paresthesia. Compare the combining form para- having to do with a parachute or parachutist, as in parakite or parawing.

peri- from the preposition *peri* round about, all around, around. Can also occasionally mean near, as in periselenium.

pro- from the preposition *pro* before, forth. Compare the L prefix *pro-*.

pros- from the preposition *pros* on the side of, in the direction of, at, to. Not recorded as a prefix in all dictionaries. Also translates as near (= toward), as in prosenchyma; and in front or forward of, as in prosencephalon.

syn- from the preposition *syn* with, together. Appears in these assimilated forms: *sy-* before z and before s plus a consonant, as in syzygy and systole; *syl-* before l, as in syllable; *sym-* before b, m, or p, as in symbol, symmetry, sympathy. These situations are not spelled out in most dictionaries.

II. Discussion of Bases

BALL-, BOL-, BLE- from *ballein* to throw, throw as to hit, cast, or hurl. There are many English words not connected with this base, such as ball, ballad, ballet, balloon, ballot, bole, bollard, bolster, bolt, and the L adjective suffix *-ble*, a variation of *-able*. From this base come amphibole, metabolism (and from this, anabolism), catabolism, epiboly, hyperbole, devil (from *diaballein* to slander—*dia-* across + BALL- to throw), diabolic. Also, the five doublets (or quintuplets) parable, palaver (through Portuguese), parabole, parabola, and parole; the changes here involve the bilabial /b/ going to its near neighbor the labiodental /v/, and the liquids 'r' and 'l' suffering metathesis (both of these affecting palaver), with parole being a contraction.

DERM- from *derma* skin, hide; DERMAT- from the stem *dermat-*. This is actually from a base *der-* with the suffix *-ma*, *-mat* (see Lesson XI). Derm-, dermo-, derma-, dermat-, dermato-, -derm, -derma, -dermatous, and -dermis are all generally listed as combining forms, as in dermal, dermographia (= an irritable condition of the skin), dermatome (TOM- to cut), dermabrasion (and the recent dermaplaning), dermatogen, dermatoplasty, dermatosis, dermatotherapy, ectoderm, hypodermic, scleroderma, sclerodermatous, epidermis, endodermis. Also, derm, derma, dermis. Compare derma, meaning kishke, from Yiddish.

DOX- from *doxa* expression, opinion, glory, splendor, etc; DOG- from *dogma* (genitive *dogmatos*) opinion, from *dokein* to seem right. Also, doxology and paradox.

GNO- from *gnosis* inquiry, investigation, and the reduced form of the reduplicative verb *gignoskein* to know—which are cognate with the English verb 'know' (from OE *cnawan*, where the 'c' was pronounced as /k/, later to drop out in speech but kept as 'k' in writing). Some words from this base are direct lifts, as diagnosis (from *diagnosis* a distinguishing or discerning), prognosis (from *prognosis* foreknowledge), gnosis, gnome (= maxim; from *gnome* opinion, judgment), and gnomon (from *gnomon* indicator, i.e. one who knows).

HOM- from *homos* same; homo- is the generally recognized combining form here (hom- as preferred main entry in WNCD) with some 90 words beginning with homo-. Many words are of Gk origin, as homograph, homology, homophone; others are constructed analogically, as homophile, homophobe, homoplastic, homotransplantation. HOME(o)- (from *homoios* like, similar), sometimes found as a combining form, has whelped homeomorphism, -pathy, -stasis, -therm, -typical. Homo is also a derogatory clip for homosexual. HOMAL- (from *homalos* even) is found in homalographic (= homolographic). Compare the L *homo* man, found in Latin expressions, such as Homo sapiens, and in homage and homunculus.

MORPH- from *morphe* form, figure, shape. Morph-, morpho-, and -morph (as in isomorph) are occasionally found as combining forms. Also, anamorphosis, apomorphine, diamorphine (= heroin), endomorph, ectomorph, mesomorph (these last three represent hypothetical body types), epimorphosis, paramorphism, morphine, Morpheus (= god of dreams, coined by Ovid), morphogenesis, morpheme (patterned on phoneme), morphophoneme, morphosis.

ONYM- from *onyma* (the Aeolian and Dorian form of *onoma*, as in onomastics, onomatopoeia) name. Also, antonym, eponym, metonym, paronym, allonym, caconym, toponym, pseudonym.

PHER- from *pherein* to carry; PHOR-, which appears as a combining form -phore, is from the Gk adjective combining form *-phoros*. Also pheromone, anaphora, cataphoresis, diaphoresis, dysphoria, euphoria, exophoria, metaphor ("to carry across"). Compare apheresis (*aph-* + *airesis* a taking).

TACT- from *taktikos* suitable for arrangement; TAX- is from *taxis* arrangement; both ultimately from *tassein* to arrange. Tax- (as in taxeme), taxo- (as in taxonomy), taxi- (as in taxidermy), -taxy (as in heterotaxy, a variant of heterotaxis), and -taxis (as in heterotaxis) are all variously recorded as combining forms. Also, taxis, taxon, hypotaxis, parataxis, syntax, syntactical, epitaxy. Compare tact, tactful, tactile, tactual, etc., from the L base TACT- touch; also compare tax (from L *taxare* to evaluate, estimate), and taxi (from taximeter cab).

III. Definition of Words Showing the Force of the Prefix

1. hypersonic: (*hyper-* excessive) of speed five times or more in excess of the speed of sound (in the air, at least 5,435 feet per second).

2. parallel: (*par-* beside) said of lines of planes running beside one another and always the same distance apart, as railroad tracks.

3. syllable: (*syl-* together) a word or part of a word in which two or more letters are taken together and pronounced as a unit. (A syllable may also consist of a single vowel.)

4. hypertension: (*hyper-* excessive) excessively high blood pressure.

5. hypothyroidism: (*hypo-* below) an activity of the thyroid gland abnormally below its normal functioning.

6. proscenium: (*pro-* in front of) that part of a stage out toward the audience in front of the curtain.

7. periscope: (*peri-* around) a tubular optical instrument that allows those in a submarine, or other place where surface view is obstructed, to see all around the surface.

8. sympathy: (*sym-* with) harmony or agreement in feeling with someone else.

9. paranoia: (*para-* disordered) a disordered state of mind characterized by delusions of persecution or grandeur.

10. perimeter: (*peri-* around) the measure around a figure or an area.

11. symphony: (*sym-* together) a musical composition in sonata form for (usually the four choirs of) an orchestra in which musicians play together.

12. prosthetic: (*pros-* in addition to) an artificial device added to the body to replace a missing part, such as a limb or a tooth.

IV. Analysis and Definition of Words

1. *syn-* together + TAX- to arrange: word order in sentences; sentence construction.

2. *meta-* after + PHOR- to bear: an implied comparison between two different things.

3. *hypo-* under + DERM- skin: injected (or for injecting) under the skin.

4. *an-* not + (H)OMAL- same: any abnormal departure from a general rule.

5. *para-* contrary to, aside + DOX- opinion: pertaining to a statement that may be true but seems contrary to common sense.

6. *hyper-* over + TROPH- to nourish: excessive development of a bodily organ or part.

7. *a-* not + GNO- to know: of one who holds that the existence of God is unknown and probably unknowable.

8. *eu-* well + PHOR- to go: a feeling of elation, well-being, or happiness.

9. from *metabole* a change, from *meta-* changed + BOL- to put: having to do with the process of the building up and destruction of protoplasm; pertaining to the process by which all living things turn food into energy and living tissue.

10. from *synodos* meeting, assembly, from *syn-* together + OD- way: a church council.

11. *meta-* changed + MORPH- form: changed; transformed.

12. *para-* beside + *pherne* dowry (PHER- to bear): personal belongings.

13. *pro-* before + GNO- to know: to foretell from signs or symptoms; predict.

14. *peri-* near + GE- earth: the point in the orbit of the earth's moon or any other earth satellite that is closest to the earth. (Opposite of apogee.)

15. from *hyperbole* extravagance, from *hyper-* excessive + BOL- to throw: an extravagant exaggeration used for effect.

16. *ant-* against + ONYM- word: a word opposite in meaning to another word.

17. *en-* in + DEM- people (also, district) here, a substantive, an animal that is indigenous (L *indigena* a native .m *in-* + GEN- be born) to a certain locality and, often, not found elsewhere.

18. *peri-* around + PHER- to go: the outside boundary.

19. from *syllogismos* computation, calculation, conclusion, from *syn-* together + LOG- reasoning: a specious or deviously crafty argument.

20. HOM- same + ONYM- word: two words having the same pronunciation or spelling but not the same meaning or origin. (Bore and boar are also homophones.)

V. Antonyms Formed Through Prefixes

1. exoskeleton—endoskeleton
2. sympathy—antipathy
3. aphelion—perihelion
4. proslavery—antislavery
5. atheism—theism
6. anabolism—catabolism
7. ectoparasite—endoparasite
8. epilogue—prologue
9. hypertonic—hypotonic
10. euphoria—dysphoria

LESSON VII

LOAN WORDS

As seen in Latin Lesson XXV and the assignments of Greek Lesson XIX, EW's consideration as to what constitutes a loan word is narrower in scope than some of the considerations and examples in the discussion of loan words in this lesson. Conformity to English inflections (e.g. -s and -es for plural; -ed, etc., for verbs), and conformity to English pronunciation, hodge podge that it is, together with tenure in the language and the extent of alteration of spelling presumably constitute much of the criteria for deciding what is "English" and what is "foreign." The word 'miasma' has been used in English for more than 300 years; if I pronounce it the English way and give it the -s plural (rather than the Greek -ata), is the word now "English"? If I pronounce it the Greek way and give it the -ata plural, is it then "foreign"? American dictionaries consistently prefer both the English pronunciation and the -s plural. British dictionaries (including the OED) rather consistently prefer both the foreign pronunciation and the -ata plural. The OED even labels it a foreign word. From this we may assume that the Americans consider the word to be English, and the British consider the word to be foreign. It should be pointed out to the students that the trend in the United States in the 1970s and 1980s leaned heavily in favor of English inflections. The trouble is that for some cases the foreign plural got attached to certain meanings (or vice versa), such as phalanges, which is the preferred plural for bones of the finger or toe.

The point of this topical section in EW on loan words is not directed toward any special attempt to define 'loan word' but to stimulate some discussion as to what constitutes foreignness and nonforeignness in the English vocabulary. Even so, it is not supposed that the matter is going to be settled once and for all in your classroom, or in anyone else's. The discussions of loan words in EW and IM are meant to give the students an educated feel for the great melting pot that is English and to make them aware that many of the "foreign" words that have not gained the rite of passage into naturalization are thereby not accorded all the rights and privileges that are granted to "English" words.

ASSIGNMENT

I. Discussion of Suffixes

-ic (*-ac* after the letter i), *-tic*. For a full discussion of this suffix, see Latin Lesson IX in IM. The 'a' is in original Greek nouns, as LL *maniacus*,

165

from L *mania*, from Gk *mania* madness; or L *cardiacos*, from Gk *cardiakos*, from *cardia* heart; or from analogical constructions as *aphrodisiakos* (an adjective), from *aphrodisios* concerning *Aphrodite* Aphrodite (= the Greek goddess of love and beauty). In substantive use, the suffix means one who is skilled in, as a mechanic (= one skilled in machines).

-*ics*, -*tics*   the plural of -*ic*, representing L -*ica*, from Gk -*ika*, as in *mathematika* mathematics, or *physika* physics. EW's definition 'art' can be extended to actions or activities of, acrobatics (= the activities of an acrobat), or gymnastics. Another meaning is the operations, workings, or phenomena of, as mechanics (= the workings of a machine).

-*oid*   from -*oeides* in the form of (as in *sphairoeides* spheroid), from *eidos* form. Also used substantively, as in humanoid, spheroid, globoid, anthropoid.

II. Discussion of Bases

AESTHE-, ESTHE-   from *aisthanesthai* to perceive. The 'ae' form, as in aesthete or aesthetics, is still given first place in preference, with the 'e' form as a variant. Occasionally found is the combining form esthesio-, aesthesio-, also from this base, meaning sensation, as in esthesiology, esthesiometer (and here the 'e' form is preferred). Dictionaries differ in their choice of anaesthesia; some give first choice to anesthesia.

ANTHROP-   from *anthropos* man. Both anthrop- (before vowels, as in anthropoid) and anthropo- are generally recorded as a combining form. Also, anthropocentric, anthropogenesis, anthropogeny, anthropogeography, anthropography, anthropometer, anthropomorphism, and several others.

ARCHA(E), ARCHE-   from *archaios* ancient, from *arche* a beginning. Archaeo- (as in archaeopteryx), archeo-, arche- (as in archespore), and archi- (as in archiplasm) are variously recorded as combining forms. The 'ae' is generally preferred in learned journals and many books, and in England; the 'e' form (which Collins often signals as "especially U.S.," as in Archean and Archeozoic, but without signaling archeo- as being American) is widely used in American periodicals. Compare arch (= a curved structure) from L *arcus*; also, the prefix arch- (as in archbishop), or archi- (as in architecture), meaning chief or principal, from Gk *archos* ruler. Compare also the combining form -arch in Lesson XIII.

AST(E)R-   from *astron* star. Also the popular combining form astro-, in some words of original Greek, as astrolabe, astrology, astronomy, but many more of recent coinage, as astrobotany, astrochemistry, astrodynamics, astrometeorology.

GEN(E)- through *-gene*, which represented the Gk *-genos*, itself from *-gen*, which is the root of the verb *gignesthai* to be born, to beget. The gi- is a reduplication in Gk that was clipped off for derivatives. The combining form -gen (usually listed) has two meanings: (1) something that produces, as allergen (produces an allergy), androgen (produces male characteristics), nitrogen (a necessary part of plant growth and animal tissue); and (2) something that has been produced or is growing, as acrogen, cultigen (= a cultivated plant), phosgene (= a gas or liquid formed from other constituents). The corresponding adjective form is -genic. The GON- comes from *gonos* descent, begetting, from the above *gignesthai*. Also, anagenesis, antigen, endogen, epigone, exogen, oxygen, metagenesis. Compare agony (from *agonia* a struggle, from *agon* contest), paragon (*para-* beside + *akaina* point, barb), diagonal (*dia-* through + *gonia* angle). Also, compare words from the Latin base GEN-, GENER- race, kind, the Latin base GEN- to produce, and the Greek base GEN(E)- race, kind.

GER- from *geron* old man; GERONT- from its stem *geront-*. Both geront- (as in gerontics) and geronto- (as in gerontology) are usually recorded as a combining form. Compare words from the Latin base GER-, GEST- to carry, to produce.

HOL- from *olos* (*holos*) all, whole. Hol- (before vowels) and holo- are generally listed as a combining form, used especially in new formations such as holoenzyme, hologram, holography, holometabolism, holophone, holophrase, holoplankton, holoscope. Compare hole (from OE *hol*) and holiday (from OE *haligdaeg* holy day).

IATR- from *iatros* a healer, a physician, from *iasthai* to heal. As combining forms in initial position (not generally found), there is iatr- (as in iatric) and iatro- (as in iatrochemistry, iatrogenic, iatrophysics). In final position, the forms are -iatry, -iatric, -iatrics (all variously recorded), as in psychiatry, psychiatric, pediatric, geriatrics.

PEP- is from *pepsin* digestion; PEPT- from *peptos* cooked, digested; both from *peptein* to cook. Also, peptidase, peptide, peptize, peptogen, peptonize, and the trade name Pepto-Bismol. Compare peplum (a kind of overskirt, from Gk *peplos*), and pepper (Gk *piperi*) and its clip pep.

TECHN- from *techne* art, skill, method. Techno- is generally found as the combining form. The base means art or skill (as in technography and technique), or technical (as in technology and technocracy).

III. Analysis and Definition of Words

1. GE(o)- earth + CENTR- center + -*ic* pertaining to: that is measured (or as if seen) from the center of the earth. (Not generally etymologized in dictionaries.)

2. ANTHROP(o)- human being + MORPH- form, shape + -ic pertaining to: described or thought of as having human form or human characteristics.

3. GENE- origin + -tics science or study of: the branch of biology concerned with the principles of heredity and variation. (Not generally etymologized in dictionaries.)

4. CRYPT- hidden + -ic pertaining to: obscure; mysterious; having a hidden meaning.

5. ANTHROP- human being + -oid like: (of human beings) apelike. (When the words refers to apes, it means 'resembling human beings.')

6. GER- old age, old people + IATR- medicine + -ics science of: the branch of medicine dealing with the study of aging, the elderly, and their debilities and diseases. (Compare gerontology—GERONT- + -logy: the scientific study of aging and of the special problems of the elderly.)

7. PYR(o)- fire + TECHN- art + -ics science of: here, figurative, brilliant or spectacular music.

8. AESTHE- to feel, perceive + -tic pertaining to: artistic; pertaining to beauty.

9. ANTHROP(o)- human being + CENTR- center + -ic pertaining to: pertaining to an interpretation of the world in terms of human values and experiences.

10. ASTER- star + -oid having the shape of: here, substantive use, one of thousands of small objects or planets chiefly between Mars and Jupiter.

11. exo- outside + -tic pertaining to: here, substantive use, a thing from a foreign country.

12. dys- bad + PEPT- to digest + -ic pertaining to: suffering from poor digestion.

13. ARCHA- ancient + -ic pertaining to: out-of-date; old-fashioned.

14. CHRON- time + -ic pertaining to: continuing for a long time.

15. DEMON- evil spirit + -iac pertaining to: raging; fitful.

16. eu- good + PEPT- digest + -ic pertaining to: here, figurative, optimistic.

17. cat- very, in accordance with, with respect to, etc. + HOL- whole + -ic pertaining to: comprehensive; broad-minded.

18. eu- good + GEN- race (or stock) + -ic pertaining to: having to do with the improvement of the human race.

19. an- without + ESTHE- to feel + -tic pertaining to: here, substantive, something that relieves pain.

20. CYCL- circle + -*ic* pertaining to: pertaining to a time period that repeats itself in the same order.

IV. Words Easily Confused

1. **Amnesia** is a loss of memory. **Anamnesis** means the recalling of things in the past recollection.

2. **Anesthesia** is the loss of sensation (heat, cold, pain, etc.). **Paresthesia** is an abnormal sensation, as itching, prickling, with no objective cause.

3. (An) **anti-Christian** means (a person) opposed to Christianity. **Ante-Christian** means before the time of Christ.

4. (An) **antiseptic** means (something) used for preventing infection. (An) **aseptic** also means (something) used for preventing infection, but also means (something) free from the living germs that cause disease, fermentation, or putrefaction.

5. **Hypocritical** pertains to a person who pretends to be what he is not. **Hypercritical** means excessively critical.

6. **Immoral** means morally wrong, wicked, licentious. **Amoral** means without a sense of morality, being neither moral nor immoral.

7. **Supersonic** means greater than the speed of sound at normal pressure and temperature (about 1,100 feet per second). **Hypersonic** refers to speed five or more times that of sound.

8. **Symbolism** means the use of, or the organized set or pattern of, symbols. **Embolism** means the blocking of a blood vessel by some substance; also, the insertion of one or more days in a calendar; intercalation.

9. **Sympathy** means harmony or agreement in feeling between two (or more) people; also, the sharing of another's feelings, as of pain or trouble. **Empathy** also means such sharing, but more strongly, such as complete intellectual identification with, or participation in, another's attitudes, feelings, etc.; also, the imaginative ascribing to an object, either natural or man-made, one's own thoughts, feelings, or attitudes.

10. A **synonym** is a word that has the same meaning as another word. A **homonym** is a word spelled and pronounced like another word but with a different meaning.

V. Loan Words

1. angst—from German (akin to L *angustus* narrow, petty, limited): a feeling of anxiety or fear.

2. apparat—from Russian: a political or party organization or an underground political movement.

3. au jus—from French: served in its own gravy or juice (as in, roast pork au jus).

4. autostrada—from Italian (*strada* = street): in Italy, an expressway (superhighway, turnpike).

5. baksheesh—from Persian *bakhshish* gift: money given as a tip or bribe, especially in certain Near East countries.

6. enchilada—from Mexican Spanish (ultimately from L *in-* + Nahuatl *chilli* chili): a rolled tortilla filled with meat (usually beef or chicken) and served heated with grated cheese and chili sauce. Also in the phrase 'the whole enchilada' = the whole lot; the whole bit; everything.

7. enfant terrible—from French (literally, terrible child): a child whose language or behavior embarrasses older people; or, a person, group, or organization that is unconventional, responsible, or indiscreet.

8. gemütlich—from German: congenial; cozy; comfortable; agreeable.

9. machismo—from Spanish *macho* male, strong man, he-man (from L *masculus,* diminutive of *mas* male): strong sense of maleness; virility (L *vir* man); manly self-assurance.

10. samizdat—from Russian (*samo-* self + *izdat elstvo* publishing house): a system practiced by Soviet writers of publishing, as by typewriter and carbons, literature banned by the government.

11. subito—from Italian (from L *subitus* sudden, from *sub-* + IT- to go): as a direction in music, quickly or suddenly.

12. table d'hôte—from French (literally, host's table): a meal served at a fixed time with a fixed price. This is also called prix fixe (= fixed price). Compare à la carte (= according to the bill of fare), served with a fixed price for each item or dish.

LESSON VIII

ASSIGNMENT

I. Discussion of Adjective-Forming Suffixes

For these Latin suffixes the instructor is referred to EW's notes at Latin Lesson VIII and IM's notes to accompany.

II. Discussion of Bases

CHROM- from the noun *chroma* color; CHROMAT- is from the stem *chromat-*. Chrom- (before vowels, as in chromize) and chromo- (as in chromosome) are generally found as a combining form. Chromat- (before vowels, as in chromatid) and chromato- (as in chromatography) are generally listed separately as another combining form. In addition, -chrome is used as a noun and adjective combining form, as in monochrome and polychrome. Also, apochromatic, Cibachrome (= a modern trade name involving a direct positive printing process), Agfachrome, Ektachrome, Fujichrome, Kodachrome (all color film trade names), euchromosome, metachrome, metachromatism. This EW base is actually from a base *chro-* with the suffix *-ma, -mat* of Lesson XI.

CRI- from *krinein* to judge, choose, pick out, separate, distinguish, etc. In critic, CRI- means to judge; in crisis, it can mean decide, judge, or separate; in endocrine and exocrine, it means separate. Also, apocrine, criterion, criticism, critique (through F).

ETHN- from *ethnos* a number of people living together, nation, people, tribe. Ethno- is generally found as the combining form, as in ethno-astronomer, -botany, -grapher, -graphy, -history, -linguistics, -musicology, -psychology. Ethnic and ethnicity came in through *ethnikos* national, foreign, gentile.

LECT- ultimately from *legein* to speak, choose, gather, is from derivatives of this verb that contain the base *-lekt-*, as in analects (from *analekta*), dialect (from *dialektos*), eclectic (from *eklektikos*), catalectic (from *katalektikos*). Notes on LOG(UE) and other forms of this base are in Greek Lesson IV at LOG-.

PHA(N)- from *phainein* to show. Phantom, phantasm, phantasma (all doublets) came in through *phantasma* image. Fantasy and fantasia (the 'f' came in through F and It respectively), both doublets, stem from *phantasia* appearance, image. The English noun fancy (= inclination) is a contraction of fantasy. Also, fantastic, diaphanous. Compare the Greek base PHA- to speak.

PHIL- from *philos* loving. Phil- (as in philanthropy), -phil (eosinophil), -phile (Anglophile), -philia (pedophilia), -philiac (hemophiliac—in which PHIL- means, medically, a tendency), -philous (acidophilous) are all variously recorded as combining forms. Also, Philadelphia, philander, philanthropize, philately (*ateleia* exemption or freedom from charges—i.e., by the postage stamp that showed prepayment of the postal tax), philhellenic (*Hellen,* meaning Greek), Francophile, necrophilia, dendrophilous (DENDR- tree), hydrophilous (HYDR- water).

PHON- from *phone* sound, voice. Three combining forms are usually listed: phon- (before vowels) and phono-, as in phonic, phonation, phonautograph, phoneme, phonemics, phonology, phonography and its clip phono; -phony (or the variant -phonia), as in telephony, euphony, symphony, tautophony, dysphonia and its adjective dysphonic, cacophony (*kakos* bad) and its adjective cacophonous; and -phone, as in diaphone, euphone and its adjectives euphonious and euphonic, homophone, hydrophone (= an underwater microphone), megaphone, microphone, saxophone, sousaphone, xylophone, telephone, and its clip phone. Also, antiphon, euphonism, euphonistic, etc.

POLY- from *polys* much, many. This is generally listed as a combining form, which has generated some 250 words in English.

TAUT- from *tauto* same. Tauto- is the combining form, giving tautochrome, tautologize, tautomer (-ic, -ism), tautonym (-ic, -y), tautophony.

THERM- from the noun *therme* heat. The combining form is thermo- (therm- before vowels), giving close to 100 words. Also generally listed as a combining form is -therm, giving diathermal, ectotherm and ectothermy, endothermal (and -thermic), epithermal, exothermal (-thermic), hyperthermia, hypothermia, homeotherm, heterotherm.

III. Analysis and Definition of Words

1. CHROMAT- color + -*ic* pertaining to: of colors.
2. POLY- much + PHON- sound + -*y* quality of (Lesson X): music containing two or more voices harmonizing; counterpoint.
3. *syn*- together + ONYM- name + -*ous* like: alike in meaning.
4. ETHN- race + -*ic* pertaining to: pertaining to races or groups of people having common customs, language, characteristics, etc.
5. BIBLI(o)- book + PHIL- to love: a lover of books.
6. ASTR- star + -*al* pertaining to: of the stars.
7. TAUT(o) the same + LOG- to speak + -*ic* pertaining to + -*al* like + -*ly* E adverb suffix: in a manner characterized by redundancy or repetition.
8. CHROMAT- color + -*ic* pertaining to: of tones in music, progressing only by half steps. (Chromatic scale is a scale that proceeds by semitones.)
9. *dia*- through + PHAN- to show + -*ous* having the character of: sheer; light; transparent; translucent.
10. *dia*- between + LECT- to speak + -*ics* art of: the art or practice of logical discussion or debate as the means of examining the truth of an opinion or theory.

11. THERM- heat + -al pertaining to: having to do with heat.

12. *hyper*- excessive + CRI- to judge + -*tic* pertaining to + -*al* characteristic of: excessively critical.

13. POLY- many + GAM- marriage + -*ous* practicing: having more than one wife at the same time.

14. from *diakritikos* piercing, penetrating, from *dia*- through + CRI-separate + -*tic* pertaining to + -*al* characteristic of: marks meant to distinguish. (Diacriticals, a term more commonly thought of as applying to phonetics, here refers to marks in music to signify up or down bowing, spiccato, louré, martelé, jeté, tremolo, left-hand pizzicato, separate bowing, phrasing, trills, diminuendo, staccato, crescendo, an octave higher or lower, triplets, glissando, etc. Some of these diacritics of music have slightly different applications and meanings when applied to different instruments. Some of them, such as the martelé, spiccato, and up and down bowing, apply only to strings.)

15. *eu*- good + PHON- sound + -*ious* full of: pleasant or agreeable to the ear.

16. ETHN(o)- race + CENTR- center + -*ic* pertaining to: characterized by the practice of regarding one's race or culture as being superior to all others.

17. PHIL(o)- love + LOG- word + -*ic* pertaining to + -*al* characteristic of: having to do with literary classical scholarship.

18. PHIL- love + ANTHROP- human being + -*ic* pertaining to: having to do with the showing of kindness and goodwill to humanity.

19. *a*- without + MORPH- form, shape + -*ous* having the character of (amorphy, an obsolete noun): having no definite shape or form.

20. *ec*- out + LECT- to choose + -*ic* pertaining to: composed of selections from various sources.

IV. Division of Words into Syllables

1. a/mor/phous
2. as/tral
3. di/a/crit/i/cal
4. di/aph/a/nous
5. ec/lec/tic
6. eu/pho/ni/ous
7. po/lyg/a/mous
8. syn/on/y/mous
9. tau/to/log/i/cal
10. ther/mal

LESSON IX

PLACE NAMES

The study of place names has had its fair share of avid adherents over the past hundred years or so. Many scholars have published books on the subject: well over a thousand publications on geographical names, from Arabia to Wyoming, await the eyes of eager students who might be interested in doing individual or group projects, mini or grand, on their favorite city, county, province, department, state, island, country, or continent. Many are of Latin or Greek origin, but many more have histories as colorful as EW's Baton Rouge and Berkeley. Following are a few reference books on the subject.

Place Names in the United States by Henry Gannett (G.P.O., Washington, 1905); *Illustrated Dictionary of Place Names (United States and Canada)* by K. B. Harder (Van Nostrand, 1976); *American Place Names* by A. H. Holt (Crowell, 1938); *Scratch Ankle, U.S.A.* by M. J. Quimby (A.S. Barnes, Cranbury, New Jersey, 1969—a colorful selection); *American Place Names* by G. R. Stewart (Oxford, 1970); *Handbook of French Place Names in the U.S.A.* by R. Coulet du Gard (Adams Press, Chicago, 1974); *Place Names of the World* by A. Room (Rowman and Littlefield, New Jersey, 1974—a good list of elements that are non-English); *A Dictionary of Place-Names (Giving Their Derivations)* by C. B. Blackie (John Murray, London, reprinted by Gale Research Center, Detroit, 1968).

Some or all of these should be available in a good library, which may also have other references on the subject.

ASSIGNMENT

I. Discussion of Noun-Forming Suffixes

-ician   from the OF suffix *-icien*, a combination of *-ic* and *-ien* (= *ian*). Other examples are physician, beautician, magician, logician, optician, politician. Some words are formed by analogy, as academician, algebrician, geometrician.

-ism   sometimes through L *-ismus* or F *-isme* (*communisme, optimisme*), ultimately from Gk action nouns ending in *-ismos* or *-isma* that derive from verbs, as *barbarismos* barbarism, from *barbarizein* to barbarize. The suffix also attaches to nouns, giving these meanings: the action or conduct of a particular kind of person, as heroism and despotism (from hero and despot); an abnormal condition caused by, as alco-

holism; the name of a system of practice or theory, as Darwinism, Quakerism, and Republicanism; and, related to this, class-names for doctrines or principles, as agnosticism, paganism; also, terms denoting a language or characteristic of language, as Americanism, dialecticism. The suffix -istic forms the corresponding adjective for some of these nouns, as atheistic, egotistic. Some of these nouns admit two adjectives, as natural and naturalistic, pagan and paganistic.

-ist from the suffix -istes, either directly or through L -ista, as antagonist, from L antagonista, from Gk antagonistes. Also defined as an expert in, as a botanist or chemist; also, one who plays a musical instrument, as a flutist, guitarist, lutanist and lutenist (from lute), sitarist, percussionist; also, a writer of, as a novelist, librettist, essayist.

-ite from the Gk suffix -ites, sometimes directly, sometimes through L, as Sybarite, from L Sybarita, from Gk Sybarites a Sybarite, a person from Sybaris. Dynamite was built on analogy.

II. Discussion of Bases

AGOG(UE)- from the Gk suffix -agogos leading, from the verb agein to lead, as pedagogos pedagogue (PED- boy). Variously recorded as a suffix and combining form. The clipped form, -agog, is often preferred in the U.S.

CHIR- from cheir hand. Chir- and chiro- are often found as the combining form. Also, chirography, chiromancy (MANC- to divine by means of), chironomid, chiropody (POD- foot), surgeon (from AF surgien, from OF cirurgien) and its doublet chirurgeon, an archaic word for a surgeon. CHEIR- is a variant spelling; CHIR- is generally preferred.

COSM- from kosmos order, world, universe. Cosmo-, often listed as a combining form, is found in original Greek words, as cosmography (from kosmographia), and in words built on analogy, as cosmonaut (COSMO- + NAUT- sailor). Also, appearing in final position is the combining form -cosm, as in microcosm and macrocosm.

HETER- from hetero the other of two, different, another. Hetero- is the combining form (heter- before vowels) found in close to 100 English words.

NE- from neos new. The combining form is neo- (ne- before vowels), appearing in current formations, as neo-Christianity, neocolonialism, neo-Dadaism, Neo-Darwinism; in words from other languages, as neologism (from F), neophilia and neon (from L); and with clips, as neomycin (neo- + streptomycin), and neoprene (neo- + chloroprene). The word new is from OE.

ODONT- from the stem odont- of the noun odous tooth. Odonto- (odont- before vowels) is one combining form, as in odontology, odontitis, odontoblast, odontograph, odontalgia (= a toothache); also, -odont as a combining form in final position, meaning having teeth of a certain type, as in acrodont, mesodont. Compare the L *dens, dentis* tooth, which has given dentist, dental, etc.

OP(T)- from the stem *op-* of *opsomai,* future of the verb *horan* to see. Various combining forms spring from this base. One is -opsy, an examination (not found in many dictionaries), as in autopsy and biopsy. Also, -opsis, resembling or having a likeness to (something else), as in caryopsis and coreopsis. Also, -opia, signifying a condition of vision (as in diplopia, a disorder of the eyes in which objects are seen double, from *diplos* double), or a condition of · ɑl defect (as in hyperopia). Also, here, myopia, hemeralopia. Optu- (from *optos* seen) is also occasionally found, as in optometrist, optɔelectronics, optophone. Compare opt and option (from L *optare* to choose, oppose), optimism (from F *optimisme,* from L *optimus* best), and optimum (from L, the neuter form of *optimus*). Related to OPHTHALM- eye (in Greek Lesson XXIII).

ORTH- from *orthos* straight, right, correct. Orth- (before vowels as in orthicon) and ortho- are usually found as the combining form. Also, orthodontist, orthopedics (PED- child), orthography. There are also two meanings in chemistry: (1) specifying a compound, usually an acid, containing the greatest possible number of hydroxyl groups, as orthophosphoric acid; and (2) specifying a benzene derivative in which the substituted atoms or radicals occupy neighboring positions, as in orthoxylene.

PED- from the stem *paid-* of the noun *pais* boy, child. Paedo-, pedo- (with paed- and ped- before vowels, as in pederasty, from PED- + *eran* to love) are generally recorded as the combining form, the 'ae' spelling being preferred in England and the 'e' form generally preferred in the U.S. Also, pedodontics, pedophile, pedology. More words opening with ped-, however, come from the Latin base PED- foot, as in pedigree, pedometer, peduncle.

PEDIA- from *paideia* education, from *paideuein* to educate, from the above PED-. PAEDIA- is an alternate spelling not generally preferred in the U.S.

POL-, POLIS- both forms are ultimately from *polis* city-state. Police, polity, and policy (= a plan of action) are all doublets from *polis.* Also, politico (= politician), its clip pol, and its combining form politico-, as in politico-military. The combining form -polis is usually listed, as in metropolis (from *meter* mother) megalopolis (MEGAL- large), Minneapolis (from the Sioux *minne-* water—here, the Mississippi River).

III. Analysis and Definition of Words

1. CHIR(o)- hand + POD- foot + -*ist* one engaged in: one who treats various troubles of the feet. Another name for podiatry (see sentence 20).

2. POL- city + -*ite* inhabitant of + -*ic* pertaining to: prudent; tactful.

3. ORTH(o)- correct + PAED- child + -*ic* pertaining to: having to do with surgery that deals with skeletal deformities and diseases. (Some dictionaries add to this, "especially in children.")

4. HETER(o)- different + DOX- opinion, teaching: contrary to or differing from an acknowledged standard; unorthodox.

5. GNOS- to know + -*tic* pertaining to + -*ism* belief in: a mystical and philosophical doctrine of early Christian times which claimed that matter was evil, that spiritual knowledge rather than faith was essential to salvation, and which denied that Christ had a corporeal existence.

6. PED- child + -AGOGUE to lead: a pedantic, dogmatic, dull teacher.

7. POLY- many + THE- god + -*ist* one who believes in + -*ic* pertaining to: having to do with the belief in more than one god.

8. ORTH- straight + ODONT- tooth + -*ist* an expert in: a dentist who specializes in straightening teeth.

9. COSM(o)- universe + POL- state + -*ite* inhabitant of: one having wide international sophistication who feels at home in any part of the world.

10. *peri*- around, near + ODONT- tooth + -*ist* one engaged in, an expert: a dentist who specializes in the treatment of diseases of the supporting tissues of the teeth, as the bone, gums and other connective tissue.

11. DEM- people + -AGOGUE to lead: a leader who appeals to the emotions and popular prejudices of the people in order to gain power and/or money for himself.

12. NE(o) new + LOG- word + -*ist* an expert, or one engaged, in: a person who introduces new words, or existing words with new meanings, into a language.

13. (a) PAN- all + THE- god + -*ism* belief in: the doctrine that God is the transcendent reality of which the material universe and man are only manifestations; (b) PAN- + THE- + -*ist* one who believes in + -*ic* pertaining to: having to do with pantheism (above).

14. PED- child + IATR- physician + -*ics* science of: the branch of medicine dealing with the care, development, and diseases of babies and children.

15. GE(o)- earth + POL- state + -*ite* inhabitant of + -*ics* study of: the study of the influence of geography, and perhaps other considerations such as demography, on the politics (especially the foreign policy) of a state.

16. *syn*- together + OPT- to see + -*ic* pertaining to: having to do with, or furnishing a general view of, some subject.

17. TAX(i)- to arrange, put in order (the 'i' came in from the Gk *taxis* taxis [= a change of place]) + DERM- skin + -*ist* one working with: one who prepares, stuffs, and mounts the skins of animals.

18. from L *ballista* (whence the E noun ballista), from BALL- to throw. The -*ist* suffix does not apply here in any EW sense. Ballist is an old form of ballista, the machine for throwing stones. Add -*ics* (the science of) for ballistics: the science of projectiles, such as bullets, rockets, bombs.

19. ORTH(o)- correct + DOX- opinion: conforming to established doctrine or procedure (here, in religion).

20. POD- foot + IATR- physician + -*ist* an expert in: a doctor who treats ailments of the feet.

IV. Common Nouns Derived from Place Names

1. bantam—from Bantam, a village in west Java in Indonesia, where this chicken is supposed to have originated.

2. bayonet—from the F *baionette,* from the French city of Bayonne, where the weapon was first made or used. Occasionally questioned as the authentic etymology. Other possible derivations are discussed in the OED.

3. bungalow—from Hindustani *bengla*, which means belonging to Bengal, or Bengalese.

4. bunk—a clip from bunkum; also spelled buncombe, from Buncombe County, North Carolina, whose congressman F. Walker, of the 16th Congress (1819 – 21), made tiresome speeches "for Buncombe."

5. currant—originally *raisins de Corauntz*, through AF, from F *raisins de Corinths*, which means raisins of Corinth.

6. dollar—from German *taler*, a clip of *joachimstaler* (or -*thaler*; the German 'th' is pronounced like 't'), a coin minted at Joachimsthal in Bohemia. The unvoiced /t/ went to the voiced /d/.

7. gypsy (also British gipsy)—a shortened and altered form of Egyptian, from a belief that gypsies originally came from Egypt.

8. magenta—from the town of Magenta in northern Italy where the French and Sardinians defeated the Austrians in the Battle of

Magenta in 1859, the same year the dye was discovered. Apparently the dye was given this name for no other reason.

9. milliner—a variant of the now obsolete Milaner, a dealer in goods from Milan, Italy, a city that was known for women's finery in the 16th century.

10. peach—through F *peche*, from L *persica*, neuter plural of *persicum* (*malum*), meaning a Persian (apple), from Gk *persikos*.

11. spaniel—from OF *espagneul* Spanish, from L *Hispania* Spain. The OF *espaignol* meant a Spanish dog.

12. spruce—from OF *Pruce*, from ML *Prussia*, an area in Germany famous for this timber.

13. tarantula—from Italian *tarantola*, from the Italian city Taranto, near which the spider is found.

14. turquoise—from ME *turkeis*, from MF *turquoyse* from (*pierre*) *turqueise*, meaning a Turkish (stone).

15. tuxedo—from Tuxedo Park, New York, where the garment was reputedly first worn.

LESSON X

EXPRESSIONS

As with place names in the previous chapter, the study of special expressions has fascinated wordsmiths for many years, and research has poured dozens of books into print. Dictionaries fare poorly in this area. Editors feel, no doubt rightly, that it is not the function of a dictionary, especially a contemporary one, to record all the expressions of a language. Indeed, to do so would swell a dictionary to several volumes. In fact, contemporary dictionaries cannot even hope to record the large majority of idioms in the language—much less the cliches, common phrases, catch phrases, and other expressions. For these expressions both instructor and student must go elsewhere.

Any reasonable town or city library should have reference books on the history of common expressions which can provide plenty of fodder for a dittoed handout as material for a brief research project or a simple home-work assignment. Five good books on the subject are the following: *Long-man's Dictionary of English Idioms* (Longman Group Ltd., Harrow and Lon-don, 1979); *Dictionary of Catch Phrases* by Eric Partridge (who also has several other books out on cliches, slang, etc.); *Picturesque Expressions, A Thematic Dictionary*, edited by L. Urdang and N. LaRoche (Gale Research, Detroit, 1980); *Dictionary of Word and Phrase Origins*, Vols. 1–3, by William and Mary Morris (Harper & Row, 1962, 1967, 1971); and (mentioned in EW) *A Hog on Ice* by Charles E. Funk (Harper, 1948).

ASSIGNMENT

I. Discussion of Noun-Forming Suffixes

-ast, -st   through the L suffix *-astes*, from Gk *-astes*, from verbs ending in *-azein*, as *gymnastes*, from *gymnazein* to do gymnastic exercises, train, exercise. The *-ast* is occasionally listed.

-t, -te   Words with this suffix usually came into English through L *-ta* (*poeta, propheta, athleta, pirata*), from Gk *-tes* (*poietes, prophetes,* etc.). Not generally recorded in dictionaries.

-y, -ia   from L *-ia*, from Gk *-ia*, as in *agonia* agony, and *philanthropia* philanthropy. It also means territory (as Micronesia, Polynesia, and Rumania), and society (as in suburbia and slurbia). The *-y* can also be added to English words of Latin or Greek origin, as jealousy and delivery, from jealous and deliver. The *-ia* also appears in loan words from Latin, as insignia and militia.

   The Gk neuter plural of the adjective ending *-ios* also gives an English suffix *-ia*, denoting a higher taxon of (plants and animals), as Sauria and Reptilia (both through NL); also things derived from, as in tabloidia.

II. Discussion of Bases

ALL-   from *allos* other. Allo- and all- (before vowels, except in chemistry) are listed as a combining form in most dictionaries, meaning other, different, atypical, as in allonym, allogamous, allomerism, allegory. In chemistry this combining form is used to denote the more stable of two geometric isomers. Also, allocentric, allochromatic, allogamy, allogenic, allograph, allometry, allomorph, and several others. Com-pare allocate, from L (*ad-* to + LOC- place) and allocution from L (*ad-* to + LOCUT- to speak).

CAC-   from *kakos* bad. Caco- (cac- before vowels, as cacodorous) is sometimes listed as a combining form, as an element occurring in words from Greek, such as cacodemon and cacodoxy, and, by analogy, in the formation of new words, such as cacodorous, cacogastric, cacogenesis, cacography.

CAU- from *kauter* a burner (as a branding iron), from *kaiein* to burn. CAUS- from *kaustikos* capable of burning (from *kaiein*), as in caustic. Also, cauter, cauterize (in medicine, as with a silver nitrate stick), and cautery. Compare cautel and caution from L *cautela* and *cautio* respectively, both from *cavēre* to beware (not in EW).

CLA- from *klas(is)* breaking, fracture, from the verb *klan* to break. Listed in some dictionaries is the combining form -clase, meaning a (specified) type of cleavage (as euclase, a silicate of aluminum and beryllium, a brittle metal that is easy to break). Another combining form is -clasis, as in anaclasis. Also, the adjective form -clastic, as in synclastic, in which broken is taken as bent, i.e., curved, like a ball or an egg. Also, clastic, cataclasm, clasmatocyte.

DO- from the noun *dosis* a dose, a giving, and a reduced form of the reduplicative verb *didonai* to give. Antidote is from *antidoten* given as a remedy. Also, dosimeter, epidote (*epi-* in addition to, over + DO- + -*te* that which, "because it is longer in the base of the crystal than allied minerals"—WBD).

DYN- from *dynasthai* to be powerful; DYNAM- from *dynamis* power. Dyna-, dynam-, and dynamo- are occasionally listed as combining forms. Also, dynatron, dyne, dynode, dynamite, dynamism.

ERG-, URG- from *ergon* work. Ergo- and erg- (before vowels) are both generally found as a combining form, as in ergometer. Also, ergon, ergonomics, surgeon. Also occasionally listed as combining forms are -urgy and -urge, with much the same sense, as in dramaturgy and dramaturge.

LAT(E)R- from *latreuein* to serve (with prayer). Usually listed as a combining form is -latry, meaning worship, as in bibliolatry, cosmolatry, demonolatry, hierolatry, Mariolatry. The corresponding combining form -later denotes the person, as an idolater.

PATH- from *pathos* feeling, emotion, experience. The combining form -pathy is generally listed with three meanings: (1) feeling or suffering, as in empathy, sympathy; or, being acted upon, as in telepathy; (2) a disorder of a (specified) kind or part, as in neuropathy; (3) a system of medicine based upon a (specified) factor, as in osteopathy. The form -pathia is listed as an obsolete variant, as in psychopathia. Also listed are the corresponding adjective suffix -pathic, as in psychopathic; and the agent noun suffix -path, as in psychopath. Also, path- (before vowels, as in pathic) and patho- are generally found, as in pathology, pathophysiology, pathogen, pathogenesis.

PHY- from *phyein* to grow, bring forth. Phyt- (before vowels, as in phytin) and phyto- are usually listed as a combining form, meaning plant (from *phyton* a plant, i.e., something that has grown), as in phytochemistry, phytogeography. Also as a combining form in final position is -phyte, meaning a plant having ` (specified) characteristic or habitat, as xerophyte, lithophyte, tog .:r with its corresponding adjective form -phytic, as in holophytic. Neophyte began its life in transferred senses, referring to a beginner in various contexts.

PHYSI- from *physis* nature, a derivative of *phyein* (above). The combining form is physi- (reduced to phys-, meaning 'physical,' in physiatrics = physical therapy) and physio-, as in physiognomy, physiography, and physiotherapy. Physico- (= physical), not usually listed, appears in physicochemical.

STA- from *sta-*, the stem of the verb *histanai* to cause to stand. Generally listed is the combining form -stat, used with the names of (specified) instruments that maintain something in a stable or constant state, as a thermostat or rheostat. Occasionally listed is the combining form -stasis, meaning a maintaining, a stopping, a slowing, as in hemostasis (or hemostasia). The L STA- to stand, and the E word 'stand' (from OE *standan*) are both related to this base. Also, catastasis, diastase, diastasis, ecstasy, epistasis, eustatic, hypostasis, metastasis, prostate.

THE- from *tithenai* to place, put down. Also, antithesis, diathesis, epithet, hypothesis, metathesis, parenthesis, prothesis, prosthesis, synthesis, and (where there is one) their corresponding adjective forms -thetic(al), as hypothetical, synthetic.

III. Analysis and Definition of Words

1. *apo-* away + STA- to stand + *-te* one who: one who renounces his religion.
2. *em-* in + PATH- to feel + *-y* state or quality: the quality or process of entering fully into the meaning of (the situation).
3. *meta-* after + PHYSI- nature + *-(i)c* pertaining to + *-al* character of: pertaining to the branch of philosophy that tries to explain reality and knowledge or the real nature of things.
4. DYNAM- force, power + *-ism* condition of (not 'belief in' in this meaning): energetic quality; forceful power; forcefulness.
5. *epi-* on, in addition to + THE- to put, place + *-t* that which: a descriptive word or phrase expressing some quality or attribute.
6. HOL(o)- whole + CAUS- to burn + *-t* that which: a thorough destruction of (here, human beings) by fire. (The instructor might wish to point out that the phrase "the Holocaust," with a capital,

refers specifically to the mass destruction of European Jews by the Nazis during World War II, a phrase that was not in general use until the latter half of the 1960s.)

7. ALL- other + ERG- to work + -y that which: a pathological reaction to substances that do not affect the average individual.

8. DEMON(o)- evil spirit + LATR- to worship + -y state, act: the worship of evil spirits.

9. (a) ICON(o)- image + CLA- to break + -st one who does: one who attacks established beliefs or institutions because he thinks them wrong or foolish; (b) the above + -ic pertaining to: pertaining to an iconoclast (here, presumably, a less severe transfer of the sense of one who breaks or destroys images to one who defiles, desecrates, or defaces an image).

10. anti- against + PATH- to feel + -y state of: a feeling of dislike, hatred, or aversion.

11. NE(o)- new + PHY- to grow + -te one who: here, an attributive noun, one who is new at something; a beginner.

12. THERM(o)- heat + STA- stand, stop, + -t that which: here, a figurative transfer, a mechanism for regulating temperature (i.e. here, anger).

13. COSM(o)- universe + GON- to originate + -al pertaining to: pertaining to the origin of the universe. (Neologist Thoreau was one of the first, and apparently one of the few, people to have used this word, which is not often found in contemporary dictionaries. It means cosmogonic, the more favored word.)

14. AESTHE- to perceive + -te he who: one who has or affects a high degree of sensitivity to the beautiful, as in art, music, poetry, etc.

15. an- not + ec- out + DO- to give + -te that which (= Gk anekdota things not published): a usually short narrative of an interesting, amusing, or biographical incident.

16. CAUS- to burn + -tic pertaining to (in Gk kaust- + the suffix -ic): here, figurative, sharp, biting, or sarcastic.

17. ICON(o)- image + LATR- to worship + -y state of: the worship of images.

18. CAC(o)- bad + PHON- sound + -y state of: harsh, dissonant sound.

19. a- without + PATH- to feel + -y state of: a lack of interest in, feeling for, or desire for anything.

20. DYN- power + -ast one who does + -y state of: here, figurative, a line or succession of individuals who attain distinction or prominence in a family over several generations.

LESSON XI

ASSIGNMENT

I. Discussion of Noun-Forming Suffixes

-ma, -m, -me   from nouns ending in *-ma*, as *drama* drama, *problema* problem, *diadema* diadem, *thema* theme. Not recognized as a suffix in dictionaries. EW's *-mat-* suffix is from the gentive stem of these nouns, as *dramat(os)*, *problemat(os)*, *themat(os)*. Some dictionaries record the suffix *-eme* (from Gk *-ema*), as *phonema* phoneme.

-sis, -se, -sy, -sia   The first two came in through nouns ending in *-sis*; the *-sis* words are direct loans, as *analysis* analysis, *prognosis, diagnosis, diapedesis,* etc.; the *-se* form, as in dose, got switched in F from Gk *dosio*. Words with *-sia* are either loan words, as amnesia, or modern constructions, as paresthesia and paramnesia. The *-y* form is an alteration of *-ia* as *autopsia* autopsy. The corresponding adjective suffix *-tic* is from the adjective stem *-tik-*, as in *theoretik(os), diagnostik(os), pathetik(os)*, for theoretic(al), etc.

II. Discussion of Bases

ANDR-   from *andr-* the stem *aner*man. Andr- (before vowels, as androecium—*oec-* house—and android) and andro- are the combining form, as in androphobia, androgen, androgyny, androcracy, androsterone, androconium (*con-* dust). Also as combining forms are -andry, as in polyandry, monandry, and its corresponding adjective form -androus, as in polyandrous, monandrous.

KINE-, CINE-   from *kinema* motion. Also, kine, kinema (the older, British spelling for the now preferred cinema), kinescope, kinesiology, kinesthesia, kinetography, kinetoscope, cinematic, cinemagoer, cinematize, cinematographer, *cinéma vérité* (F). Also, in medicine, kinase; and streptokinase (Gk *strephein* to twist), an enzyme used for dissolving blood clots, also called fibrinolysis.

GEN(E)-   from *genos* race (as in genocide), or *genea* race, family (as in genealogy).

GYN(E)   from *gyne* woman. GYNEC- is the stem of this noun, with GYNAEC- being a variant spelling. Gyno- (as in gynophore), gyn- (before vowels, as in gynarchy), gyneco- (as in gynecology), gynec- (before vowels, as in gynecoid), -gyny (as in androgyny and misogyny) and its corresponding adjective form -gynous (as in androgynous and

184

misogynous) are all variously listed as combining forms, meaning woman or female. The combining form -gyne, meaning woman or female, or ovary (as in androgyne, pseudogyne, trichogyne) is also sometimes found.

IDI-   from *idios* (one's) own, private. Idio- is usually listed as the combining form, as in idiocy, idiograph, idiolect, idiom, idiomatic, idiomorphic, idiopathic. Compare the base IDE- thought, idea, as in ideology.

LITH-, -LITE   from *lithos* stone. Litho- (as in lithography, lithology, lithophile, lithophyte, lithotomy, lithosphere), lith- (before vowels, as in lithic), -lith (as in megalith, eolith, acrolith, paleolith) and its corresponding adjective form -lithic (as in paleolithic, etc.) are all generally listed as combining forms. The combining form -lite is also usually found, having to do with names of minerals and fossils, as aerolite, chrysolite.

MIS-   from *misein* to hate or *misos* hatred. Miso- (as in misogamy, misogyny, misology, misoneism) and mis- (before vowels, as in misanthrope) are the combining form for this base. Compare mis-, the Germanic prefix meaning bad, wrongly, as in misunderstanding, misuse, misbehave.

PHE-, PHA-, (PHEM-, voice)   from the verb *phanai* to speak. The combining form is -phasia (or -phasy), used in forming words referring to speech disorders (such as aphasia, dysphasia). Also, apophasis, dysphemism, euphemism. Compare two other Gk bases: PHA- to show, appear, and PHAG- to eat; also, ephemeral (*ep-* upon + HEMER-day).

SCHIZ-, SCHIS-   from *schizein* to split. Both schizo- and schiz- (before a vowel) are generally listed as a combining form, as in schizoid, schizomycete, schizophrene, schizothymia, and several words connected with biology. SCHIS- comes from *schistos* a cleft, giving schismatic, schismatize, schistocyte, schistosome, schistosomiasis, and others. Also the clip schizo, for schizophrenic.

STERE-   from *stereos* solid. Stereo- and stere- (before vowels, as in stereopsis) are the combining form, as in stereobate, stereochemistry, stereogram, stereography, stereoisomer, stereology, stereometry, stereophony, stereophotography, stereoscope, stereotape, stereotype.

TYP-   from *typos* impression, a depression or dent, from *typtein* to impress, form, mold, stamp. Typo- is a combining form in some dictionaries, giving typology and the informal clip typo (= a typographical error). Also appearing occasionally is -type, representing the word type, as in prototype and ferrotype. Also, atypical, ectype, typify.

III. Analysis and Definition of Words

1. MIS(o)- hatred + GYN- woman, female + -y state of: a hatred of women.

2. KINE- to move + ESTHE- to feel + -tic pertaining to: pertaining to the sensation of body movement, especially in muscles, tendons, and joints.

3. NE(o)- new + LITH- stone + -ic pertaining to: pertaining to the latest period of the Stone Age and characterized by polished stone instruments, agriculture, and animal husbandry.

4. HETER(o)- other, different + GENE- kind, race + -ous having the character of: consisting of dissimilar kinds.

5. POLY- many + ANDR- man, husband + -y state of: the condition of having more than one husband at the same time.

6. ana- up + THE- to place, put, set + -ma result of: (a) anything that is condemned or completely detested; (b) a curse. (Anathema in Greek means 'a thing devoted to evil.')

7. pro- before + GNO- to know + -sis state of: the prospect of recovery as forecast from the course of a disease.

8. eu- well + PHEM- to speak + -ism condition (or an instance): a mild or indirect word or expression that is used in place of one that is harsh or too direct.

9. apo- from + THE(o)- god + -sis state of: a glorified or deified ideal.

10. SCHIS- to split + -m result of: a division into hostile groups.

11. ARCHE- beginning + TYP- model: the original model of which all things of the same type are copies.

12. STERE(o) three-dimensional + PHON- sound + -ic pertaining to: giving a lifelike sound of three-dimensional effect.

13. IDI(o)- one's own, peculiar + -m result of: here, the language of a particular group.

14. syn- together + THE- to put, place + -sis result of: the combination of elements into a whole.

15. DOG- opinion + -mat result of + -ism belief in: a definite, authoritative opinion; an emphatic assertion of opinion.

16. HOM(o)- same + GENE- kind + -ous pertaining to: of a culturally uniform structure or composition.

17. hypo- below, under + THE- to put, place + -tic pertaining to + -al belonging to: involving a set of assumptions provisionally accepted as a basis of reasoning, experiment, or investigation.

18. anti- against + THE- to put, place + -sis result of: the direct opposite

19. MIS- hatred + ANTHROP- human being + -*ic* pertaining to: pertaining to one who distrusts or dislikes people in general, characterized by a marked hatred or contempt of humanity.

20. STERE(o)- solid + TYP- model: here, figurative, a fixed character; a conventional type.

IV. Etymological and Current Definitions

1. bead—(a) from OE *bed* prayer; (b) a small ball or piece of glass, plastic, etc., with a hole through it so it can form part of a necklace; also, a string of beads, especially for keeping count in saying prayers. The first sense in (b) is the common meaning in singular; the second meaning is always in plural.

2. gossip—(a) from OE *godsibb* a godparent; (b) idle, often untrue talk about other people and their affairs.

3. abominate—(a) from the deponent verb *abominari* to loathe or deplore an unfavorable or ill omen; (b) to hate strongly; to feel disgust or loathing for.

4. cretin—(a) from Swiss F *crestin* a Christian even though a deformed idiot, from L *Christianus* Christian; (b) a person suffering from retardation caused by deficiency of the thyroid gland; also, a fool or stupid person.

5. pittance—(a) from OF *pitance* a donation to a monastery; a food allowance for a monk; (b) a very small allowance of money; scanty wages.

6. contemplate—(a) from *contemplari* to survey or observe (an augury), from *com-* with + *templum* a restricted area in the heavens marked off for observing auguries; (b) to observe thoughtfully; to think about for a long time.

LESSON XII

COMBINING FORMS

For more than a century the expression 'combining form' has been used to describe linguistic forms that are used with other words or other combining forms to make new words. Among contemporary dictionaries, however, the term is not used by AHD and not always by RHD, although both offer the expression as a main entry. RHD uses *hemato-* as its example there, but under hemato- calls it "a learned borrowing from Greek," as it calls hemi-, hemo-, and others. It calls -trophy "a combining form," -tropal "a suffix identical in meaning with -*tropic*," -tropic "a combination of -*trope* and -*ic*," -trope, "var. of tropo-, occurring as the final elements in compound words," and tropo- "a learned borrowing from Greek." These are fine lines here, and it is doubtful if these differences are going to have much meaning to the lay user or even your average student. Any of these terms would certainly seem preferable, however, if only more instructive, to AHD's blanket "prefix," which is applied to all combining forms in initial position as well as to your everyday prefixes, and "suffix," which is applied to all combining forms in final position as well as to your everyday suffixes. As examples under its headword 'combining form,' it offers -logy, macro-, and Sino-, but at these three main entries they are called suffixes. Its definition of a 'suffix' reads "An affix added at the end of a word or stem, serving to form a new word or as an inflectional ending, such as -*ness* in *gentleness*, -*ing* in *walking*, or -*s* in *sits*." It calls its 'affix' "a word element, such as a prefix or suffix, that can only occur attached to a base, stem, or root." Therefore, according to all this, a common formation like anaplastic is not possible in that it calls -plastic a 'suffix,' but a suffix can only occur attached to a base, stem, or root, which ana- is not. This also applies to (the conventional) base + suffix situation: it calls a 'prefix' an 'affix'; an affix can only occur attached to a base; it calls trop- a prefix; therefore the word tropism cannot exist since a prefix cannot attach to a suffix to form a word (discounting the few and unusual situations like country, outrage, and soprano that are discussed in the topical section of Latin Lesson IV on prefixes). At any level of instruction it would seem helpful to the students to be aware of this information, especially since EW and all other dictionaries (that I have seen) use 'combining form' for such as trop- and -logy.

ASSIGNMENT

I. Discussion of Combining Forms

-*logy*   is discussed in IM at LOG-, at Lesson IV. AHD users should be alerted to the fact that AHD does not use the term 'combining form.' See discussion of this above.

-*nomy*   from L -*nomia*, from Gk -*nomia* law, from *nemein* to manage or distribute. Usually entered as a combining form. Also taxonomy, autonomy, gastronomy.

-*cracy*   from LL -*cratia*, from Gk -*kratia*, from *kratos* power, strength. Usually listed as a combining form. Also, monocracy, mobocracy, technocracy, gerontocracy, theocracy, plutocracy, pantisocracy, heirocracy, isocracy.

-*crat*   from F -*crate*, called (in WNCD) a back formation from F -*cratie* -cracy, from Gk -*kratia* (above). Generally listed as a combining form.

II. Discussion of Bases

AUT-   from *autos* self. Listed, with auto-, as a combining form (aut- before vowels, as in autism, autarchy; or before h, as in authentic). Auto- as a combining form (a clip from automobile), meaning self-propelling, is usually listed as a separate entry, giving autobus, autobike (= British motorbike), autotruck, automen (= people concerned with the automobile industry), auto court (= motor court or motel), autodom, autoette, autocade, autodrome; this same auto- can also mean automatic, as in autopilot and autoscan (as on radios with electronic tuning). There are many more spinoffs from the first meaning, however, as autotoxin, autobiography, autochthon, autoclave, autocracy, autodidact, autoeroticism, autogiro, autoimmune.

GASTR-   from *gaster, gastros* belly, stomach, Gastr-, gastro-, gastri- are variously listed as combining forms, with gastr- usually appearing before vowels, as in gastral, gastrectomy. From gastro- comes gastroenteritis, gastrogenic, gastronomy, gastrology, gastroscopy.

HELI-   from *helios* sun. Heli- (before vowels, as in helianthus) and helio- are generally listed as the combining form. Also, heliograph, heliometer, helioscope, heliostat, heliotaxis, heliotherapy. Compare heli(c)- and helico-, from Gk *helix* spiral, as in helix, helical, helicoid, helicopter; and the popular combining form heli- (= helicopter), as in helipad, heliport, helilift, heliborne, heliambulance, helibus, helicab.

IDE-   from Gk *idea,* from *idein* to see. Ideo- appears as the combining form, as in ideograph, ideography, ideology. Compare the base IDI- one's own.

MANC-, MANT-   from *mantis* prophet, diviner, with -mancy (which came in through OF -*mancie*) usually found as the combining form. Also necromancy, oneiromancy, hydromancy.

MICR-   from *micros* small. Micro- and micr- (before vowels) are the combining form. Many micro- words, as microorganism, are a clipped form of microscopic. WNCD gives six definitions of this combining form. Some 275 words spring from this base.

NECR-   from *nekros* dead body. Both this and necro- are generally found as the combining form. Also, necrogenic, necrology, necromancy, necrophagia, necrophilia (= necrophily), necropsy, necrotomy.

PALE-   from *palaios* ancient. Pale- (before vowels, as in palearctic, paleethnology) and paleo- are the combining form. PALAE- is the preferred British spelling. Some 60 words derive from this base.

PSEUD-   from *pseudes* false, and from *pseudein* to deceive. Pseud-, which usually appears before vowels as in pseudepigraphy, and pseudo- are the combining form. This also has a chemical sense meaning resembling or related to, as in pseudomorph (in the sense of a mineral which has the form of another mineral), pseudosalt. There are some 60 compounds with this base, including the free-standing pseudo (adjective and noun).

PSYCH- from *psyche* mind, soul, life. Psycho- and psych- (usually before vowels, as in psychic, psychiatry) are the combining form. Beginning around the 1970s there began a run in popular usage on psycho-, appearing in such words as psychometric, -metrician, -biography, -cultural, -linguistics, -stimulant, -sexual, -social, -active, -history, etc.

TROP- from *trope* a turn, change, from *trepein* to turn. There are various combining forms. Trop- (before vowels, as in tropic, tropism) and tropo- appear initially, as in tropology, troposphere, tropotaxis. In final position there is -trope, as in heliotrope; -tropism, as in heliotropism; -tropy, meaning a condition of turning or curving, as in phototropy; and the adjective forms -tropous (anatropous) and -tropic (geotropic) and -tropal. Compare -trophy, a combining form meaning nourishment or growth, from the Gk base TROPH- to nourish, grow, as in atrophy. Trophy, through ME *trophee*, is ultimately from TROP-.

III. Analysis and Definition of Words

1. THE(o)- god + -crat one who practices rule by + -ic pertaining to: having to do with a government in which God, or a god, is recognized as the supreme ruler; or, pertaining to a government run by officials who are regarded as being divinely guided.

2. GASTR(o)- stomach + -nomy science of + -ic pertaining to + -al pertaining to: pertaining to the art or science of good eating.

3. DERMAT(o)- skin + -logy study of + -ist expert in: one skilled in the branch of medicine dealing with the skin and its diseases.

4. PSEUD- false + ONYM- name: a fictitious name; a name used by an author in place of his real name; a pen name.

5. GYNEC(o)- woman + -logy study of: the branch of medicine that deals with the health and diseases of women.

6. ANDR- man, male + -oid like: an automaton in the form of a human being. (Some dictionaries give 'man' as the meaning of ANTHROP- while others and EW use 'human being.')

7. CHRON(o)- time + -logy study of + -ic pertaining to + -al pertaining to: according to the order of time.

8. ARCHAE(o)- ancient, primitive + -logy science of + -ist expert in: an expert in the scientific study of the people, customs, and life of ancient times.

9. HELI(o)- sun + TROP- to turn + -ic pertaining to: turning, bending, or growing in response to light.
10. BI- life + OP- to see + -sy act of: the removal of a piece of living tissue for examination and diagnosis.
11. IDE(o)- thought + -logy study of + -ic pertaining to + -al pertaining to: pertaining to a systematic body of concepts, opinions, or doctrines that people have about human life and its customs.
12. MICR(o)- small + COSM- universe: a unity that is a miniature of a larger one. (The word came in through OF *microcosme,* ultimately from Gk *mikros kosmos* little world.)
13. TAX(o)- arrange, put in order + -nomy science of: the science of classifying plants and animals.
14. NECR(o)- the dead + MANC- to divine by means of + -y state of: magic or enchantment.
15. PSYCH- mind + IATR- physician (also means to cure, from *iatreia*) + -y act of: the science of treating mental disorders.
16. ANTHROP(o)- human being + -logy study of + -ist expert in: a specialist in the science of man, especially physical characteristics, origin, culture, customs, beliefs, etc.
17. PALE(o)- old + LITH- stone + -ic pertaining to: pertaining to the earliest period of the Stone Age.
18. AUT(o)- self + -nomy system of laws: independence; self-government.
19. ETHN(o)- race, cultural group + -logy study of + -ist expert in: a specialist in the branch of anthropology that deals with the origin, distribution, customs, institutions, and general culture of various ancient or contemporary cultural groups.
20. AUT(o)- self + -crat one who practices rule by + -ic pertaining to: having absolute power or authority.

IV. Derivation and Meaning of Given Names

Some desk and college dictionaries do not give derivations of given names. If a student's dictionary does not have given names, any public or school reference librarian will be able to help. Two books that are especially good are: *History of Christian Names,* by Charlotte M. Yonge (Macmillan, London, 1884), which gives both meanings and derivations; and *Oxford Dictionary of English Christian Names,* Third Edition, by E. G. Withycombe (Oxford, 1977), which gives meanings only.

While students are searching for words in this assignment, all of which are from Greek, they might also search for their own names and report to the class on their findings. Some students find the meaning of their given names presumptuous, or funny, or otherwise ill-suited to themselves. Such a report could make for a light-hearted break.

1. Alexander: helper of man—from *alexein* to help, assist, defend + ANDR- man.
2. Anastasia: resurrection—from *anastasia,* from *ana-* up + *stasia* cause to stand (from STA- to stand).
3. Christopher: bearer of Christ—from Christo (= Christ, from *chriein* to touch, rub, anoint) + PHER- to bear.
4. Dorothea (and Dorothy): gift of God—an arbitrary inversion of *theodora* gift of God, from THE(o) God + *doros* gift. *Theodora* is the feminine form of the masculine *theodoros.* Compare Theodore below.
5. Eugene: well-born—from *eu-* well + GEN- to originate.
6. George: farmer, tiller of the soil—from the noun *georgos.*
7. Peter: a stone—from the noun *petros*.
8. Philip: a lover of horses—from *phillipos,* from PHIL- to love + (H)IP(P)- horse.
9. Sophia: wisdom—from the noun *sophia.*
10. Theodore: gift of God—from THE(o) God + *doros* gift.

V. Etymological and Current Definitions

1. pagan—(a) from L *paganus* (substantive adjective) a peasant; a rustic; a country dweller; (b) in LL, a heathen; worshipper of false gods; currently the same, including a person who is not a Christian, Jew, or Moslem.
2. providence—(a) from L *provident-,* present participle stem of *pro-video* to look forward to; see at a distance—whence, a looking forward to, etc.; (b) God's care and protection over his creatures; (in capital) God, especially when thought of as exercising such care and protection.
3. psalm—(a) from Gk *psalmos* a song sung with harp accompaniment; a performance on or the plucking of a stringed instrument; (b) a sacred song or poem; (in capital) any one of the 150 songs, hymns, or prayers in the Book of Psalms of the Old Testament.
4. Satan—(a) ultimately from Hebrew *shatan* adversary; (b) the Devil; the enemy of goodness; the chief evil spirit; the adversary of both God and man.
5. pilgrim—(a) ultimately from L *peregrinus* foreigner (compare the doublet peregrinate, 'to wander or travel about'); (b) a person who

journeys, usually a long distance, to some sacred or holy place as an act of devotion.

6. cathedral—(a) from Gk *kathedra* (*kata* + *hedra*) seat; (b) the official church of a bishop, or any other large or important church. (Chair and chaise are doublets of this.)

7. paradise—(a) from Gk *paradeisos* a park; garden; pleasure ground, from Iranian (cf. Avestan *pairidaeza* enclosed park, from *pairi-* around + *daeza* wall); (b) heaven; the abode of God and the angels and the final abode of the righteous; Eden.

LESSON XIII

SEA TERMS

Additional Examples of Sea Terms

The following expressions,* all of which derive from the sea, could also be used in this lesson.

To *run down*, originally meant to collide with, and still does mean this, as well as to disparage. To *bear down upon*, from the naval maneuver of attacking down the wind, has come to mean to be severe with or persist in an argument. To *come down on*, that is, to attack from the windward, now means to censure or rebuke. To *press into service* refers to the press-gangs in the British navy during the War of 1812.

Son of a gun was originally a term of admiration, a "thoroughbred." It is said to derive from the days when wives were permitted to travel on their husbands' ships in the British navy, with the result that sometimes children were born at sea. A vessel at anchor wishing to escape an enemy or harbor officers would *cut and run*, that is, cut her cable and slip away unobserved. On shore the term means to decamp or leave hastily.

Ships that could sail *by and large* could sail either by, or close to, the wind, with sheets close-hauled (= having the sails set nearly fore-and-aft) when the wind was ahead. *Large* in this phrase is the French nautical term *largue*, meaning slacked off, or sheeted out, and in time became confused with the pronunciation of 'large.'

---

*Adapted in part from G. D. Chase's *Sea Terms Come Ashore* (Maine Bulletin, vol. XLIV, No. 8, Orono, February 20, 1942).

To raise sails with a quicker motion, sailors attached blocks to the halyards for hoisting. These blocks, not far apart, would eventually all come together and were then *chock-a-block* and could go no further.

In times of war a ship showed her colors as a challenge to a hostile ship. If she was victorious, she came off *with flying colors*. One or two men hauled directly on the halyards *hand over hand,* or *hand over fist*; today John makes money hand over fist—that is, fast and easily.

ASSIGNMENT

I. Discussion of Combining Forms

-archy   from *archein* to rule. Generally listed as a combining form (a "word element" in RHD). Also, patriarchy, oligarchy, squirearchy.

-arch   also from *archein*. Both this and EW's arch- are combining forms. Another -arch, akin to this base, means having (such) a point or (so many) points of origin, as in endarch. EW's arch- also means extreme, as in archconservative, archrogue, archenemy, archfiend; also, early or primitive, as in archencephalon and archespore. Compare the base ARCHA(E)- primitive, beginning (Lesson VII).

-mania   from *mainesthai* to be mad (insane), to rage. Occasionally listed as a combining form. Also, megalomania, bibliomania, nymphomania, metromania (= mania for meter), melomania (music), Anglomania (things English); and the free-standing mania, whence maniac, maniacal, and manic.

-maniac   from the above. Not generally considered a combining form.

-phobia   from *phobos* panic, fear. Where this is found it is called a combining form (suffix in AHD), and defined as an abnormal fear or hatred of. The combining element -phobia, from Gk through LL, as in hydrophobia, has been freely used with other elements, several of which the students will recognize. The following list constitutes a sampling of combinations: acrophobia (fear of heights), agora- (open spaces), ailuro- (cats), algo- (pain), andro- (men), astra- (thunder, lightning), batho- (depth), cyno- (dogs), demo- (crowds), dromo- (crossing streets), geno- (sex), gyno- (women), hapte- (being touched), hemo- (blood), homo- (= homosexual), hypno- (falling asleep), muso- (mice), myso- (contamination), neo- (the new), nycto- (night, darkness), ophidio- (snakes), photo- (light), sito- (eating, food), taphe- (being buried alive), thanato- (death), toxico- (poison), xeno- (strangers, foreigners), zoo- (animals). Some of these neither student nor instructor is likely to come across again, but an exercise that would give the students practice in recognizing Greek word elements could be made from the list. Another exercise is in the following lesson.

-phobe   from the above. Generally recorded as a combining form, as one who has a (specified) fear, hatred, or dread, as a xenophobe.

II. Discussion of Bases

ACR-   from *akros* at the farthest point, topmost, outermost. Acro- and acr- (before a vowel, as in acronym) are generally found as the combining form. Also, acrodont, acrocarpous, acromegaly, acrophobia, acrophony, the Acropolis (-POLIS city, state). Compare acre and acreage from OE *aecer* field, and acrid and acrimony from the L base ACR- sharp.

EGO-   this is the pronoun 'I' in Latin. Also egocentric, egomania, ego trip.

HIER-   from *hieros* holy, sacred. Hier- (before vowels, as in hierachy) and hiero- are usually found as the combining form. Also, hieroglyph, hierograph, hierolatry, hierocracy, hierology, hierophant.

HYDR-   from the combining form hydr-, from the noun *hydor* water. Hydr- (before vowels, as in hydrant, hydrangea, hydraulic, hydria) and hydro- are the combining form. Also, dihydric, hydrobiology, hydrobomb, hydrocarbon, hydrodynamics, hydroelectric, hydrogen, hydrology, hydrolysis, hydroplane, hydroponics, and some 150 other words.

MEGA-   from *megas* great, large, vast, powerful. Meg- (before vowels, as in megohm) and mega- are a combining form, which also means a million, as in megabar (= a unit of pressure equal to a million bars), megabucks (= a million dollars), megacycle and megadeath. MEGAL- (before vowels) and megalo-, from the genitive singular *megalou*, are another combining form from this base, as in megalomania, megalopolis.

OLIG-   from *oligos* few. Olig- (before vowels, as in oligarchy) and oligo- are the combining form. Also, Oligocene, oligochrome, oligoclase, oligomer, oligophrenia, oligopoly.

PATR-   from the stem *patr-* of the noun *pater* father. Since many English words come from the Latin (with or without the 'i'), it would seem unnecessary at most levels to have students separate the English words that derive from these two bases.

PATRI-   from *patria* fatherland, native land, substantive use of adjective *patrius* relating to a father, paternal, a derivative of *pater* (above).

SOPH-   from *sophos* wise. Also, sophic, sophism, sophisticated, sophistry.

TELE-   from *tele* far off. This combining form also means having to do with television as in telecast, telecopter, telecourse, telediagnosis, the trademark TelePrompTer, teledrama, telefilm, teleplay, telerecording, telethon, teleview, televiewer. From EW sense, also, telecommunication, telegony, telekinesis (= psychokinesis), telemeter, telephoto, telephotography. Compare teleology and teleomony, from Gk *telos* end, goal.

XEN-   from *xenos* stranger, guest, host. Xeno- and xen- (before vowels) are the combining form. Also, xenodiagnosis, xenogenesis, xenolith, xenomania, xenon, xenophilia, xenophobia.

ZO-   from *zoion* animal. Zo-, before vowels as in zooid (*-oid* like), and zoo- (some 80 words) are the combining form in initial position. In final position is -zoon (plural -zoa), as in hematozoon, spermatozoon, protozoan, Metazoa; and -zoic, an adjective combining form, meaning having a (specified) animal mode of existence, as in holozoic, endozoic, saprozoic.

III. Analysis and Definition of Words

1. HIER- sacred + -*archy* rule by: (a) a group of church officials of different ranks; (b) an organization arranged into higher and lower ranks.

2. PATR- father + ONYM- name + -*ic* pertaining to: here, substantive use, a name derived from that of a father or paternal ancestor, usually with the addition of an affix, as -son in Johnson, or Mac- in MacDonald. (Here, not referring to Poe but the character William Wilson in Poe's short story of the same name in which the narrator Wilson is a Doppleganger.)

3. ACR(o)- highest + POLIS city, state: the citadel of Athens on which the Parthenon was built.

4. EGO- I + -*maniac*: an extremely conceited person.

5. PATR- father + -*ist* an expert in + -*ic* pertaining to: pertaining to the writings of the fathers of the Christian church.

6. PYR(o)- fire + -*maniac*: a person with an irresistible desire to start fires.

7. TELE- afar + PATH- to feel + -*y* state or activity: apparent communication of one mind with another otherwise than through speech, sight, or any of the other senses.

8. ACR(o)- highest + -*phobia* abnormal fear of: an abnormal fear of being in a high place.

9. *an*- without + -*arch* one who rules + -*y* state of, act of: lack of a system of government; or, disorder, confusion, and lawlessness.

10. THE(o)- god + SOPH- wise + -*y* quality of: any system of philosophy or religion that claims to have mystical insight into the divine nature.

11. XEN(o)- foreigner + -*phobia* abnormal fear of: a hatred or fear of foreigners.

12. HYDR(o)- water + DYNAM- force, power + -ics science of: the branch of science that deals with the forces exerted by water and other liquids in motion.

13. EGO- I + CENTR- center + -ic pertaining to: self-centered; selfish; having little regard for interests, beliefs, or attitudes other than one's own.

14. HOM(o)- same, similar + LOG- proportion + -ous having the character of: corresponding in position or structure.

15. OLIG- few + -archy rule by: a form of government in which the ruling power is vested in a few persons.

16. NECR(o)- the dead + -logy a systematic study of: a list of the recently dead; an obituary.

17. PATRI- family + -arch one who rules + -al pertaining to: appropriate to the male head of the family or clan; suitable to a venerable old man.

18. MEGAL(o)- large + -mania passion for: a mental disorder marked by delusions of great personal importance.

19. ACR(o)- the extremities + MEGAL- large + -y condition of: a chronic malfunction of the pituitary gland marked by abnormal, progressive enlargement of hands, feet, and face.

20. PALE(o)- old + ZO- animal + -ic pertaining to: pertaining to the geological era (between 220 million and 600 million years ago) whose insect, reptile, and fish fossils represent early forms of life.

IV. Formation of Words by Combining Greek Elements

1. hatred of marriage: misogamy—from MIS(o)- hatred + GAM- marriage.

2. rule by women: gynarchy (not in WNCD)—from GYN- woman + -archy rule by; or gynecocracy—from GYNEC(o)- woman + -cracy rule by; also gyneocracy—from GYN(eo)- + -cracy. (The instructor may expect any of these on papers.)

3. madness for books: bibliomania—from BIBLI(o)- book + -mania madness about.

4. having a love for animals: zoophilic—from ZO(o)- animal + PHIL- to love.

5. palmistry, i.e., the art of divination by means of the hand: chiromancy—from CHIR(o)- hand + MANC- to divine by means of.

6. a scientist who studies water: hydrologist—from HYDR(o) water + -logy systematic study of + -ist one engaged in. This is usually found as an add-on to hydrology.

7. condition of hating new things: misoneism—from MIS(o)- hatred + NE- new. Neophobia, although not generally listed, may be given by some students since -*phobia* is sometimes defined as hatred.

8. having many forms: polymorphous or polymorphic—from POLY- many + MORPH- form.

9. study of the teeth: odontology—from ODONT(o)- tooth + -*logy* study of.

10. abnormal fear of pain: algophobia—from ALG(o)- pain + -*phobia* abnormal fear of.

LESSON XIV

WORDS FROM OTHER SOURCES

As this lesson and the next few lessons open with discussions of words that come from sports and games, the military, the arts, literature, etc., the instructor may wish to consult two excellent books that cover this type of material and would enhance the supplementary material to this course. Both books were, at this writing, still in print in a reprint edition. A good library should also have them. Both could be useful for oral reports, extra-credit assignments, or other special projects, depending, as always, upon the level of instruction, time, etc.

Names and Their Meaning, by L. Wagner, reprinted by Gale Research Company, Detroit, 1968. Subjects include countries, creeds, royal surnames, national nicknames, birds, religious orders, flowers, the Bible, wines, counties of England and Wales, carriages, dances, textiles, class names, and precious stones.

More About Names, by L. Wagner, reprinted by Gale Research Company, Detroit, 1968. Subjects include nicknames of American states, firearms, matrimony, articles of attire, insects, the sea, music, fishes, liquor, animals, plants, weaponry, the church, fruits and vegetables.

ASSIGNMENT

I. Discussion of Combining Forms

-meter from Gk *metron* measure. Also, barometer, altimeter, meter, pedometer, odometer, speedometer, kilometer, tetrameter, hexameter,
heptameter, octameter, decameter, hectometer, millimeter. (The
Greek numbering system is in EW at Lesson XVI.)

-metry through the Gk suffix *-metria* a measuring, from *metron* measure.
Also, biometry, chronometry, photometry, anthropometry. The corresponding adjective combining form is -metric, as in geometric, trig-
onometric, etc., and the adjective metric. The *-y* drops after the form
-metrist, the person.

-graph from *graphein* to write, draw. Also, apograph, diagraph, digraph,
epigraph, paragraph, pictograph, monograph, stereograph. This item
could also be introduced in this lesson as a base, GRAPHO- (or
GRAPH- before vowels) or as a combining form in initial position, in
such words as graph, grapheme, graphic(s), graphite, graphoanalysis,
graphology, graphoscope, graphospasm (= writer's cramp), graph-
otherapy. The combining form -grapher, the person, is also usually
found in contemporary dictionaries, as in geographer, photographer,
telegrapher, paragrapher, monographer.

-graphy from the Gk combining form *-graphia*, from *graphein* to write,
draw. Also, biography, filmography, discography, stereography, choreography, orthography. The corresponding adjective form -graphic also
usually appears as a combining form, as in biographic, telegraphic,
photographic, etc.

-gram from *gramma* something written or drawn, from *graphein* to write.
Also, chromogram, cardiogram, digram (= digraph), anagram, epi-
gram, program, stereogram, kilogram, radiogram (= British, a radio
phonograph), phonogram (= a phonograph). This item could also be
treated as a base GRAM(M)-, as in gramophone, grammar, gram-
matical, grammaticize, gramradio (= South African, a radio phonograph). The combining form -gram can also refer to the unit of
weight, as in kilogram, hectogram, dekagram, decigram, centigram,
milligram, and gram or (British) gramme.

-scope ultimately from *skopein* to look at, consider, examine. Also
stethoscope, stereoscope, proctoscope (*proktos* anus). The combining
form -scopy (not usually listed), meaning a viewing or an observation,
could also be added here, as in cranioscopy, radioscopy, proctoscopy,
telescopy; also the corresponding adjective form -scopic. EW touches
on these two forms.

II. Discussion of Bases

BAR- from *baros* weight. This base can stand free, as bar (= a unit of pressure), or as a combining form -bar (not generally recorded), as in millibar, isobar, isallobar. Dictionaries do, however, generally list the forms bar- (before vowels, as in bariatrics) and baro- (as in barometer, baroscope, barotropy). *Barys* heavy (akin to *baros*) gives baritone. Many orthographic similarities are not connected with this base, as barbarian, barbecue, barber, barcarole, bargain, barley, baron, baroque, and others.

CAL(L)-, KAL(L)- from *kallos* beauty. Also calligraphy, calliope (*ops* voice), callipygian (*pyge* buttocks), callithumpian (E thump). Compare callus and callisection from L *callus* hard skin.

IS- from *isos* equal. Is- (before vowels, as in isacoustic and isallobar) and iso- are the combining form. Also, isobar, isobath, isocracy, isodynamic, isogeotherm, isogloss, isotherm, isoline, and about 150 others. Compare isolate, through F *isole* from L *insula* island.

MACR- from *makros* large, long. Macro- and macr- (before vowels) are the combining form, as in macroeconomics, macroevolution, macroinstruction (of a computer), macrophysics, and some 60 others. Compare the Gk base MICR- small, one millionth part of.

ORA- from *horama* a view, sight, from *horan* to see. Also, the F loan word diorama.

PETR- from *petra* rock and *petros* stone. The popular combining form here is petro-, with petr- before vowels, as petrous. Also, petrochemical, petrodollars, petrogenesis, petroglyph, petrography, petrol, petrolatum, petrolize, petrology.

PHOT- from the stem *phot-* of the noun *phos* light. Photo- is the combining form, with occasional listings of phot-. There are well over 200 words built with photo-, in addition to many that combine with the nominative form *phos*; the combining form phos-, not generally found, gives phosgene, and spinning off from this is phosphorus, which has its own combining forms, phosphoro- (or phosphor- before vowels, as in phosphorate) and phospho- or phosph- before vowels, as in phosphide.

TOP- from *topos* place. The combining form is topo-, with top- before vowels as in toponymy. Also, topology, topography, topos.

III. Analysis and Definition of Words

1. TOP(o)- place + -*graph* to write + -*ic* pertaining to + -*al* character of: concerning the art of detailed mapping or description of the features of an area, region, or locality.

2. PAN- all + ORA- to see + -*ma* result of: un unobstructed view in all directions of a surrounding region.

3. IS(o)- equal + TOP- place: any of two or more species of atoms of a chemical element having the same atomic number but different atomic weights and different physical properties.

4. CHRON(o)- time + -*meter* instrument for measuring: an instrument for measuring time accurately.

5. *sym*- with, together + -*metry* science of measuring + -*ic* pertaining to + -*al* having the character of + -*ly* E adverb suffix: in a manner pertaining to balanced proportions or regularity of form.

6. IDE(o)- thought, idea + -*graph* writing + -*ic* pertaining to: pertaining to a picture or symbol used in writing that represents a thing or an idea but does not represent sound.

7. CYCL- circle + ORA- to see + -*ma* result of: a large pictorial representation (here, of a battle) surrounding the spectator and often having real objects, such as miniature trees and people, as the foreground.

8. OPT(o)- eye, to see + -*metry* science of measuring + -*ist* expert: an expert (although not a doctor) in the science of examining eyes and prescribing eyeglasses.

9. PETR(o)- rock + -*graphy* science of writing: the science dealing with the description and classification of rocks.

10. MACR(o)- large + -*scopic* pertaining to viewing: large enough to be observed by the naked eye.

11. *epi*- on + -*gram* thing written: a terse, witty, sometimes paradoxical, saying.

12. *archi*- chief, principal, one who rules + -*epi* over + -*scope* to view + -*al* pertaining to: pertaining to an archbishop or an archbishopric.

13. TELE- afar, operating at a distance + -*metry* the art or science of measuring + -*ic* pertaining to: pertaining to the measurement of some quantity and the sending of it to some distant receiving station (here, earth).

14. ORTH(o)- correct + -*graphy* art of writing: correct spelling based on accepted usage.

15. BAR(o)- pressure + -*meter* instrument for measuring: an instrument for measuring the pressure of the atmosphere, used in predicting probable changes in weather.

16. MIM(e)- to imitate + -*tic* pertaining to: that mimics; imitative.

17. HOL(o)- whole + -*graph* writing: a document or other manuscript written entirely in the handwriting of the person in whose name it appears.

18. PHOT(o)- light + -*meter* instrument for measuring: an instrument for measuring the intensity, distribution, etc., of light.

19. from *kalligraphia*, from CALL(i)- beauty + -*graphy* writing: beautiful or elegant handwriting.

20. IS(o)- equal + BAR- pressure: a line on a weather map connecting places where the atmospheric pressure is the same at a given time or for a given period.

IV. Matching Exercise Using -*phobia*

In this exercise, and in those like it that follow in later exercises, students are largely on their own since the majority of these words are not recorded in contemporary dictionaries. Even W3 does not list all of them. Most of the roots are in EW, but for those that are not—such as entom(o)- (in No. 10 below), a combining form meaning insect—the students could search in their dictionaries for such combining forms. If their dictionaries do not have a combining form for that root, they could look for a word containing this root, as entomology, where in the etymology they will find that the Gk *entoma* means insect. By having the students break down each word, the instructor could have them substantiate their answers. To break down entom- into *en*- into + TOM- to cut, would not, of course, be helpful.

1. *scopo*- to view (compare -*scope* an instrument for viewing): f.
2. *dys*- disordered + MORPH(o)- body: i.
3. PED(o)- child: a.
4. from L *ballista* ballista, from BALL- to throw: h.
5. ERG(o)- work: j.
6. from hydrophobia (which here means rabies) + -*phobia*: c. Not found in any dictionary.
7. ODONT(o)- tooth: e.
8. TOP(o)- place: g.
9. ANTHROP(o)- human being: b.
10. entom(o)- insect: d.

LESSON XV

ASSIGNMENT

I. Discussion of Verb-Forming Suffix

-ize   through F *-iser* from L verbs ending in *-izare*, or through L from Gk verbs ending in *-izein*, or directly from the Gk. The spelling -ize is generally preferred in the U.S., whereas -ise is preferred in British usage. Some words, such as devise, supervise, exercise, are always spelled -ise. In addition to EW's senses, this suffix can also mean to become (as in crystallize = to become crystal), to resemble or conform to (as in Americanize), treat like (as in idolize), engage in a (specified) activity (as in philosophize), spread the teaching of (Christianize).

II. Discussion of Bases

GON-   from *gonia* angle. Used mainly with numbers, as in tetragon, pentagon, hexagon, heptagon, octagon, etc. Gonio- is generally found as the combining form, as in goniometer. Compare gon-, gono-, meaning sexual or reproductive, as in gonocyte or gonorrhea.

LAB-, LEP-, LEM-   all three originate from the verb *lambanein* to take: LAB- is from its contracted stem; LEP- is from *lepsis* a seizure; LEM- is from *lemma* anything taken. Also, analemma, analeptic, epilepsy, lemma, prolepsis, syllepsis. Compare collaborate (L *com-* + *laborare* to work).

MES-   from *mesos* middle. Mes-, before vowels as in meson and mesencephalon, and meso- are the combining form. Also, Mesoamerica, mesoblast, mesocephalic, Mesolithic, mesosphere.

PHRA-   from *phrazein* to say, speak, tell, explain. Also, paraphrasis, antiphrasis. Compare diaphragm and epiphragm, from *phragma* a fence; and euphrasy, from PHREN- mind.

STROPH-   from *strephein* to turn. Also, anastrophe, apostrophe, diastrophism.

III. Analysis and Definition of Words

1. *anti-* against + *-nomy* system of laws governing + *-an* pertaining to + *-ism* practice or condition of: the practice pertaining to the contradiction between two laws which seem equally desirable, logical, or reasonable.

2. *anti-* opposite + PHON- sound, voice + *-y* act of: an act or instance of having verses or passages sung by two choirs.

3. COSM(o)- universe + *-logy* systematic study of + *-ist* one engaged in: one who studies the universe and its laws.

4. *para-* beside + PHRA- to speak + *-se* result of: a restatement of written material (as a passage, sentence, or an entire text) giving the meaning in another form or other words.

5. *apo-* away from + STROPH- to turn + *-ize* verbal suffix: to stop, as in a speech in a play, and address the audience.

6. *a-* not + TYP- model + *-ic* pertaining to + *-al* character of: not typical; irregular.

7. *meta-* changed + THE- to set, put + *-sis* act of: the transposition of sounds, syllables, or letters in a word.

8. *par-* beside + *en-* in + THE- to place, put + *-tic* pertaining to + *-al* character of: serving or helping to explain or qualify.

9. *peri-* around + PHRA- to speak + *-sis* (here, plural, *-ses*) act or instance: an expression phrased in a roundabout way; circumlocution (L *circum-* around + LOCUT- to speak).

10. LITH(o)- stone + *-graph* writing: a print made from a plane surface, as of stone or a metal plate, on which the image to be printed is ink-receptive and the blank places ink-repellent.

11. *meta-* changed + STA- to stand + *-sis* (here plural, *-ses*) act or instance: the transference of a disease from the diseased site to other parts of the body.

12. POLY- many + GON- angle(s) + *-al* pertaining to: having many (strictly, three or more) angles and straight sides.

13. *sym-* together + BI(o)- life + *-sis* act: the intimate living together of two dissimilar organisms in a mutually beneficial relationship.

14. *epi-* upon + LEP- to seize + *-tic* pertaining to: pertaining to a disorder in the electrical rhythms of the central nervous system manifested by partial or complete loss of consciousness and sometimes by convulsions.

15. *cata-* down + STROPH- to turn + *-ic* pertaining to: caused by widespread calamity, misfortune, or other extraordinary disaster.

16. CANON- rule + *-ize* to make: here, figurative, to treat as a saint; to glorify.

17. AUT- self + OP- to see + *-sy* act: the act of examining a dead body to determine the cause of death or the character and location of disease the person died from; a post-mortem.

18. *en-* in + ERG- work + *-ize* treat with (energy): to apply voltage to

(the best response, although not many dictionaries give this sense); apply or impart energy to.

19. MES(o)- middle + ZO- animal + -*ic* pertaining to: pertaining to the geological interval between the Permian and the Tertiary periods, of the era occurring between 70 million and 220 million years ago.

20. *syn*- together + CHRON- time + -*ize* to make: to cause to go at the same rate.

LESSON XVI

ASSIGNMENT

I. Discussion of Numerals Bases

HEMI-   from the Gk element *hemi*- a half. Generally considered a prefix. Found in some 50 words. Compare the Gk base HEM- blood.

MON-   from *monos* single, one, alone. Mon-, before vowels as in monacid, and mono- are the combining form, throwing off some 250 words, including monocle, monocracy, monody, monolith, monologue, monoplane, monopoly.

PROT-   from *protos* first. Prot-, before vowels as in protamine and protagonist, and proto- are the combining form, as in protocol, protofascism, Proto-Germanic, protohistory, protolanguage, proton, protoplasm, prototype, protozoa, and others. Compare other pro- words with 't' following, as protect (L *pro*- + *tegere* to cover) and protract (L *pro*- + TRACT- to drag).

DI-   from *dis* twice. Also spelled dis- before 's' as in dissyllable, although nearly all dis- words are from different roots, as the L *dis*- prefix (= not, in different directions, apart). Most of the words using the Gk combining form are concerned with science.

DICH-   from *dicha* in two, asunder. Dicho- is the combining form; sometimes dich- is found. Most words beginning with dich- are not connected with this base, as dichloride (DI- + chloride), dichromatism (DI- + CHROMAT- color).

DEUTER-   from *deuteros* second. Deut-, deuto- (as in deutonymph, deutoplasm), deuter- (as in deuteron), and deutero- (as in deuterogenesis, deuterocanonical, Deuteronomy, deutrogamy) are the combining forms, which are usually found.

TRI- from *treis* three or *tris* thrice. Listed as a combining form. Also, triad, triarchy, Triassic, tribrach, trichord, trichotomy, and others. Triangle, triceps, and tricorn (hat) come from L TRI- three. Since, for many words, most contemporary dictionaries do not distinguish between those English words that derive from L TRI- and those that derive from Gk TRI-, it would seem unnecessary at most levels to expect students to. There are also many words that have no connection with either of these bases, such as triage, trial, tribe, tribometer, tribulation, tribunal, tributary, tribute.

TETR(A)- from *tetra-*, the Gk combining form of the numeral *tetteras* four. Listed as a combining form is tetr- before vowels (as in tetracid), otherwise tetra-. Modern formations with this base are chiefly scientific and technical words. Also, tetrachord, tetrachotomy, tetracycline, tetrad, Tetragrammaton, tetrahedron, tetralogy, tetrameter, tetrapolis, tetrarchy, trapeze (TETRA- + *peza* foot).

PENT(A)- from *pente* five. Entered as a combining form, with pent- before vowels (as in pentane), otherwise penta-. In modern English, used chiefly in technical terms and words concerned with chemistry, as in pentacarbon. Also, pentachord, pentad, pentagram, pentahedron, Pentagonese (= military jargon), pentameter, pentarchy. Pentecost, the Christian festival, is the English equivalent of the Gk *pentekoste* (*hemera*), fiftieth (day); it is also the gentile name for the Jewish harvest festival (Shabuoth, Shabuot, or Shavuot) observed on the fiftieth day after Passover. Compare penthouse, from ML *appendicum* an attached building; formerly pentice (from F), formed by apheresis and /d/ to /t/, and altered by folk etymology.

HEX(A)- from *hex* six. Hex- (before vowels, as in hexane) and hexa- are the combining form. Modern formations are often concerned with chemistry. Also, hexachord, hexad, hexagon, hexagram, hexahedron, hexameter, hexapod, hexarchy. Compare hex (= a witch or magic spell), from German *Hexe* witch.

HEPT(A)- from *hepta* seven. Hept- (before vowels, as in heptane) and hepta- are listed as the combining form. Appears in hybrids, such as heptangular and heptavalent, chiefly on account of the inconvenience of the L *septem* seven, but combines usually with Greek elements. Also, heptad, heptagon, heptahedron, heptameter, heptarchy, Heptateuch.

OCT(A)- from *okto* eight. Oct- (before vowels, as in octad, octane, octarchy), octa- (as in octachord, octahedron, octagon, octamerous, octameter), and octo- (as in octopod, octopus) are variously listed as combining forms. WNCD does not record octo-. RHD calls octo- a variant of octa-. WBD lists octo- separately, etymologizing it from both L *octo* and Gk *okto*. For certain levels of instruction it would seem unnecessary to distinguish between those English words that derive from Greek (as above) and those that derive from Latin (as October, octodecimo, octogenarian).

DEC(A)   from *deka* ten. Dec- (before vowels, as in decare and decathlon), deca-, dek-, and deka- are generally recorded as combining forms, the last two usually called variants of the first two, as in dekagram, dekaliter, dekameter, and dekastere, for decagram, etc.; also, the British spellings decalitre and decametre. Also, decade, decad, decagon, decahedron, decalogue (or decalog), Decameron (= the 100 tales of Boccaccio, so called because 10 tales were told on each of 10 days; from *deka* + HEMER- day), decapod, decastich, decastyle, decathlete (= one who performs 10 athletic contests in the decathlon; a blend of decathlon and athlete). Compare other deca- words, such as decadent (from L *de*- apart, down + L CAD- to fall).

HECT-   from F *hecto*-, an alteration of the Gk *hekaton* hundred. Hect- (before vowels as in hectare) and hecto- are the combining form, and occasionally found as variants are hekt- and hekto-, as in hektogram, hektograph, hektoliter, hektometer, for hectogram, etc.; also the British hectolitre and hectometre.

KILO-   from the F *kilo*-, an alteration of the Gk *chilioi* a thousand. Variously called a prefix and a combining form. Also, kiloampere, kilobar, kilobit, kilocurie, kilocycle, kilodyne, kilogauss, kilogram, kilohertz, kilohm, kilojoule, kiloliter (Brit. kilolitre), kilometer (Brit. kilometre), kiloton (Brit. kilotonne), kilovolt, kilowatt.

   The combining form -*ploid*, "used in cytology and genetics to indicate the number of chromosomes" (RHD), or "having or being a chromosome number that bears (such) a relationship to or is (so many) times the base chromosome number of a given group" (WNCD), is covered by most dictionaries. Like -*gate, -thon, -aholic* (and other such 'false combining forms' presented in Blends at Latin Lesson XXI), -*ploid* is similarly abstracted, from haploid—which is really the combining form haplo- (hapl- before vowels, as in haplosis, haplopia, haploid) + -oid, like, of Lesson VII. All other ploid forms (diploid, tetraploid, etc.) are analogical.

II. Analysis and Definition of Words

   1. MONO(o)- one + -*mania* passion for: a dominant (strong, overpowering, obsessive) interest.
   2. MON(o)- one + THE- god + -*ist* one who believes in + -*ic* pertaining to: pertaining to a belief in only one God.
   3. PENT(a) five + GON- angle + -*al* pertaining to: having five sides and five angles.

4. MON(o)- one + GAM- marriage + -ous committing or practicing: having only one mate during a lifetime.

5. POLY- many + syl- together + LAB- to take + -ic pertaining to + -al like + -ly E adverb suffix: in a manner using words of more than three syllables.

6. HOMO(o)- same + GEN- kind + -ize verbal suffix + -d E past participial suffix: here, figurative, to make similar or uniform.

7. HEX(a)- six + -meter measure: a line of poetry consisting of six metrical feet. (Statius and Ausonius were both Roman poets.)

8. PROT- first + AGON- struggle, contest + -ist one who: the main character in a poem, story, or (here) a play. (There are other definitions of this, as extensions or general senses, but these should not be allowed.)

9. (a) MON(o)- one, single + LITH- stone: here, literal, a single large stone as would form a monument or sculpture; (b) the above + -ic like: here, figurative, like such a large (powerful, imposing) stone.

10. PROT(o)- first + TYP- model: the first of anything; an original model on which something is patterned; a first, full-scale, and usually functional form of a new type or design of a construction, as a hydrofoil or airplane.

11. MON(o)- one, single + CHROM- color: a mass of a single color.

12. STERE(o)- three-dimensional + -scope instrument for viewing + -ic pertaining to: three-dimensional, pertaining to an instrument that allows pictures to be seen in depth.

13. MON(o)- one, single + -gram thing written: a person's initials combined into one design (commonly one's initials but not always).

14. DI- two + LEM- to take + -ma result: a situation involving a choice between two equally unsatisfactory alternatives.

15. TRI- three + LOG- speech, word, story + -y quality of: here, a concrete use, three plays written by the same person that are closely related and develop a single theme.

16. DICH(o)- in two + TOM- to cut + -y state of: division into two parts.

17. MON- single, alone + -ast one who does (although monast is not recorded in the OED) + -ic like: like (the quiet and seclusion of) the life of a nun or monk in a convent.

18. PROT(o)- first, primitive + ZO- animal + -an pertaining to, like: here, substantive use of the adjective, any animal pertaining to the phylum Protozoa, consisting of animals having only one cell.

19. MON(o)- one, single + -graph writing: a scholarly treatise (book, article, etc.) about one particular subject.

20. MON(o)- one, single + *-logue* speech: a speech (here, a dramatic soliloquy) that monopolizes conversation. The phrase dramatic monologue is usually listed as a main entry, meaning a literary work, often poetic, in which a character reveals himself ("and the dramatic situation"—RHD), usually to another person.

III. Matching Definitions With Religious Terms

These words are generally listed in desk dictionaries.

1. DEC(a)- ten + *logue* speech: e.
2. DEUTER(o)- second + *-nomy* law: h.
3. Di- twice, double + THE- god + *-ism* belief in: a.
4. HEPT(a)- seven + Gk *teuchos* book: j.
5. HEX(a)- six + Gk *teuchos* book: b.
6. MON(o)- one, single + PHYSI- nature + *-te* one who: i.
7. PENT(a)- five + Gk *teuchos* book: d.
8. PROT(o)- first + Gk *martyr* witness: f.
9. TETR- four + *-arch* ruler: c.
10. TRI- three + THE- god + *-ism* belief in: g.

LESSON XVII

ASSIGNMENT

I. Discussion of Bases

CHORE- from *choreia* dance. Choreo- is occasionally listed as the combining form, as in choreodrama, choreography and its back-formed verb choreograph, chorea (= St. Vitus's dance). Chorus is from *choros* a band of dancers. Can also appear as the final element, as in Terpsichore (*terpein* to delight). Choir (through F) is a doublet of chorus.

ER- from *eros* sexual desire; EROT- from *erot-*, the stem of *eros*. Eroto- is occasionally found as a combining form. Also, erogenic (= erogenous), erotica, erotology, erotomania.

GLYPH- from *glyphein* to carve, cut out. Also, glyphic, glyphography, glyptic, glyptodont, glyptograph—the last 3 from the combining form glypt(o)-, from *glyptos* carved.

NAUT- from *nautes* sailor, from *naus* ship. Also, nautiloid, nautilus.

NES- from *nesos* island. Also, Polynesia, Peloponnesus (also Peloponnese), Micronesia.

II. Analysis and Definition of Words

1. PATH(o)- disease + *-logy* science of + *-ic* pertaining to + *-al* like: dealing with or concerned with disease.

2. OD(o)- way + *-meter* measure: a device for measuring distance traveled by a vehicle.

3. MICR(o)- small + NES- island + *-ia* territory*: a group of small islands in the Pacific, east of the Philippines. ("The name, modelled after *Polynesia*, was intended to mean 'the region of small islands'"—OED.)

4. PETR(o)- rock + GLYPH- to carve: a carving or inscription on a rock (usually prehistoric).

5. POLY- many + CHROM- color: a combination of many colors.

6. POLY- many + NES- island + *-ia* territory* + *-(a)n* pertaining to: pertaining to Polynesia, a group of islands in the Pacific east of Australia.

7. DEM(o)- people + *-grapher* (*-graph* + *-er*) one who writes: one engaged in the statistical study of human populations, especially with regard to density, size, distribution, and vital statistics.

8. PALE(o)- old + *-graph* writing + *-ic* pertaining to + *-al* characteristic of: pertaining to the study of ancient writings and inscriptions to determine dates, origins, etc.

9. HIER(o)- sacred + GLYPH- to carve + *-ics* study of: here, figurative, any writing that is difficult to read.

10. (a) *a-* without + PHA- to speak + *-sia* state of, condition: loss or impairment of the power to use or understand words, caused by a brain lesion; (b) *a-* without + TAX- to arrange, put in order + *-ia* state of, condition: loss of normal coordination, especially of the voluntary movements of the muscles.

11. PSYCH(o)- mind + *-metry* science of measuring + *-ist* one who: a person skilled in the science of measuring mental facts and relations; one skilled in measuring mental traits, abilities, and processes.

---

*See IM's discussion of the suffix *-an* at Latin Lesson VIII.

12. THE- god + -ist one who believes in + -ic pertaining to: concerning a believer in God.

13. KINE- to move + -tic pertaining to: having to do with motion.

14. ACR- tip, end, extremity + ONYM- word: a word formed from the initial letter or letters of the words, or the important words, in a compound term. (Acronyms are discussed in the topical essay of Latin Lesson IV.)

15. syn- with, together + ESTHE- to feel, perceive + -sia condition: a phenomenon in which the stimulation of one sense evokes the sensation of another sense, as when a certain sound causes a person to visualize a certain color.

16. CHORE(o)- dance + -graphy writing: the dancing composed and arranged for a stage performance.

17. MORPH(o)- form, shape + -logy science of + -ic pertaining to + -al characteristic of: relating to the form and structure of plants without regard to function.

18. EROT- love + -ic pertaining to: concerning sexual passion or love.

19. (a) COSM(o)- universe + NAUT- sailor: in Russian space travel, a pilot or member of a crew of a spacecraft; (b) ASTR(o)- star + NAUT- sailor: a pilot or member of a crew of a spacecraft. (In the U.S.A. the term cosmonaut is used only in reference to Soviet space travelers. In Great Britain the two terms are used interchangeably for either Americans or Russians.)

20. PATH(o)- disease + GEN- to produce + -ic pertaining to: producing disease.

LESSON XVIII

LITERARY TERMS

Additional Exercise on Words from Literature

The following words also arose in connection with literature. Students could trace the source and give the meaning of these words for additional work. Answers follow the dash.

1. bowdlerize—after Thomas Bowdler (1754 – 1825), an English editor who published an expurgated edition of Shakespeare. Here, with the -*ize* verbal suffix, meaning to remove objectional material from a text.

2. Gargantuan—after the good-natured gigantic king (giant) in Rabelais's satire *Gargantua*, who had a great capacity for food and drink. Here, with -*(a)n* adjective suffix, meaning enormous, huge, gigantic.

3. Lilliputian—from the imaginary island of Lilliput in Jonathan Swift's *Gulliver's Travels*, an island inhabited by small people (about six inches tall) called Lilliputians. Hence, meaning tiny, very small, miniature, or petty, with -*ian* adjective suffix.

4. Mrs. Grundy—from the character Mrs. Grundy in Thomas Morton's play *Speed the Plough* (1798), a lady who supervises and censors the morals and manners of others. The word refers to a person of prudish conventionality in personal conduct.

5. pamphlet—from OF *Phamphilet,* popular name for a Latin poem of the 1100s (from PAN- all + PHIL- to love). It means an unbound printed booklet sometimes with a paper cover.

6. Pollyanna—from Pollyanna, the heroine of several novels by the American writer Eleanor Porter (1868 – 1920). It means a person characterized by excessive optimism and a tendency to find good in everything, even in the face of trouble or disaster.

7. Rabelaisian—from the French writer Francois Rabelais (1494? – 1553). Here, with the -*ian* adjective suffix, it means characterized by broad robust humor, extravagance of caricature, or bold naturalism.

8. sadism—from the Count or Marquis Donatien de Sade (1740 – 1814), who first wrote of the disorder. It means the practice of a person who takes delight in hurting someone else; an unnatural love of cruelty; a sexual behavior in which pleasure is obtained by inflicting pain upon one's sexual partner. The noun is reduced to sado- in sadomasochism.

9. simon-pure—from the character Simon, a Quaker, whose identity is questioned through impersonation but eventually proven genuine, from the comedy *A Bold Stroke for a Wife* (1718) by the English dramatist Susanna Centlivre (1667? – 1723). The word refers to anything or anyone real, genuine, or morally pure.

10. yahoo—from one of the race of brutes in Swift's *Gulliver's Travels* who had the form and vices of man. The word means any crude, coarse, or uncouth person.

ASSIGNMENT

I. Words with Literary Origins

1. catastrophe—the outcome (usually death or ruin in a tragedy, usually a happy marriage in a comedy) of a literary or dramatic work; dénouement.

2. elegaic—in classical prosody, a dactylic hexameter couplet (dactylic: 3 syllables—1 long and 2 short; hexameter: a line consisting of six feet).

3. catharsis—the purging of an audience's emotions through a work of art. (This is a figurative transfer of the original meaning, a purgation, from Gk *katharos* pure, clean.)

4. onomatopoeic—the adaptation of the sound of a word to its meaning, for rhetorical effect; the use of a word whose sound suggests the sense. Examples: the tintinnabulation that so musically wells from the bells (Poe); The double double double beat of the thundering drum (Dryden).

5. panegyric—a speech or writing in praise of a person or thing; a formal eulogy.

6. prosaic—characteristic of prose (as opposed to poetry).

7. parable—a brief story used for teaching some moral lesson or attitude or a religious principle.

8. prosody—the study or science of poetic meters and versification, from *pros* in addition to + OD- song.

II. Analysis and Definition of Words

1. ASCE- exercise (from *askein* to exercise) + -*tic* pertaining to: refraining from pleasure and comforts; practicing strict self-denial as a measure of personal and, especially, spiritual discipline.

2. BUCOL- cowherd (from *boukolos* herdsman, from *bous* cow) + -*ic* pertaining to: pertaining to shepherds; relating to or typical of rural life.

3. *cata-* down + CLYS- to wash (from *klyzein* to wash) + -*m* result of + -*ic* pertaining to: extremely sudden and violent; pertaining to a momentous and violent event marked by overwhelming upheaval and demolition.

4. CYNOS- dog (from *kynos*, the genitive of the noun *kyon* dog) + UR- tail (from *oura* tail), which combined into *kynosoura* (= dog's

tail) in Greek, and into Cynosura in Latin. In Greek mythology, Cynosura, a nurse of Zeus and a nymph of Mount Ida, metamorphosed into Ursa Minor (L smaller bear), the constellation also referred to as Cynosure (OED 1596), a word that immediately took on figurative uses, one of which means a center of attraction, interest, or attention—which it means here.

5. DIDAC- to teach (from *didaskein* to teach) + -*tic* pertaining to: meant to instruct; intended to convey instruction and information as well as pleasure and entertainment.

6. HEDON- pleasure (from *hedone* pleasure) + -*ism* belief in, practice of: the belief or doctrine that pleasure or happiness is the sole or chief good in life; devotion to pleasure as a way of life.

7. HEGEMON- leader (from *hegeisthai* to lead) + -*y* state of: superior leadership or authority, especially of one nation over others.

8. IDI(o)- one's own + *syn*- together + CRA- to mix + -*sy* act or instance: a characteristic peculiarity or habit, as of taste, behavior, or opinion. Some dictionaries give *cras*- a mixing, as the stem, from *krannynai* to mix, in which case this would read CRAS- + -*y* act of.

9. *peri*- around + PATE- to walk (from *patein* to walk) + -*tic* pertaining to: traveling about or from place to place in connection with some occupation. (The general sense of this word derives from Peripatetic, the adjective, pertaining to the philosophy of Aristotle, in reference to his custom of walking while teaching.)

10. POLEM- war (from *polemos* war) + -*ic* pertaining to: here, a noun, an argument or controversy; an aggressive attack on the opinions or principles of others.

III. Definition of Words

Etymologies are also given here because some of them are interesting and can offer further insights into semantic development.

1. from the stem *adamant*- of the noun *adamas* the hardest metal, from *a*- not + -*damant*- verbal adjective stem of *daman* to conquer: any extremely hard substance; any hard substance that is impenetrable.

2. *ap*- from + *horos* boundary + -*ism* belief in, which combined in Gk to form *aphorismos* definition: a concise statement expressing a general truth; a piece of practical wisdom, etc.

3. from *axios* worthy -*m* result of: a self-evident truth; a statement widely accepted as being true on its own merit (without proof).

4. ultimately from *deleesthai* to hurt + ⁀*us*: pertaining to: having a harmful effect; injurious.

5. *dia-* away + *tribein* to wear: a harsh and bitter speech or writing; denunciation; invective; tirade.

6. *em-* in + *peira* experiment + *-ic* pertaining to + *-al* characteristic of: based on experiment and observation without regard for system and theory.

7. from *epoche* a fixed point in time, *epi-* upon + *echein* to hold: a time marked by an event that begins a new period or development; a period of time; an era.

8. from *esoterikos* inner, from *esotero* inner, comparative of *eso* within: designed for or understood by a specially initiated few.

9. from *aither* upper air + *-eal* (variant of *-al*) pertaining to: lacking material substance; light; airy; delicate.

10. from *lethe* oblivion + *argos* lazy (*an-* not + *ergon* work) + *-y* quality of: abnormal drowsiness; lack of energy.

11. *an-* without + *odyne* pain: a medicine that relieves or lessens pain. (Nepenthe is also of Greek origin—*nepenthes* sorrowless, dispelling sorrow, from *ne-* not + *penthos* sorrow, grief—a drug or drink used by the ancients, according to legend, for bringing forgetfulness of sorrow or trouble.)

12. *para-* beside, beyond + *oxynein* to provoke, goad (from *oxys* sharp): a sudden fit; an attack.

13. from the stem *pragmat-* of the noun *pragma* deed, act + *-ic* pertaining to (or: prag- + *-ma* result + *-tic*): concerned with practical results or values; relating to matters of fact or practical affairs.

14. from *sardonios* of bitter or scornful smiles or laughter + *-ic* pertaining to: bitterly contemptuous; disdainfully humorous; derisively mocking.

15. from *sykophantes* informer, slanderer + *-tic* pertaining to + *-al* like + *-ly* E adverb suffix: in the manner of a servile or self-seeking flatterer.

LESSON XIX

ASSIGNMENT

I. Definition of Greek Loan Words

1. from Gk *akme* point, highest point: the highest point or stage.
2. from Gk *aroma* spice: a pleasant, often spicy or sweet, smell.

3. from Gk *aura* breeze, breath: a distinctive atmosphere surrounding someone or something; a subtly pervasive quality seeming to emanate from a person, place, or thing.

4. from Gk *bathos* depth: overdone or insincere pathos; sentimentalism.

5. from L *colossus*, from Gk *kolossos* gigantic: anything huge or gigantic.

6. from New L *cosmus*, from Gk *kosmos* order, world, universe (COSM- universe): an orderly, harmonious, systematic universe.

7. from Gk *kriterion*, from *krinein* to judge (CRI- to judge): a standard for making a judgment or decision.

8. from L *emporium,* from Gk *emporion*, from *en-* on + *poros* voyage: a large store that sells a great variety of articles.

9. from L *encomium*, from Gk *enkomion* laudatory, from *en-* in + *komos* revelry: glowing and elaborately enthusiastic praise.

10. from L *aenigma*, from Gk *ainigma*, from *ainos* fable or riddle: a baffling or puzzling situation.

11. from L *aeon*, from Gk *aion* lifetime, age: any very long period of time; in geologic terms, two or more eras (as Cenozoic, Mesozoic, etc.).

12. from Gk *hoi polloi* the many (people): the general populace; ordinary people; the masses.

13. from L *iota*, from Gk *iota* iota, the smallest letter in the Greek alphabet: an infinitesimal part or amount; bit; jot; whit.

14. from Gk *lexikon*, from *lexis* word: the vocabulary of a particular group.

15. from New L *miasma*, from Gk *miasma* pollution: a bad-smelling, perhaps poisonous, vapor rising from decaying matter on the earth.

16. from New L *nostalgia,* from Gk *nostos* homecoming + ALG- pain: a longing or wistful yearning for things belonging to the past.

17. from L *panacea* from Gk *panakeia*, from PAN- all + *akos* cure, remedy: a remedy for all difficulties.

18. from Gk *pathos* suffering, experience, emotion (PATH- to suffer): a quality or element that arouses a feeling of pity, sadness, or compassion.

19. from L *phalanx,* from Gk *phalanx* line of battle: here, figurative, a number of persons united for a common purpose.

20. from LL *phaenomenon* appearance, from Gk *phainomenon* appearing, apparent (PHA- to show): a fact or event that can be observed. The *-a* is the plural of *-on.*

21. from LL *plethora*, from Gk *plethora* fullness: superabundance; excess; superfluity; oversupply.

22. from *prolegomenon* anything said beforehand, from *pro-* before + *legein* to say: preliminary material in a book; introduction, preface.

23. from L *stigma*, from Gk *stigma* mark, puncture: a mark of disgrace or discredit.

24. from L *thesaurus*, from Gk *thesauros* storehouse, treasure: here, probably, any book filled with information. The *-i* is the L plural of *-us*.

25. from Gk *trauma* a wound: an emotional shock which has a lasting effect on the mind; any abnormal physical or mental condition produced by shock or injury; also, any bodily injury or wound.

II. Plurals

Some dictionaries do not, in all instances, record both plurals where there are two, and the grading of papers should accommodate this. Where they do record both, there is occasional inconsistency in preference, although, as pointed out in IM at Lesson VII, the general tendency in the 1980s was in favor of English plurals, where they exist. Where there are two plurals, the English will indiscriminately be given first here. Some of the words came into English through Latin, where they picked up a Latin plural.

1. colossuses, colossi (Latin).
2. cosmoses, cosmos (singular for plural).
3. criterions, criteria (Greek).
4. diagnoses (Latin).
5. emporiums, emporia (Greek).
6. encomiums, encomia (Latin).
7. enigmas, enigmata (Greek).
8. lexicons, lexica (late Greek).
9. miasmas, miasmata (Greek).
10. octopuses, octopi (Latin), octopodes (Greek).
11. phalanxes, phalanges (Latin and Greek).
12. prolegomena (Greek).
13. stigmas, stigmata (Greek).
14. syntheses (Latin).
15. thesauruses, thesauri (Latin).
16. traumas, traumata (Greek).

LESSON XX

ASSIGNMENT

I. Discussion of Suffixes

-itis   from the suffix *-itis*, the feminine form of the adjective suffix *-ites*. There are various figurative extensions of this suffix in common usage: abnormal states or conditions (as vacationitis), excesses (as televisionitis), tendencies or proneness to (accidentitis), infatuations with (jazzitis, discoitis), excessive advocacy of or reliance on (educationitis). Plural forms are -itises, -itides, -ites.

-oma   from the noun suffix *-oma*. Also, glaucoma, sarcoma, adenoma, fibroma. Plural forms are -omas, -omata.

-osis   from the L suffix *-osis*, from Gk *-osis*. Also, mononucleosis, neurosis, trichinosis, thrombosis, leukosis, leukocytosis, metamorphosis. Plural form is -oses.

II. Discussion of Bases

In this lesson through Lesson XXV, for the additional words offered here that have more than one base, IM gives the foreign words for any stems that are not covered in EW.

ARTHR-   from *arthron* joint. Also arthralgia, arthrodia, arthromere, arthroplasty, arthrosis.

CARDI-   from *kardia* heart. Both cardi- (before vowels, as in cardialgia) and cardio- are generally listed as a combining form. Also, cardiogram (= electrocardiogram), cardiomegaly, cardiomyopathy, cardiopulmonary (*pulmo* lung), cardiovascular (L *vas* vessel). Also occasionally listed is the combining form -cardia, denoting a (specified) heart action or location, as in dextrocardia, tachycardia.

CHONDR-   from *chondros* grain, cartilege. Chondr-, chondri-, and chondro- (as in chondrocranium) are the combining forms. Also, chondriosome (= mitochondrion—*mitos* thread), chondrite, chondroitin, chondrule, chondrichthian.

CYAN-   from *kyanos* dark-blue color or substance. Cyan- (as in cyanic, cyanhydrin) and cyano- are the combining form. Also, cyanometer, cyanotype, cyanosis, and other compounds, such as cyanoacetylene (acetyl = the univalent radical of acetic acid), cyanoethylate (ethyl = the univalent radical in various organic chemical compounds).

218

CYT- from *kytos* receptacle, container, body, anything hollow. Cyt- (as in cytase) and cyto- are a combining form. Also, cytogamy, cytogene, cytokinesis, cytokinin, cytolysis, cytopathology, cytopathy, cytoplasm, cytotoxin, cytotropism, cytoskeleton. As a final element, -cyte is also listed as a combining form, as in leucocyte or leukocyte, phagocyte; and the corresponding adjective form -cytic, as in phagocytic.

ENTER- from *entera* intestines. Enter- (as in enteritis, gastroenteritis) and entero- are the combining form. Also, enterology, enterocolitis (*kolon* colon), enterograph, enterohepatitis, enterostomy, enterotomy.

HEPAT- from *hepat-* the stem of *hepar* liver. Hepat- (as in hepatic, hepatitis) and hepato- are the combining form. Also, hepatectomy, hepatization, hepatocirrhosis (*kirrhos* orange-yellow—because of the diseased liver's appearance), hepatoma, hepatotomy. Also, from the nominative form of the Greek noun comes hepar, heparin, and heparinize.

MELAN- from *melan-* the stem of *melas* black. Melan- (as in melanism, melanic, melanin) and melano- are the combining form. Also, melanite, melanize, melanocyte, melanoid, melanoma (-*ma* result of), melanosis.

MYC- from *mykes* mushroom, fungus; MYCET- from the stem *myket-*. Myc- (as in mycosis, mycelium) and myco- (as in mycology, mycophagous, mycoplasma) are usually recorded as a combining form. Less so is myceto-, as in mycetozoan, mycetoma. Also occasionally listed is -mycin, as the final element, as in the trademark Aureomycin (*aur-* gold), erythromycin, neomycin. The combining form -mycetes is also occasionally found, used especially to form class names of fungi, as in Basidiomycetes, Myxomycetes; with the variant form -mycete, as in Basidiomycete.

NEPHR- from *nephros* kidney(s). Nephr- (as in nephrectomy, nephric) and nephro- are usually listed as the combining form. Also, nephrite (= a kind of jade that was formerly worn as a remedy for kidney diseases), nephritis, nephrogenic, nephropathy.

OST(E)- from *osteon* bone. Oste- (as in osteal, osteitis) and osteo- are the combining form. Also, osteocyte, osteogenesis, osteoblast (BLAST- embryonic cell), osteochondritis, osteoclasis, osteology, osteoma, osteoplasty.

SCLER- from *skleros* hard, from *skellein* to dry up. Scler- (as in scleral, scleroid, sclerite, scleritis) and sclero- are the combining form. Also, scleroderma, scleroiritis (ir[is of the eye]), scleroma, sclerometer, scleroscope, sclerose, sclerosed, sclerous.

III. Analysis and Definition of Words

These words in this exercise, the exercise that follows, and the corresponding exercises in the remaining lessons are not in the Index of Words Appearing in Context that follows Chapter XXV.

1. *endo-* within + CARD(I)- heart + *-itis* inflammation of: inflammation of the endocardium (the membrane that lines the cavities of the heart).

2. *peri-* around + OST- bone + *-itis* inflammation of: inflammation of the periosteum (the dense fibrous membrane that covers the surface of bones except at joints).

3. OSTE(o)- bone + CLA- to break (from *klastos* broken): (a) one of the large multinuclear cells found in growing bone which absorb bony tissue; (b) an instrument for the surgical breaking of a bone to correct deformity. EW's *-st* suffix does not cover this. Should probably read OSTE(o)- + CLAS- + *-t* that which.

4. SCLER(o)- hard + DERMAT- skin + *-ous* like: having a hard body covering, as plates or scales.

5. CYT(o)- cell + LY- to loosen + *-sis* state of: the destruction or disintegration of cells.

6. *par-* beside + ENTER- intestine + *-al* pertaining to: not entering or passing through the intestines. (An intravenous injection provides parenteral nourishment.)

7. *ex-* out + OST- bone + *-osis* diseased condition of: a spur or bony growth on a bone or cartilage.

8. MELAN- dark + *-ism* condition of: a condition of having a high amount of dark pigment granules in the skin, hair, eyes, plumage, etc.

9. MYC- fungus + *-osis* diseased condition of: the presence of fungus in or on any part of the body; also, the disease caused by this fungus.

10. HEPAT- liver + *-itis* inflammatory disease of: inflammation of the liver; also, a contagious virus disease characterized by such inflammation.

11. SCLER- hard + *-oid* like: hard; indurated.

12. MACR(o)- large + CYT- cell: an abnormally large red corpuscle found in the blood, chiefly in anemias.

13. ENTER- intestines + *-itis*: inflammation of the (usually small) intestines, often accompanied by diarrhea and fever.

14. CYAN- dark blue + *-osis* diseased condition of: a bluish or purplish discoloration of the skin and mucous membranes caused by lack of

oxygen in the blood, associated with high altitudes, suffocation, shock, and some forms of heart disease.

15. CARDI(o)- heart + -graph instrument for writing: an instrument that registers graphically the movements of the heart. (Often cross-referenced to electrocardiograph.)

16. en- in + ARTHR- joint + -osis process: in anatomy, a ball-and-socket joint.

17. NECR- dead tissue + -osis diseased condition of: usually localized death of living body tissues, caused by a degenerative disease, lack of oxygen supply, infection, or destructive freezing or burning. (Another word for mortification or gangrene.)

18. dia- through + THERM- heat + -y act of: the production or generation of heat in body tissue by electric currents, for medical, therapeutic, or surgical purposes.

19. HEM(o)- blood + PHIL- here, medically, a tendency + -ia quality of: a sex-linked inherited disorder of the blood characterized by a tendency of the blood not to clot normally, resulting in difficulty in controlling hemorrhaging even after minor injuries.

20. em- in + BOL- to throw + -ism condition of: an obstruction of a blood vessel by a clot (called an embolus).

IV. Matching Definitions with Medical Terms

Except for hepatoma, which is sometimes recorded, the following words are generally not listed in desk dictionaries.

1. HEMAT(o)- blood + CYT(o)- cell + LY- to loosen + -sis act of: f.
2. an- without + ENTER- intestine + -ous pertaining to: e.
3. a- not + CYAN- dark blue + OP- to see + -sia state of: a.
4. MEGAL(o)- large + CARDI- heart + -ia state of: g.
5. HEPAT- liver + -oma tumor: h.
6. LITH(o)- stone + NEPHR- kidney + -itis inflammation of: b.
7. dys- bad, disordered + OST- bone + -osis diseased condition of: i.
8. dys- bad, disordered + ARTHR- speech articulation + -ia state of: c.
9. ACR(o)- extremities + MYC- fungus + -osis diseased condition of: j.
10. MELAN(o)- dark + DERM- skin + -ic pertaining to: d.

LESSON XXI

Discussion of Combining Forms

-ectomy   from New L *-ectomia*, from Gk *-ektome* a cutting out, from the prefix *ec-* out + TOM- to cut. Also, gastrectomy, enterectomy, hepatectomy, nephrectomy, adenectomy.

-tomy   from *-tomia* a cutting; also related to the base TOM- to cut. Also, enterotomy, hepatotomy, nephrotomy, ostomy, colostomy, osteotomy. This combining form also means a cutting off or a casting off, as in autotomy (= the act or process of casting off a part of the body, such as a leg or tail, as by certain crustaceans and lizards when disturbed or in danger). The combining form, -tome, refers to a surgical instrument for cutting, as in microtome and osteotome, and might also be introduced here, along with -tomic, (and -tomical), as in microtomic (= of or having to do with a microtome and microtomy), as well as -tomous, as in dichotomous (= divided or dividing into two parts; in botany, branching by repeated divisions into two).

-rrhea (with variant British preference *-rrhoea*)   from the Greek combining form *-rrhoia*, from the noun *rhoia* a flow. Also, leukorrhea (or leucorrhea), gonorrhea.

ASSIGNMENT

I. Discussion of Bases

ADEN-   from *aden* nut, gland. Aden- (as in adenitis) and adeno- are the combining form. Also, adenine (= one of the purine bases in DNA and RNA), which was originally found in glands. Also, adenocarcinoma (*karkinos* crab), adenology, adenoma, adenotomy.

ANGI-   from *angeion* vessel, blood vessel, container. Angi- (as in angiitis) and angio- are the combining form. Also, angiography, angiology, angioma. The sense of a container is found in botany, as in angiocarpous (= having a fruit enclosed in an external covering), and angiosperm (= a plant having seeds in a closed ovary). Also, in medicine, angioplasty (see PLAST- in Lesson XXIV), a medical procedure for breaking up accumulated plaque in blood vessels in coronary artery disease, and alternative, whenever possible, to by-pass surgery.

CEPHAL-   from *kephale* head. Cephal- (as in cephalad and cephalic) and cephalo- are the combining form. Also, cephalometry, cephalagia (= a

222

headache), cephalocaudal (= from head to tail), cephalocyst, cephalo-genesis. The expression 'cephalic index' should be introduced here, since it is used in various words with CEPHAL- when measurement is indicated. It is defined as the ratio of the greatest breadth of the skull to the greatest length from front to back, multiplied by 100.

CHOL(E)-   from *chole* bile. Chol- (as in cholic acid, choline), chole- (as in cholelithiasis), and cholo- (as in chololith, a gallstone) are the combining form. Also, cholera, cholestasia, cholesterol (STER- solid, stiff).

HYSTER-   from *hystera* womb. Hyster- (before vowels, as in hysterectomy) and hystero- are the combining form, meaning both womb and hysteria. Concerning womb, there is also hysterometer, hysteropexia (*pexis* a fixing—that is, securing the uterus by suturing it to the wall of the abdomen), hysteroscope. Concerning hysteria, there is also hysteroid, hysterogenic (GEN- to produce).

LIP-   from *lipos* fat. Lip- (as in lipoid and lipid) and lipo- are the combining form. Also, lipogenesis (GEN- to produce), lipoma, lipophilic (PHIL- tendency, affinity), lipoprotein.

MAST-   from *mastos* breast. MAZ- is from *mazos* breast, as in mazology, another word for mammalogy (L *mamma* breast). Mast- and masto- are the combining form. Also, mastitis, mastoidectomy. Compare masticate, from Gk *mastax* mouth.

OO-   from *oion* egg (where the 'i' was not pronounced). Also occasionally listed is o- (before vowels) as in ooidal (-*oid* like, resembling). Also, ooblast, oocyst, oocyte, oogenesis.

OT-   from the stem *ot-* of the noun *ous* ear. Ot- (as in otic and otitis) and oto- are the combining form. Also, otocyst; otolaryngology (*laryngo-*, from *larynx* upper windpipe)—meaning the branch of medicine dealing with the ear, nose and throat, usually abbreviated ENT; otology; otosclerosis. Compare otiose, from L *otium* leisure.

PHLEB-   from the stem *phleb-* of the noun *phleps* vein. Phleb- (as in phlebitis) and phlebo- are the combining form. Also, phlebogram, phlebology, phlebotomy.

PY-   from *pyon* pus. Py- (as in pyoid) and pyo- are the combining form. Also, pyoderma, pyorrhea, pyosis (-*osis* act or process)—meaning the formation of pus.

UR-   from *ouron* urine. Ur- (as in uranalysis) and uro- are a combining form. Also, urogenital (also called urinogenital and genitourinary), urology. Also found as combining forms are urin- (as in urinary), urino- (as in urinogenital and urinometer), and, as a final element, -uria, meaning the presence of (a specified substance) in the urine, as in albuminuria and EW's melanuria, or the condition of having (such) urine, as in polyuria (= an excessive excretion of urine). Also occasionally found is -uronic, meaning connected with urine (in names of certain aldehyde acids), as in hyaluronic. Compare UR- (from *oura* tail), as in uropod, urochord, uropygium, and its adjective combining form -urous (= -tailed), as in macrurous (with the variations macrurual, macruroid, macruran)—meaning having to do with the suborder *Macrura* (lobsters, shrimp, crayfishes, prawns).

II. Analysis and Definition of Words

1. from L *diureticus*, from Gk *diouretikos*, from *di-* through + UR-urine + *-(e)tic* pertaining to (diuresis): as an adjective, causing an increase in the flow of urine; as a noun, a drug that causes an increase in the flow of urine.

2. ANGI- vessel, receptacle + *-oma* tumor: a tumor produced chiefly by the enlargement of blood vessels or lymph vessels.

3. LIP(o)- fat + LY- to loosen + *-sis* act of: the hydrolysis of fat. (Hydrolysis is from HYDR(o)- water + LY- to loosen + *-sis* act of—meaning a chemical process of decomposition involving the use of water. Lipolysis can also occur by the action of lipase—LIP- fat + *-ase* a suffix used to form the names of enzymes—an enzyme in the pancreatic and gastric juices that can change fats to fatty acids, glycerin, and sugar.)

4. *a-* without + CEPHAL- head + *-ous* like (an acephalan = a headless mollusk): headless; in zoology, lacking a distinct head, or having no part of the body specially systemized as the seat of the senses.

5. from New L *empyema*, from Gk, from *em-* in, on + PY- pus + *-ma* result of: a collection of pus in a body cavity, especially in the lungs, as in pneumonia (Gk *pnein* to breathe).

6. OO- egg + LITE- stone: a rock consisting of small round grains, usually of calcium carbonate, that resemble fish roe.

7. HYDR(o)- water + CEPHAL- head + *-ous* pertaining to (hydrocephalus): relating to, characterized by, or affected with an abnormal increase in the amount of cerebrospinal fluid that has accumulated within the cranium, usually in infancy, causing abnormal enlargement of the head.

8. *par-* beside + OT- ear + *-itis* inflammation of: inflammation of the parotid gland; mumps. (The parotid glands, one in front of each ear, supply saliva to the mouth through the parotid ducts.)

9. PHLEB(o)- vein + *-tomy* surgical cutting of: the letting of blood from a vein in the treatment of disease. (Also called venesection—L *vena* vein + *sectio* cutting).

10. MAST- breast + -oid like + -ectomy surgical removal of: removal of the mastoid (= a nipple-shaped projection of bone behind the ear).

11. from New L enuresis, from en- in, into + UR- urine + -sis act of: the inability to control urination; bed-wetting.

12. ADEN- gland + -oma tumor: a benign tumor originating in a secretory gland; also, any tumor resembling a gland in structure.

13. PHLEB- vein + -itis inflammation of: inflammation of a vein.

14. PY- pus + UR- urine + -ia condition of (or, the combining form -uria): the presence of pus in the urine.

15. OO- egg + GENE- originate + -sis result of: the formation and development of an ovum (= L egg).

16. HYSTER- uterus + -ectomy surgical removal of: surgical removal of the uterus.

17. ANGI(o)- vessel + -logy science of + -ist expert: one who studies or is an expert in blood vessels and lymphatic vessels. He/she also engages in X-ray examination of blood vessels by injecting a radiopaque (= not transparent to X-rays) substance into the blood.

18. en- in, within + CEPHAL- head + -itis inflammation: inflammation of the encephalon (= the brain), caused by injury, poison, infection, etc.

19. PY(o)- pus + -rrhea discharge: a disease in which pockets of pus form about the roots of the teeth, frequently causing the teeth to become loose. (Also called Riggs' disease, after John M. Riggs, an American dentist who lived from 1810 to 1885.)

20. POLY- much + UR- urine + -ia condition of (or, the combining form -uria): the passing of an excessive quantity of urine, as in diabetes.

III. Matching Definitions with Medical Terms

Except for hematuria, which is usually found, and hemangioma, which is occasionally found, these words are generally not recorded in desk dictionaries.

1. OT(o)- ear + MYC- fungus + -osis diseased condition of: f.

2. CHOL- bile + ANGI(o)- vessel + -graphy writing: j.

3. BAR- pressure + OT- ear + ALG- pain + -ia state of: i.

4. ADEN- gland + ec- out of + TOP- place + -ia state of: g.

5. anti- against + PY(o)- pus + GEN- to produce + -ic pertaining to: h.

6. LIP(o)- fat + HEM- blood + ARTHR- joint + -*osis* diseased condition of: c.

7. *eu*- well + CEPHAL- head + -*ous* pertaining to: a.

8. HEMAT- blood + UR- urine + -*ia* state of (or, -uria combining form): e.

9. *endo*- within + PHLEB- vein + -*itis* inflammation of: d.

10. HEM- blood + ANGI- vessel + -*oma* tumor: b.

LESSON XXII

Discussion of Combining Forms

-*path*   from *pathos* suffering. This is actually a back formation of the following combining form, -pathy. For notes on both of these, see IM discussion of the base PATH- at Lesson X.

-*pathy*   also from *pathos* suffering. See -*path* above.

-*iasis*   from the noun suffix -*iasis*, which formed nouns from denominative verbs that end in -*ian* and -*iazein*, as the Gk *psoriasis*, which derived from the verb *psorian* to have an itch, from the noun *psora* itch. It is also defined as a process, as in odontiasis (= the process of cutting teeth, or teething). As a disease, also, hypochondriasis, ancylosto-miasis (*ankylos* hooked + STOM- mouth)—meaning infestation of hookworms.

-*therapy*   from *therapeia* therapy, from the verb *therapeuein* to treat, heal, cure, from the noun *theraps* attendant. Not entered as a combining form but only as a free-standing word. The forms -therapeutic, -therapeutics, -therapeutist, -therapist, ~uld, following EW, also be considered here as combining forms, sir. ney all combine with other elements (as with psycho-) but these are not in dictionaries as combining forms either.

ASSIGNMENT

I. Discussion of Bases

BRACHY-   from *brachys* short. Usually listed. Also brachycephalic (= having a short skull of excessive breadth), also appearing with -*ous*; a brachycephal is the person, and brachycephaly is the condition. Also, brachydactyly, brachypterous, brachyuran (UR- tail, here also referring to animals with a reduced abdomen). Compare the combining form brachi- (as in brachial, brachiate) and brachio-, as in brachiotomy, brachiopod, where brachi- means arm, from Gk *brachion* arm.

BRADY- from *bradys* slow. Only sometimes listed. Very few elements combine with this form.

CHLOR- from *chloros* light green, greenish yellow. Chlor- (before vowels) and chloro- are usually found as the combining form, associated with scientific terms. Also, chloride, chlorine, chloroform (formyl = the radical HCO occurring in formic acid and formaldehyde), chlorosis.

DOLICH- from *dolichos* long. Dolich- and dolicho- are generally listed as the combining form. Also, dolichomorphic, dolichocranial.

ERYTHR- from *erythros* red. Generally listed as the combining form with erythro-. WBD also records the form as meaning a red blood cell, with erythrogenic (= producing red blood cells) as an example.

EURY(S)- from *eurys* wide. Generally listed, but not with 's'. Also, eurybathic (or eurybenthic), eurycephalic (of -*ous*)—meaning broadheaded, eurygnathous (*gnathos* jaw), euryon, euryphagous, eurypterid, eurystomatous, eurythermal. Compare eurythmic, a variant of eurhythmic, from *eu*- well + rhythmic.

LEUC-, LEUK- from *leukos* white. These two forms, together with leuco- and leuko-, are generally listed as combining forms. Dictionaries vary in their preference of leuc- or leuk- in several words, so expect both spellings to show on assignments. Leukemia, leukemic, leukemogenic, and leukoplakia (*plak-* something flat) are, however, generally listed only with a 'k', with leukaemia and leukaemic listed as (preferably British) variants.

MER- from *meros* a part, division. Not listed by many dictionaries. The combining form -mer (= denoting a member of a particular group) as in isomer, dimer, tautomer, is sometimes found. Also sometimes listed is -mere (= a part or division), as in blastomere; and -merous (MER- + -*ous*, for an adjective) often occurs, as in trimerous and pentamerous, frequently written 3-merous, 5-merous. Also, meroplankton (*plankt-* to wander), meroblast, merogenesis. Compare the combining form mer-, meaning sea (akin to L *mare* sea), as in mermaid.

PLATY- from *platys* flat. Only occasionally listed. Also, platypus, platyrrhine.

STEN- from *stenos* narrow. With steno-, this is generally recorded and variously defined in English as tight, narrow, contracted, close, little. Also, stenobathic (*bath-* deep)—meaning living within narrow limits of depth, stenophagous (= eating few kinds of foods), stenomorph, stenophyllous, stenorynchous (*rhynchos* snout).

TACHY- from *tachys* swift. Usually listed. TACH- is not often found; tacho- (as in tachometer) and tachisto- (as in tachistoscope) are sometimes found. Also, tachycardia, tachygraphy, tachylyte (LY- to loosen)—meaning black, glassy basalt (see sentence 4 below).

XANTH- from *xanthos* yellow. Xanth- (as in xanthate, xanthous, xanthene, xanthic, xanthine, xanthism) and xantho- are the combining form. Also, xanthochroid (*ochros* pale)—meaning white persons having light hair and fair skin, xanthophyll, xanthoma, xanthopterin, xanthophyll.

II. Analysis and Definition of Words

1. BRACHY- short + CEPHAL- head + -*ic* pertaining to: having a breadth of head at least four-fifths as great as the length from front to back; short-headed or broad-headed with a cephalic index of over 80.

2. LEUC(o)- white + CYT- cell + -*osis* diseased condition of: an increase in the number of leucocytes (= white blood cells).

3. HEM(o)- blood + STA- to stop + -*t* that which: a clamp that compresses the ends of small blood vessels in order to stop hemorrhage. (This is a back formation of the adjective hemostatic.)

4. TACHY- swift + LY- to loosen + -*te* that which (or, the combining form -lite, meaning stone, rock, mineral): a black, glassy basalt of volcanic origin that is easily fusible (i.e., loosened). (Also spelled tachylite.)

5. ERYTHR(o)- red + CYT(o)- cell + -*meter* measure: an instrument for counting red blood corpuscles.

6. STEN- narrow + -*osis* diseased condition of: the contraction or constriction of a passage, duct, or canal.

7. HYDR(o)- water + -*therapy* treatment by: the scientific treatment of disease by means of water.

8. ERYTHR- red + -*ism* condition of: a condition of abnormal redness, as of plumage, skin, or hair.

9. DOLICH(o)- long + CEPHAL- head + -*ic* pertaining to: having a relatively long head with a cephalic index of less than 75; having a breadth of head small in proportion to the length from front to back; having a breadth of skull less than four-fifths of the length from front to back.

10. PENTA- five + MER- part + -*ous* pertaining to: consisting of or divided into five parts.

11. HOME(o)- same + -*pathy* treatment of disease by: a method of treating disease by administering small doses of a remedy that

would, in larger doses, produce symptoms of the disease in a healthy person.

12. ARTHR(o)- joint + MER- portion, part: one of the divisions of the body of an articulate (= with joints) animal.

13. *an*- up + EURYS- wide + *-m* result of: a permanent cardiac or arterial blood-filled dilatation (= swelling), caused by pressure of the blood on a weakened spot.

14. TACH(o)- speed + *-meter* measure: in medicine, an instrument for measuring or indicating the speed of the blood. (A similar instrument can measure the speed of a river, etc.; another such instrument measures the speed of rotation, as of a shaft or a wheel.)

15. PHYSI(o)- nature + *-therapy* treatment of + *-ist* one who: one who treats disease or physical defects by physical and mechanical means (massage, regulated exercise, water, heat, electricity) rather than by drugs. (Dictionaries generally award this term second place over the more popular term physical therapy.)

16. OSTE(o)- bone + PHY- to grow + *-te* that which: a bony outgrowth.

17. CHLOR- yellowish-green + *-osis* diseased condition of: an iron-deficiency anemia in young girls at or about puberty, characterized by a yellowish-green complexion and irregular menstruation. (Also called greensickness. Also used in botany, designating blanched or yellow leaves owing to lack of chlorophyll.)

18. IS(o)- equal + MER- part + *-ous* pertaining to: having an equal number of parts, markings, or ridges; in botany, of a flower, having the same number of members in each whorl.

19. IDI(o)- one's own, peculiar + *-pathy* disease + *-ic* pertaining to: arising spontaneously or from an unknown cause.

20. UR(o)- urine + LITH- stone: a calculus in the urinary tract. (A calculus is a concretion, usually of mineral salts that collect around organic matter, forming such as gallstones or kidney stones.)

III. Matching Definitions with Medical Terms

Some of these words are not recorded in some desk dictionaries.

1. EURY- wide + THERM- heat + *-ic* pertaining to: d.

2. ERYTHR(o)- red + *-phobia* fear of: g.

3. ORTH(o)- straight + DOLICH(o)- long + CEPHAL- head + *-ous* pertaining to: i.

4. ANGI(o)- vessel + STEN- narrow + *-osis* diseased condition of: h.

5. BRADY- slow + ARTHR- speech articulation + *-ia* state of: c.

6. XANTH(o)- yellow + PHOR- to bear: b.
7. MER(o)- part + -*tomy* a cutting: a.
8. PLATY- flat + CEPHAL- head + -*ic* pertaining to: j.
9. CHLOR- green + OP- see + -*sia* state, result of: e.
10. TACHY- swift + CARD- heart + -*ia* state of: f.

IV. Formation of Medical Terms

This exercise might best be done orally. The instructor should insist the students not look at the answers at the end of Lesson XXV until, with the instructor's help if necessary, they have made good effort.

1. a tumor composed of fatty tissue: lipoma—LIP- fat + -*oma* tumor.
2. pain in a joint: arthralgia—ARTHR- joint + ALG- pain + -*ia* state of.
3. narrowing of the heart: cardiostenosis—CARDI(o)- heart + STEN- narrow + -*osis* diseased condition of.
4. blueness of the extremities: acrocynosis—ACR(o)- the extremities + CYAN- blue + -*osis* diseased condition of.
5. a fungus infection of the skin: dermatomycosis—DERMAT(o)- skin + MYC- fungus + -*osis* diseased condition of.
6. surgical incision into the liver: hepatotomy—HEPAT(o)- liver + -*tomy* surgical operation or cutting.
7. inflammation of the ear: otitis—OT- ear + -*itis* inflammation of.
8. smallness of the heart: microcardia—MICR(o)- small + CARD- heart + -*ia* state of.
9. condition of having a black tongue: melanoglossia—MELAN(o)- black + GLOSS- tongue + -*ia* state of.
10. the study of bones: osteology—OSTE(o)- bone + -*logy* study of.

LESSON XXIII

Discussion of Combining Forms

-*emia*   from HEM-, HEMAT- blood. Variously listed as a suffix and combining form, with -*aemia* as the (preferably British) variant. Also, bacteremia, pyemia, hyperemia, toxemia.

-hedron from *hedra* seat, side, surface. Usually found as a combining form. Also, dodecahedron (*dodeka* twleve), rhombohedron (= a solid bounded by six rhombic planes), tetrahedron (= a solid figure having four faces, as a pyramid), trapezohedron, pentahedron. The corresponding adjective combining form, -hedral, is also usually found (dihedral, polyhedral, etc.) and could be introduced here, from *-hedron* + *-al*.

ASSIGNMENT

I. Discussion of Bases

ACOU-, ACU-   from *akouein* to hear. Not found as a combining element. Occasionally listed is acousto-, meaning of sound or acoustic waves, as in acoustoelectronics. Also, catacoustics, diacoustics, hyperacusia.

MENING-   from the stem *mening-* of the noun *meninx* membrane. Seldom found as a combining form. More frequently found are meningo-, as in meningococcus and meningoencephalitis, and meningi-, as in meningioma. The meninges (Gk plural of *meninx*) are the three protective membranes (pia mater 'tender mother,' arachnoid membrane 'cobweblike membrane,' dura mater 'hard mother,' i.e., hard source) that cover the brain and spinal cord.

MY-, MYS-, MYOS-   from *mys* (nominative) and *myos* (genitive) mouse. Only my- (as in myalgia) and myo- are recorded as a combining form. Also, myosin, myoblast, myocardiograph, myocarditis, myocardium, myocyte, myogenic (GEN- to originate)—meaning originating from the muscles, myoma, myopathy, endomyocarditis, epimysium, myosin, paramyosin, perimysium. Compare myosis (variant of miosis), mystic, and mystery, from Gk *myein* (of the eyes) to be closed. Note that muscle itself is from L *mus* mouse. The connection between mouse and muscle is due to the supposed appearance of certain muscles.

MYEL-   from *myelos* marrow, from *mys* mouse, muscle. Usually found as a combining form, together with myelo-. Also, myeloblast, myelocyte, myelogenic, myelography.

NEUR-   from *neuron* nerve. Both neur- and neuro- are listed as the combining form. There are well over a hundred words connected with this base, including neuritis, neuralgia, neurectomy, neuroleptic, neurology, neuron, neuropathology, neurosurgery.

OPHTHALM-   from *ophthalmos* eye. Ophthalmo- is usually listed as a combining form. Compare *op* eye, to which it is related, and *thalamos* chamber—in which the 'p' (pi) became in *ophthalmos* a 'ph' (phi). Also, ophthalmitis (another word for ophthalmia), ophthalmoscopy.

PHREN- from *phren* diaphragm, midriff; also mind, spirit. Usually recorded as a combining form, with phreno-. Associated with the mind are phrenetic (a doublet of frantic, from L via F), phrenology; and the combining form -phrenia, indicating a mental disorder, as in schizophrenia, and EW's hebephrenia and bradyphrenia. Associated with the diaphragm is phrenic and phrenitis, the latter also meaning inflammation of the brain.

PLEG- from *plege* stroke, from *plessein* to strike; PLEX- is from a related noun *plexis* a stroke, percussion, also from *plessein*. Neither form is listed in dictionaries, but -plegia, meaning paralysis, is usually found as a combining form, as in paraplegia and diplegia. Also, plectrum (from *plektron* a thing to strike with, from *plessein*), plexor, apoplexy, apoplectic.

RHIN- from the stem *rhin-* of the noun *rhis* nose. Both rhin- and rhino- are occasionally found as a combining form, as in rhinitis, rhinolith, rhinology, rhinoplasty (*-plasty* = plastic surgery), rhinorrhea, rhinoscope. Also sometimes listed as a combining form is -rrhine (with the variant -rhine), meaning having a (specified kind of) nose, as in platyrrhine.

SOM- from *soma* body (earlier, corpse), with SOMAT- coming from the stem *somat-*. Only somat- and somato- are listed as a combining form in initial position, as in somatic, somatogenic, somatoplasm, somatopleure (*pleura* side), somatopsychic, somatotropin. The combining form -some is generally found, as in monosome. Also sometimes listed is the combining form -soma (a variant of -some), used especially in the formation of names of zoological genera, as in Schistosoma. Also, somascope.

STHEN- from *sthenos* strength. Not found as a combining form. Also, sthenia (patterned on asthenia, from *a-* without + STHEN-), asthenosphere.

THYM- from the Gk combining form -thymia, from *thymos* mind. Not listed, although -thymia is occasionally found as a combining form, meaning a condition of the mind and the will, as in dysthymia. Also, enthymeme. Compare thyme (the plant) from the verb *thyein* to burn as a sacrifice; and thymus (the gland), from *thymos* a warty excrescence.

TON- from the noun *tonos* tension; tone, vocal pitch, raising of the voice; hence, the various definitions of tonic—a medicine that stimulates, having to do with muscular tension, and having to do with a tone or tones in music. Not found as a combining form. Also tonometry (also called tonography), tonoplast.

II. Analysis and Definition of Words

1. MENING- membrane + -itis inflammation of: an infectious and sometimes fatal disease characterized by inflammation of the membranes surrounding the brain or spinal cord.

2. ex- out + OPHTHALM- eye + -ic pertaining to: characterized by an abnormal protrusion of the eyeball from the orbit and caused by disease or suffocation.

3. PLATY- flat + -RRHIN- nose + -ian pertaining to: having a broad, flat nose. (Not in all dictionaries, and when it is, it is usually cross-referenced to the preferred platyrrhine, which also carries an additional, taxonomic sense.)

4. UR- urine + -emia condition of the blood: an abnormal condition resulting from an accumulation in the blood of waste products that are normally disposed of through the urine.

5. NEUR- nerve + a- without + STHEN- strength + -ia state of: a neurosis accompanied by various physical ailments (as headaches, disorders in digestion or circulation, other pains) with no discernible organic cause, and characterized by impaired functioning of interpersonal relationships, fatigue, depression, and feelings of inadequacy.

6. a- without + TON- tension + -y state of: lack of muscular tone, especially in a contractile organ, enervation, debility; also, in phonetics, lack of stress. (Contractile here means capable of contracting, as a muscle.)

7. OPHTHALM(o)- eye + -scope instrument for viewing: an instrument for examining the interior of the eye or the retina.

8. HEMI- half + PLEG- paralysis + -ia state of: paralysis of only one side of the body resulting from injury to the motor centers of the brain.

9. CYCL(o)- circle, wheel + THYM- mind + -ia state, condition of: alternation of lively and depressed moods.

10. RHIN(o)- nose + -scope instrument for viewing: an instrument for examining the nasal passages.

11. CAL(i)- beauty + STHEN- strength + -ics the art of: the practice or art of performing systematic rhythmic exercises for health, strength, and grace. (Also spelled callisthenics.)

12. MY(o)- muscle + CARD- heart + -itis inflammation of: inflammation of the muscular part of the heart (the myocardium). WNCD defines myocardium as the middle muscular layer of the heart.

13. SCHIZ(o)- split + PHREN- mind + -ia state of: a psychotic disorder in which the patient dissociates himself from his environment and deteriorates in character and personality, expressed as a disorder of thought, feeling, and conduct; also, the condition of having or showing inconsistent or contradictory qualities; a split personality.

14. PSYCH(o)- mind + SOMAT- body + -ic pertaining to: having to do with the interaction and interdependence of bodily disorders and mental disturbances; or, noting a physical disorder caused by or influenced by an emotional state (RHD).

15. DECA- ten + -hedron solid figure with a (specified) number of faces: a solid figure having 10 faces.

16. NEUR(o)- nerve + -logy science of + -ist one who: one who studies or is a specialist in the nervous system and its diseases.

17. OSTE(o)- bone + MYEL- bone marrow + -itis inflammation: inflammation of the bone and bone marrow.

18. IS(o)- equal + TON- tension; tone + -ic pertaining to: (in physical chemistry) pertaining to solutions that exhibit equal osmotic pressure (also called isosmotic); (in physiology) pertaining to a solution containing the same salt concentration as in mammalian blood, or pertaining to the contraction of a muscle when under constant tension; (in music) characterized by equal tones.

19. PY- pus + -emia condition of the blood: a form of blood poisoning caused by pus-producing bacteria (microorganisms) in the bloodstream accompanied by multiple abscesses in different parts of the body; or (in WNCD) septicemia (= invasion of the bloodstream by virulent microorganisms) caused by pus-forming bacteria, etc.

20. cata- against + TON- tension, tone + -ic pertaining to: pertaining to catatonia (= a condition associated with schizophrenia, characterized by mental stupor and muscular rigidity. Catatonia often alternates with sudden outbursts, seizures of panic, or hallucinations—WBD); called catalepsy (LEP- take, seize) in WNCD.

III. Matching Definitions with Medical Terms

Some of these words are generally not recorded in desk dictionaries.

1. MY- muscle + a- without + STHEN- strength + -ia state of: f.
2. OPHTHALM(o)- eye + PLEG- paralysis + -ia state of: d.
3. OLIG(o)- few + PHREN- mind + -ia state of: g.
4. hyper- excessive + ACU- to hear + -sia state of: i.
5. SOMAT- body + OT- ear + OP- eye + a- not + GNO- know + -sia state of: h.

6. RHIN(o)- nose + PHON- voice + -*ia* state of: j.
7. *hyper-* excessive + LIP- fat + -*emia* condition of the blood: b.
8. MON(o)- one + PLEG- paralysis + -*ia* state or result of: c.
9. SOM- body + ESTHE- to perceive, feel + -*sia* state or act of: a.
10. *a-* without + MY(o)- muscle + TON- tone + -*ia* state of: e.

LESSON XXIV

Discussion of Suffixes

-in, -ine   from the L suffix *-ina*, the feminine form of *-inus*, meaning of or belonging to. The *-in* form is usually used to denote neutral substances such as fats, glycosides, glycerides, and proteins, as in albumin, olein, palmitin, digitoxin, stearin. The *-ine* form is usually reserved for denoting basic substances and the halogen elements, as in aniline, chlorine, fluorine. In WNCD *-in* is defined as an enzyme (as in pancreatin), an antibiotic (as in penicillin), and as a pharmaceutical product (as in niacin); *-ine* is further defined as a basic or base-containing carbon compound that contains nitrogen (as in quinine and cystine), a hydride (as arsine), and a commercial product or material (as glassine).

-ium   from the L *-ium*, a suffix on neuter nouns. Appears in English loan words from Latin, as auditorium, tedium. Specialized in chemical terminology to form names of elements, as barium; to denote a chemical radical, as in ammonium; and to indicate groups forming positive ions, as in imidazolium. Desk dictionaries do not record EW's meanings for this suffix; its plural is *-ia*. "The usage of the suffix derives from ammonium" —OED. The original and now preferred American aluminum (also originally spelled alumium) was altered to the now preferred British aluminium (five syllables) to conform to the other metals ending in -ium. The Canadians got caught in the middle: they use both. Aussies generally go British, as here.

ASSIGNMENT

I. Discussion of Bases

BLAST-   from *blastos* a sprout or shoot. Both blast- (as in blastema) and blasto- are generally listed as a combining form. As a variant in final position, both -blast and -blastic (the corresponding adjective suffix) are occasionally recorded. Also, blastogenesis, blastomere, blasto-mycetes, blastomycosis, blastophere, epiblast, diploblastic (*diploos* twofold), ecoblast. Compare blast, from OE.

COCC(US)- from *kokkos* a seed or berry. The combining form -coccus is only occasionally listed. Also, micrococcus. Also appears at the beginning of words, as in coccid, coccidiosis, coccolith, and coccosphere. Also, the freestanding coccus. Compare coccyx (= the triangular bone at the lower end of the spinal column), from *kokkyx* a cuckoo, because the bone is shaped like a cuckoo's bill.

CYST- from *kystis* pouch, bladder, ulcer (on a horse). CYST- (as in cystitis, cystic, cystine, cystiform), cysto- (as in cystolith, cystoma, cystoscope, cystotomy), cysti- (as in cysticercosis—*kerkos* tail), and -cyst (as in blastocyst, statocyst—*statos* standing, static) are all generally found as combining forms.

DACTYL- from *daktylos* finger, dactyl (= a foot in classical verse); in zoology, a finger or toe; as a modern transfer, a foot in modern English verse. As initial elements, both dactyl- (as in dactylitis) and dactylo- (as in dactylology) are usually found as a combining form. As final elements, -dactyl (as in pterodactyl), -dactylous, meaning having (so many) fingers or toes (as in didactylous, from DI- two), and -dactyly (-dactyl + -y, as in brachydactyly) are occasionally listed.

DROM- from *dromos* a running, a course, a race, flight, etc. Neither drom- (as in dromedary) nor dromo- (as in dromomania) is found as a combining form. However, in final position is the combining form -drome (abstracted from hippodrome), meaning a large space or area (as in airdrome, cosmodrome), also a race track (as in motordrome). Also occasionally found is the adjective combining form -dromous, meaning running, as in catadromous.

HIST-, HISTI- from *histos* web. Both hist- (as in histidine, histamine) and histo- are usually recorded as the combining form. Histi- is generally not listed. Also, histoblast, histoclastic, histogenesis, histography, histology, histolysis, antihistamine.

ICHTHY- from *ichthys* fish. Both ichthy- (as in ichthyic) and ichthyo- are usually recorded as the combining form. Also, ichthyography, ichthyology, ichthyophagous (= feeding on fish).

ORNIS- from *ornis* bird; ORNITH- is from its stem *ornith-*. Ornith- (as in ornithic) and ornitho- (as in ornithology, ornithopter, and ornithosis) are usually listed as the combining form.

PHAG- from *phagein* to eat. This form is used in initial position (as phagocyte, phagocytosis, phagolysis, phagosome), but phago- is not always listed as a combining form. Four combining forms appear in final position: -phage (bacteriophage); -phagia, a variant of -phagy (dysphagia); -phagous, forming an adjective (hylophagous, sarco-phagous); -phagy (geophagy, anthropophagy, exophagy).

PLAS(T)- the PLAS- is from the verb *plassein* to form, mold; PLAST- is from *plastos* formed, molded. There are several combining forms, which are variously recorded. In initial position: plasm- (plasmin); plasmo- (plasmolysis, plasmogamy); plasto- (plastometer). In final position: -plasia (hyperplasia, hypoplasia); -plasm (protoplasm, endoplasm); -plast, meaning cell (chromoplast, protoplast); -plasty, meaning formation, occurring primarily in the processes of plastic surgery (dermoplasty, neoplasty, osteoplasty); -plasy, a variant of -plasia (homoplasy). These forms with -m- are from the Gk *plasma*, the -*m(a)* being the suffix of Lesson XI.

PTER- from *pteron* wing, feather; PTERYG- from *pteryg-*, the stem of the noun *pteryx* wing, akin to *pteron*. Pter- (as in pterin, pteryla—*yl*-wood) and ptero- (pterodactyl, pteropod) are occasionally found as a combining form. Also sometimes listed are -pter (hymenopter); its corresponding adjective form -pterous (dipterous); and pterid- (pteridoid) and pterido- (pteridology), a combining form meaning fern, from the stem *pterid-* of the noun *pteris* fern, a derivative of *pteron*.

STOM- from *stoma* mouth; STOMAT- is from its stem *stomat-*. Stom- (as in stomodaeum) and stomo- are sometimes recorded as combining forms, as are stomat- (stomatitis, stomatic) and stomato- (stomatology, stomatopod). Also occasionally listed are -stome (cyclostome, pneumostome—*pneuma* wind), the corresponding adjective form -stomous (monostomous), and -stomy (cystostomy, gastroduodenostomy—*duoden-*, a contracted stem of *duodecim* twelve; here, so called because of its length, about twelve fingerbreadths). The form -stomy is generally used in medical terms, where it refers to "surgical operations for making an artificial opening" (RHD).

II. Analysis and Definition of Words

1. *peri-* around + CARD- heart + -*ium* lining: the membranous sac enclosing the heart.

2. *syn-* together + DROM- a running: a group of signs and symptoms that occur together as characteristic of a disease or abnormality, or, in a modern transferred sense, of a type of behavior.

3. ANTHROP(o)- human being + PHAG- to eat + -*ous* inclined to: feeding on human flesh; cannibalistic.

4. PROT(o)- first + PLAS- to form + -*m* result of: the living substance of all plant and animal cells; a typically translucent, colorless, semi-

fluid, complex substance regarded as the physical basis of life, having the ability to sense and conduct stimuli and to metabolize.

5. *ana-* back + STOM- mouth + *-osis* act or process: the union of parts or branches (as of rivers, blood vessels, or leaf veins) so as to communicate.

6. ERYTHR(o)- red + BLAST- embryonic cell: a nucleated cell, found in bone marrow, from which red corpuscles develop.

7. *syn-* together + DACTYL- finger or toe: (as an adjective) having certain digits formed together; (as a noun) a syndactyl animal. (Not in all dictionaries.)

8. ICHTHY- fish + *-osis* diseased condition of: a disease in which the skin becomes dry and flakes off in large, fishlike scales or plates. (Also called fishskin disease.)

9. *phyto-* combining form meaning plant (from PHY- to grow) + PHAG- to eat + *-ous* inclined to: feeding on plants; herbivorous.

10. NEUR(o)- nerve + PTER- wing + *-ous* pertaining to: pertaining to the order (Neuroptera) of carnivorous insects which have membranous wings (as the lacewings and ant lions).

11. MICR(o)- small + COCCUS- spheri   bacterium: any of certain disease-causing or fermentation-producing spherical or egg-shaped bacteria.

12. *ana-* up + DROM- a running + *-ous* pertaining to: (of fish, as salmon and shad) going up rivers from the sea to spawn. (This is the opposite of catadromous.)

13. ORNITH(o)- bird + *-logy* science or study of: the branch of zoology that deals with the study of birds.

14. OSTE(o)- bone + PLAST- to form + *-y* act of: the surgical replacement of lost or defective bone.

15. ORTH(o)- straight + PTER- wing + *-ous* pertaining to: pertaining to the order (Orthoptera) of insects which have hard, narrow forewings and longitudinally folded, membranous hindwings (as crickets, grasshoppers, cockroaches). (Not in all dictionaries, but where it is found it is preferred to the alternate orthopteran.)

16. POLY- many + DACTYL- finger, toe + *-ism* condition of: the state or condition of having more than the normal number of fingers or toes.

17. HIST(o)- tissue + *-logy* science or study of: the branch of anatomy that deals with microscopic structure of plant and animal tissue.

18. PHAG(o)- to eat + CYT- cell: a cell occurring in body fluids and tissues that is capable of absorbing and destroying foreign matter or harmful disease-producing material.

19. CHIR(o)- hand + PTER- wing: any animal of the order (Chiroptera) of mammals having forelimbs that are modified as wings; a bat (the only definition in WNCD).

20. *epi-* over + GASTR- stomach + *-ium* region: the part of the abdomen lying over the stomach.

21. PTER(o)- wing + DACTYL- finger, toe: any animal of the order (Pterosauria) of extinct flying reptiles having a featherless membrane stretching from the elongated fourth digit of each foreleg to the body. (Pterodactyls existed during the Jurassic and Cretaceous periods.)

22. OSTE(o)- bone + BLAST- embryonic cell: a bone-forming cell.

23. ICHTHY(o)- fish + *-logy* science or study of: the branch of zoology that deals with the science and study of fish.

24. NE(o)- new + PLAS- to form + *-m* result of: a new, abnormal growth of tissue (such as a tumor) serving no physiologic function.

25. HEM(o)- blood + lys- combining form of EW's LY- to loosen + *-in* chemical substance: a substance in the blood that destroys erythrocytes (= red blood cells). Hemolysin may be antibodies or material contained in bacterial toxins and snake venom.

III. Matching Definitions and Words

Very few of these are recorded in desk dictionaries.

1. RHIN(o)- nose + PLAST- form + *-y* act of (the combining form -plasty = plastic surgery): i.

2. ORNITH- bird + *-osis* diseased condition of: j.

3. LITH(o)- stone + PHAG- to eat + *-ous* inclined to: b.

4. *endo-* within + MYS- muscle + *-ium* enveloping tissue: g.

5. CHOLE- gall + CYST(o)- bladder + KIN- to move + *-in* chemical substance: h.

6. PTER(o)- wing + POD- foot: l.

7. ICHTHY(o)- fish + PHAG- to eat + *-ous* inclined to: c.

8. DI- two + PTER- wing + *-ous* pertaining to: d.

9. MACR(o)- long + DACTYL- finger, toe + *-ism* condition of: e.

10. HIST(o)- tissue + LY- to loosen + *-sis* result of: a.

11. CHOLE- gall + CYST(o)- bladder + STOM- mouth (here, an opening) + *-y* act of: f. (If students choose to use the combining form -stomy, in IM in the previous lesson, this should be acceptable.)

12. ICHTHY(o)- fish + LITE- stone: k.

LESSON XXV

Discussion of Diminutive Suffixes

-ium, -ion   The *-ium* is the L suffix *-ium,* which is the equivalent of the Gk diminutive suffix *-ion,* as bacterium (from L *bacterium,* from Gk *bakterion* little staff, from *baktron* stick). Rarely found in contemporary dictionaries with this meaning. Used mainly in modern Latin scientific names, as geranium.

-idium   through New L from the Greek diminutive suffix *-idion.* Usually recorded as a combining form. Also, antheridium and peridium. RHD also records the original Greek suffix, as in enchiridion.

-arium, -arion   from, respectively, *-arium,* the neuter suffix of Latin nouns ending in *-arius* (as New L *planetarium* planetarium, from L *planetarius* astrologer) and from the Greek diminutive suffix *-arion* (as EW's conarium from New L *conarium,* from Gk *konarion,* from *konos* cone). RHD at *-arium* refers the user to *-orium* (= denoting a place or an instrument, as in emporium and auditorium), which it etymologizes to Latin, although emporium goes back to Greek. The original Greek suffix *-arion* is not generally listed. Contemporary dictionaries do not record EW's meaning.

-isk, -iscus   from, respectively, the Gk diminutive suffix *-iskos,* and from the corresponding LL suffix *-iscus,* from Gk. Not generally recorded. Also, obelisk, from *obelos* pointed pillar.

ASSIGNMENT

I. Discussion of Bases

ACTIN-   from the Greek combining form *aktin-,* from the noun *aktis* ray. Both actin- (as in actinism, actinium) and actino- (as in actinotherapy, actinometer, actinozoan) are generally found as a combining form; also occasionally actini- (as in actiniform). Both EW senses are recorded.

ANTH-   from the noun *anthos* flower. Only antho- appears as a combining form, and this only occasionally. Also, anthocyanin, anthozoan, anthemion (*anthemon* flower + *-ion* diminutive suffix), anthophagous, anthophore, anthotaxy, anther, anthesis, anthocyanin, anthology (literally, collection of flowers, i.e., the best). Compare anthem and its doublet antiphon, both ultimately from Gk *anti-* opposed to + PHON- sound—concerning two voices or choirs singing in response to one another.

CARP- from the Gk combining form *karp-*, from the noun *karpos* fruit. Carpo- is usually found as a combining form; sometimes carp-. Also -carp (as in mesocarp, schizocarp, endocarp, pericarp); and the four corresponding adjective forms: -carpous, usually found (as in polycarpous); -carpic, usually found (as in endocarpic, polycarpic); -carpal, not found (as in endocarpal); and -carpial, not found (as in pericarpial). Compare carp(o)- from Gk *karpos* wrist, as in carpus, carpal, carpitis. Also compare carp (noun, a complaint; verb, to complain) from Scandanavia, and carp (the fish) from Germanic.

DENDR- from *dendron* tree. There are four combining forms, variously listed: dendr- (as in dendrite); dendro- (as in dendrochronology); dendri- (as in dendriform); and -dendron (as in rhododendron—*rhodon* rose, philodendron). Also, dendrograph, dendroid (*-oid* like), dendrology, dendrophile.

GON- from *gonos* seed, from *gignesthai* be born, beget, the verb that also begot the Gk base GEN- to produce, originate. Both gon- (before vowels, as in gonidium) and gono- are usually listed as a combining form, along with -gony (as in sporogony, theogony, cosmogony) and -gonium (as in archegonium). Also, gonococcus, gonocyte, gonophore, gonopod, and gonad with its extensions gonadotropin (and the less popular gonadotrophin), gonadotropic, gonadectomy. Compare the Gk base GON- angle, as in hexagon.

GYMN- from *gymnos* naked. Both gymn- (as in gymnast, gymnastics) and gymno- usually appear as the combining form. Also, gymnosperm.

HIPP- from *hippos* horse. Hipp- (as in hippic) and hippo- are usually recorded as a combining form; also -hippus, which is used in generic names especially in paleontology, as in Eohippus. Also, the name Philip (PHIL- to love + (H)IP- horse—lover of horses).

HYGR- from the adjective *hygros* wet. Hygro- is usually found (hygr- only occasionally) as the combining form, as in hygrograph, hygrometer, hygrophilous, hygroma.

PHYLL- from *phyllon* leaf. Phyll- (as in phyllome, phyllite, phyllode, and the proper name Phyllis) and phyllo- (as in phyllophore, phyllopod, phyllotaxis) are a combining form. Also, in final position, are -phyll (which RHD calls a variant of -phyl, using chlorophyl as an example), and the corresponding adjective suffix -phyllous, meaning having (a specified number of) leaves, as in diphyllous, monophyllous.

THEC(A)- from the noun *theke* case, cover, depository. The only combining form associated with this base is -thecium (not often found), as in amphithecium, endothecium, epithecium, exothecium, perithecium; the plural is -thecia. Also, theca and epitheca. Compare F *bibliotheque* from Sp *biblioteca* library.

THROMB- from *thrombos* clot, lump. Both thromb-, as in thrombin, and thrombo- are usually found as the combining form. Also, thrombocytopenia (*penia* poverty), thromboembolism (embolism = the blocking of a blood vessel by a blood clot, from *em-* in + BALL- to throw), thrombokinase, thrombophlebitis, thromboplastin, prothrombin.

TOX- from the phrase *toxikon* (*pharmakon*) bow (poison), that is, poison for use on arrows, from *toxon* bow. Tox- (as in toxemia, toxic) and toxo- (as in toxoplasmosis) are occasionally found as a combining form. More often found are toxic- (as in toxicity) and toxico- (as in toxicology). Also, toxicosis, toxigenesis, toxiphobia, toxophilite (= a lover of archery—*toxon* bow).

XYL- from *xylon* wood. Xyl- (as in xylem, xylene) and xylo- (as in xylology) are the combining form. Also, xylocarpous, xylogen (GEN- to originate), xylograph (= a woodcut), xylophage.

II. Analysis and Definition of Words

1. *peri-* around + ANTH- flower: the external envelope of a flower, including the calyx (= the outer leaves of the unopened bud) and the corolla (= the petals of the flower).

2. SCHIZ(o)- to split + CARP- fruit + -*ous* like: of or like any dry fruit that divides, when ripe, into two or more one-seeded seed vessels that do not split open, as in the carrot and celery.

3. PHYLL(o)- leaf + POD- foot: as an adjective, of or belonging to the group of small crustaceans with four or more pairs of leaflike appendages which function as both swimming apparatuses and gills; as a noun, such a crustacean.

4. GON- reproductive + -*idium* little: a reproductive cell produced asexually in algae (as a tetraspore or zoospore); also, a green chlorophyll-bearing cell within the thallus (= plant body) of lichens.

5. XYL(o)- wood + TOM- to cut + -*ous* inclined to, practicing: (of certain insects) able to bore into or cut wood.

6. ACTIN(o)- radiating structure + MORPH- form + -*ic* pertaining to: having a radial symmetry and capable of division into symmetrical halves by any longitudinal plane passing through the axis.

7. CARP(o)- fruit + PHAG- to eat + -*ous* inclined to: fruit-eating.

8. *pro-* before + THROMB- clot + -*in* chemical substance: a plasma protein produced in the liver and converted into thrombin (= the blood-clotting agent). (Also called thrombogen.)

9. HETER(o)- different + PHYLL- leaf + -ous inclined to: bearing different kinds of leaves on the same plant.

10. XYL(o)- wood + PHAG- to eat + -ous inclined to: feeding on wood (as some insect larvae) or boring into wood (as some mollusks and crustaceans).

11. TOX- poison + -emia condition of the blood: blood-poisoning caused by pathogenic bacteria entering the bloodstream or by ingested food contaminated by poison.

12. OO- egg + GON- generative + -ium little: in biology, a primitive germ cell that divides and gives rise to oocytes (= female germ cells, called ova, before maturation); in botany, the female reproductive organ in certain bacteria, algae, and fungi.

13. XANTH(o)- yellow + PHYLL- leaf: a yellow pigment present in green leaves and plants.

14. MON(o)- one + CARP- fruit + -ic pertaining to: pertaining to a plant that produces fruit only once during its lifetime.

15. OO- egg + THECA- case: a firm-walled egg case of certain mollusks and insects (as a cockroach or mantis).

16. THROMB- clot + -osis diseased condition of: coagulation of blood (= a blood clot) in a blood vessel or the heart.

17. ANTH(o)- flower + CYAN- dark blue + -in chemical substance: a pigment in the cell sap of plants that produces the red, blue, and lavender colors in flowers, leaves, roots, or fruits.

18. ACR(o)- highest, the extremities + CARP- fruit + -ous inclined to: producing fruit at the top or at the end of the main stem (as in certain mosses).

19. PSEUD(o)- false + POD- foot + -ium little: the temporary protrusion of the protoplasm of a cell that serves as a means of locomotion and a food-gathering function; also, (in WBD) the posterior extremity of a rotifer (= a microscopic water animal), serving chiefly as a swimming organ; also, (in WNCD) a slender leafless branch of the gametophyte in various mosses that often bears gemmae (= asexual reproductive bodies that become detached from a parent plant). (Also called pseudopod and pseudopode.)

20. from exanthema a breaking out, from ex- out + ANTH- flower + -ma result: an eruptive disease of the skin (as measles); also, its eruption. (Considered by some dictionaries as a variant of the preferred exanthem.)

21. DENDR- treelike structure + -ite one connected with: the branching part at the receiving end of a nerve cell (also called a dendron). In geology, a stone or mineral with branching, treelike markings, caused by crystallization of foreign minerals; also, such a marking.

22. TOX- poison + -ic pertaining to + -(o)logy science of: a science that deals with poisons and their effects, antidotes, etc., in clinical, industrial, legal, and other environments and situations.

23. PHYLL(o)- leaf + TAX- to arrange + -y state: the arrangement of leaves on a stem in relation to one another; also, the study of this arrangement and the laws that govern it. (Considered by some dictionaries as a variant to the preferred phyllotaxis.)

24. NEPHR- kidney + -idium little: a primitive excretory organ in some invertebrates and lower vertebrates (as mollusks, some annelid worms, and brachiopods).

III. Matching Definitions With Words

Most of these words are generally not recorded in contemporary dictionaries.

1. Students can figure this word out by elimination, but it will probably cause difficulties unless they search for it in an unabridged dictionary. Gonid- is a shortening of gonidium (GON- reproductive + -idium little), here, meaning any of the green chlorophyll-bearing cells found within the thallus of a lichen, with the combining form -angium (ANG- vessel + -ium little), meaning a vessel or receptacle. The word is defined in W3 as a sporangium that contains or produces gonidium. The answer in EW is h.

2. GE(o)- earth + CARP- fruit + -y act of: g.

3. MELAN(o)- dark + PHYLL- leaf + -ous characterized by: l.

4. POD(o)- foot + THECA- case: k.

5. ACTIN(o)- ray + -therapy treatment by: j.

6. epi- upon + XYL- wood + -ous inclined to: i.

7. HYGR(o)- moist + PHIL- to love + -ous inclined to: a.

8. HIPP(o)- horse + PHAG- to eat + -y act of: e.

9. CHLOR- green + ANTH- flower + -y act of: c.

10. GYMN(o)- naked + PTER- wing + -ous characterized by: b.

11. DENDR(o)- tree + CHRON(o)- time + -logy science of: d.

12. SCLER(o)- hard + PHYLL- leaf + -ous characterized by: f.

IV. Formation of Words From Meanings

As with Exercise IV in Lesson XXII, this exercise might be best done orally.

1. paralysis of the tongue: glossoplegia—GLOSS(o)- tongue + PLEG- paralysis + -ia state of.

2. having hidden flowers: cryptanthous—CRYPT- hidden + ANTH-flower + -*ous* characterized by.

3. eating only one thing: monophagous—MONO- one + PHAG- to eat + -*ous* inclined to.

4. pertaining to the formation of bone: osteoplastic, osteogenic—OSTE(o)- bone + PLAST- to form + -*ic* pertaining to; OSTE(o)-bone + GEN- to produce + -*ic* pertaining to.

5. having small wings: micropterous—MICR(o)- small + PTER- wing + -*ous* characterized by.

6. fear of flowers: anthophobia—ANTH(o)- flower + -*phobia* fear of.

7. with winged fruit: pterocarpous—PTER(o)- wing + CARP- fruit + -*ous* characterized by. (This is a genus of tropical timber trees, family *Leguminosae*.)

8. bearing leaves: phyllophorous—PHYLL(o)- leaf + PHOR- to bear + -*ous* inclined to.

9. deficient hearing: hypacusia—*hyp*- less than normal + ACU- to hear + -*sia* result or state of.

10. inflammation of the nerve of the eye: ophthalmoneuritis—OPHTHALM(o)- eye + NEUR- nerve + -*itis* inflammation of.

INDEX OF WORDS APPEARING IN CONTEXT (GREEK)

Roman numerals after the entries indicate the lesson in which the word is to be found. Words from Lessons XX through XXV are not included here.

A

academy ii
Achilles' heel i
acme xix
acromegaly xiii
acronym xvii
acrophobia xiii
Acropolis xiii
adamant xviii
Adonis i
aegis i
aesthete x
aesthetic vii
agnostic vi
allergy x
amazon i
amnesty iv
amorphous viii
amphibious iv
anachronism iv
analgesic iv
analogy iv
analytical iv
anarchy xiii
anathema xi
anatomy iv
android xii
anecdote x
anemic v
anesthetic vii
anodyne xviii
anomaly vi

antagonistic v
anthropocentric vii
anthropoid vii
anthropologist xii
anthropomorphic vii
antibiotics iv
antinomianism xv
antipathies x
antiphonies xv
antipodal iv
antithesis xi
antonym vi
apathy x
aphasia xvii
aphorisms xviii
apocryphal iv
apogee iv
apostates x
apostolic v
apostrophizes xv
apotheosis xi
apotheosized iv
Arcadian ii
archaeologists xii
archaic vii
archetype xii
archiepiscopal xiv
aroma xix
ascetic xviii
asteroids vii
astral viii
astronauts xvii
ataxia xvii

atheist iv
atlas i
atrophy iv
atypical xv
austere iii
aura xix
autocratic xii
autonomy xii
autopsy xv
axiom xviii

B

ballistic ix
barometer xiv
bathos xix
bedlam ii
bibliographical iii
bibliophile viii
biopsy xii
boycott ii
bucolic xviii

C

cacophony x
calligraphy xiv
canon iii
canonical iii
canonized xv
Cassandra i
cataclysmic xviii
catalytic v
catastrophe xviii

PREFIXES (GREEK)

The Roman numerals in parentheses indicate the lesson in which each prefix is to be found.

a-, *an-*, not, without (IV)
amphi-, both, on both sides of, around (IV)
ana-, *an-*, up, back, again (IV)
anti-, *ant-*, against, opposite (IV)
apo-, *ap-*, from, off (IV)
cata-, *cat-*, down, against, very (IV)
dia-, *di-*, through, across, between (IV)
dys-, bad, disordered, difficult (V)
ec-, out, out of (V)
ecto-, outside, external (V)
en-, *em-*, *el-*, in, into (V)
endo-, *ento-*, *end-*, *ent-*, within (V)

epi-, *ep-*, upon, to, in addition to (V)
eu-, *ev-*, good, well (V)
ex, out, out of (V)
exo-, outside, external (V)
hyper-, over, excessive (VI)
hypo-, *hyp-*, below, less than normal (VI)
meta-, *met-*, after, changed (VI)
para-, *par-*, beside, disordered (VI)
peri-, around, near (VI)
pro-, before, in front of (VI)
pros-, toward, in addition to (VI)
syn-, *sym-*, *syl-*, *sy-*, *sys-*, with, together (VI)

SUFFIXES AND COMBINING FORMS (GREEK)

The Roman numerals in parentheses indicate the lesson in which each suffix is to be found.

-ac, pertaining to, etc. (VII)
-al, pertaining to, like, belonging to, having the character of (VIII)
-an (*-ian-*), pertaining to, like, one concerned with (VIII)
-arch, one who rules (XIII)
-archy, rule by (XIII)
-arion, little (XXV)
-arium, little (XXV)
-ast, one who does (X)

-cracy, rule by, etc. (XII)
-crat, one who advocates or practices rule by (XII)
-ectomy, surgical removal of (XXI)
-emia, condition of the blood (XXIII)
-gram, thing written (XIV)
-graph, writing, etc. (XIV)
-graphy, writing, etc. (XIV)
-hedron, solid figure (XXIII)

251

-*ia*, quality of, etc. (X)
-*iasis*, diseased condition (XXII)
-*ic*, pertaining to, etc. (VII)
-*ician*, specialist in, etc. (IX)
-*ics*, art, science, or study of (VII)
-*idium*, little (XXV)
-*in*, chemical substance (XXIV)
-*ine*, chemical substance (XXIV)
-*ion*, little (XXV)
-*iscus*, little (XXV)
-*isk*, little (XXV)
-*ism*, belief in, etc. (IX)
-*ist*, one who believes in, etc. (IX)
-*ite*, one connected with, etc. (IX)
-*itis*, inflammation of, etc. (XX)
-*ium*, little (XXV)
-*ium*, part, etc. (XXIV)
-*ize*, verbal suffix (XV)
-*logy*, science of, etc. (XII)
-*m*, result of (XI)
-*ma*, result of (XI)
-*mania*, madness about, passion for (XIII)
-*maniac*, one having a madness or passion for (XIII)
-*mat*, result of (XI)
-*me*, result (XI)
-*meter*, measure (XIV)
-*metry*, art or science of measuring (XIV)
-*nomy*, science of, etc. (XII)

-*oid*, like (VII)
-*oma*, tumor, etc. (XX)
-*osis*, diseased condition of, etc. (XX)
-*ous* (-*ious*), full of, pertaining to, like (VIII)
-*path*, one who suffers from a disease of, etc. (XXII)
-*pathy*, disease of, etc. (XXII)
-*phobe*, one who fears or hates (XIII)
-*phobia*, abnormal fear or hatred of (XIII)
-*ploid*, -fold (XVI) (footnote)
-*rrhea* (-*rrhoea*), abnormal discharge (XXI)
-*scope*, instrument for viewing, etc. (XIV)
-*se*, act of, etc. (XI)
-*sia*, act of, etc. (XI)
-*sis*, act of, etc. (XI)
-*st*, one who does (XI)
-*sy*, act of, etc. (XI)
-*t*, he who, etc. (X)
-*te*, he who, etc. (X)
-*therapy*, treatment of or by (XXII)
-*tic*, pertaining to, etc. (VII)
-*tics*, art, science, or study of (VII)
-*tomy*, surgical operation on, etc. (XXI)
-*y*, quality of, etc. (X)

BASES (GREEK)

The Roman numerals in parentheses following the meanings indicate the lesson in which each base is to be found.

A

ACO(U)-, to hear (XXIII)
ACR-, highest, the extremities (XIII)

ACTIN-, ray, radiating structure (XXV)
ACU-, to hear (XXIII)
ADEN-, gland (XXI)

AESTHE-, to feel, perceive (VII)
AGOG(UE)-, to lead (IX)
AGON-, struggle, contest (V)
ALG-, pain (IV)
ALL-, other (X)
ANDR-, man, male (XI)
ANGEL-, messenger, message (V)
ANGI-, vessel (XXI)
ANTH-, flower (XXV)
ANTHROP-, human being (VII)
ARCHA(E)-, ARCHE-, ancient, primitive, beginning (VII)
ARTHR-, joint, speech sound or articulation (XX)
ASCE-, to exercise (XVIII)
AST(E)R-, star (VII)
AUT-, self (XII)

B

BALL-, to throw, put (VI)
BAR-, weight, pressure (XIV)
BI-, life (IV)
BIBLI-, book (III)
BLAST-, bud, formative substance, embryonic cell (XXIV)
BLE-, BOL-, to throw, put (VI)
BRACHY-, short (XXII)
BRADY-, slow (XXII)
BUCOL-, cowherd (XVIII)

C

CAC-, bad (X)
CAL(L)-, beauty (XIV)
CANON-, rule (III)
CARDI-, heart (XX)
CARP-, fruit (XXV)
CAU(S), to burn (X)
CENTR-, center (V)
CEPHAL-, head (XXI)
CH(E)IR-, hand (IX)
CHLOR-, green, yellowish-green; chlorine (XXII)
CHOL(E)-, bile, gall (XXI)

CHONDR-, cartilage (XX)
CHORE-, dance (XVII)
CHROM(AT)-, color (VIII)
CHRON-, time (IV)
CINE-, to move (XI)
CLA-, to break (X)
CLYS-, to wash (XVIII)
COCC(US)-, berry, seed, spherical bacterium (XXIV)
COSM-, universe, order (IX)
CRA-, to mix (XVIII)
CRI-, to judge, decide, separate (VIII)
CRYPH-, CRYPT-, hidden, secret (III)
CYAN-, dark blue (XX)
CYCL-, circle, wheel (III)
CYN(OS)-, dog (XVIII)
CYST-, bladder, sac, sac containing morbid matter (XXIV)
CYT-, cell (XX)

D

DACTYL-, digit, finger or toe (XXIV)
D(A)EMON-, spirit, evil spirit (IV)
DEC(A)-, ten (XVI)
DEM-, people (V)
DENDR-, tree, treelike structure (XXV)
DERM(AT)-, skin (VI)
DEUTER-, second (XVI)
DI-, twice, double (XVI)
DICH-, in two (XVI)
DIDAC-, to teach (XVIII)
DIPL-, twice, double (XVI)
DO-, to give (X)
DOG-, opinion, teaching (VI)
DOLICH-, long (XXII)
DOX-, opinion, teaching (VI)
DROM-, a running, a course (XXIV)
DYN(AM)-, force, power (X)

E

EGO-, I (Latin) (XIII)
EM-, blood (V)
ENTER-, intestine (XX)
ER(OT)-, love (XVII)
ERG-, work (X)
ERYTHR-, red (XXII)
ESTHE-, to fell, perceive (VII)
ETHN-, race, cultural group (VIII)
EURY(S)-, wide, broad (XXII)

G

GAM-, marriage (V)
GASTR-, stomach (XII)
GE-, earth (IV)
GEN(E)-, to originate, produce (VII)
GEN(E)-, kind, race (XI)
GER(ONT)-, old age, old people (VII)
GLOSS-, GLOT(T)-, tongue, language (III)
GLYPH-, to carve (XVII)
GNO(S)-, to know (VI)
GON-, generative, reproductive, sexual (XXV)
GON-, angle, angled figure (XV)
GON-, to produce, originate (VII)
GYMN-, naked (XXV)
GYN(E)-, GYN(A)EC-, woman, female (XI)

H

HAEM(AT)-, blood (V)
HECT-, a hundred (XVI)
HEDON-, pleasure (XVIII)
HEGEMON-, leader (XVIII)
HELI-, sun (XII)
HEM(AT)-, blood (V)
HEMER-, day (V)
HEMI-, half (XVI)
HEPAT-, liver (XX)
HEPT(A)-, seven (XVI)

HETER-, other, different (IX)
HEX(A)-, six (XVI)
HIER-, sacred (XIII)
HIPP-, horse (XXV)
HIST(I)-, tissue (XXIV)
HOD-, way, road (V)
HOL-, whole (VII)
HOM(E)-, same (VI)
HYDR-, water (XIII)
HYGR-, wet, moist (XXV)
HYSTER-, uterus, hysteria (XXI)

I

IATR-, physician, medicine (VII)
ICHTHY-, fish (XXIV)
ICON-, image (III)
IDE-, thought, idea (XII)
IDI-, one's own, peculiar (XI)
IS-, equal (XIV)

K

KAL(L)-, beauty (XVI)
KILO-, one thousand (XVI)
KINE-, to move (XI)

L

LAB-, to take, seize (XV)
LAT(E)R-, to worship excessively, be fanatically devoted to (X)
LECT-, to speak, choose (VIII)
LEM-, LEP-, to take, seize (XV)
LEUC-, LEUK-, white (XXII)
LIP-, fat (XXI)
LITE-, LITH-, stone (XI)
LOG(UE)-, speech, word, proportion, reasoning (IV)
LY-, to loosen (IV)

M

MACR-, large, long (XIV)
MANC-, MANT-, to divine by means of (XII)
MAST-, MAZ-, breast (XXI)

MEGA(L)-, large; a million (XIII)
MELAN-, black, dark (XX)
MENING-, membrane (XXIII)
MER-, part (XXII)
MES-, middle (XV)
MICR-, small, one millionth part of (XII)
MIM-, to imitate (III)
MIS-, hatred (XI)
MNE-, to remember (IV)
MON-, one, single (XVI)
MORPH-, form, shape (VI)
MY(S)-, muscle (XXIII)
MYC(ET)-, fungus, mold (XX)
MYEL-, bone marrow, the spinal cord (XXIII)
MYOS-, muscle (XXIII)

N

NAUT-, sailor (XVII)
NE-, new, new and different form of (IX)
NECR-, the dead, corpse, dead tissue (XII)
NEPHR-, kidney (XX)
NES-, island (XVII)
NEUR-, nerve (XXIII)

O

OCT(A)-, eight (XVI)
OD-, song, poem (III)
OD-, way, road (V)
ODONT-, tooth (IX)
OLIG-, few (XIII)
ONYM-, name, word (VI)
OO-, egg (XXI)
OPHTHALM-, eye (XXIII)
OP(T)-, eye; to see (IX)
ORA-, to see (XIV)
ORNIS-, ORNITH-, bird (XXIV)
ORTH-, straight, correct (IX)
OST(E)-, bone (XX)
OT-, ear (XXI)

P

PAED-, child (IX)
PAL(A)E-, old (XII)
PAN(T)-, all, every (IV)
PATE-, to walk (XVIII)
PATH-, to feel, suffer; disease (X)
PATR-, father (XIII)
PATRI-, family, clan (XIII)
PED-, child (IX)
PEDIA-, education (IX)
PENT(A)-, five (XVI)
PEP(T)-, to digest (VII)
PETR-, rock (XIV)
PHA-, to speak (XI)
PHAG-, to eat (XXIV)
PHA(N)-, to show, appear (VIII)
PHE(M)-, to speak (XI)
PHER-, to bear, go (VI)
PHIL-, to love (VIII)
PHLEB-, vein (XXI)
PHON-, sound, voice (VIII)
PHOR-, to bear, go (VI)
PHOT-, light (XIV)
PHRA-, to speak (XV)
PHREN-, mind, diaphragm (XXIII)
PHY-, to grow (X)
PHYLL-, leaf (XXV)
PHYSI-, nature (X)
PLAS(T)-, to form (XXIV)
PLATY-, flat, broad (XXII)
PLEG-, paralysis (XXIII)
PLEX-, paralytic stroke (XXIII)
POD-, foot (IV)
POLEM-, war (XVIII)
POL(IS)-, city, state (IX)
POLY-, many, much (VIII)
PROT-, first, original, primitive (XVI)
PSEUD-, false (XII)
PSYCH-, mind (XII)
PTER(YX)-, wing, fin (XXIV)
PY-, pus (XXI)
PYR-, fire (III)

R

R(R)HIN-, nose (XXIII)

S

SCHIS-, SCHIZ-, to split (XI)
SCLER-, hard (XX)
SOM(AT)-, body (XXIII)
SOPH-, wise (XIII)
STA-, to stand, stop (X)
STAL-, to send, draw (V)
STEN-, narrow (XXII)
STERE-, solid, three-dimensional
(XI)
STHEN-, strength (XXIII)
STLE-, STOL-, to send, draw (V)
STOM(AT)-, mouth (XXIV)
STROPH-, to turn (XV)

T

TACH(Y)-, swift; speed (XXII)
TACT-, to arrange, put in order (VI)
TAPH-, tomb (V)
TAUT-, the same (VIII)
TAX-, to arrange, put in order (VI)
TECHN-, art, skill, craft (VII)
TELE-, afar, operating at a distance
(XIII)
TETR(A)-, four (XVI)
THANAS-, THANAT-, death (V)

THE-, to place, put (X)
THE-, god (IV)
THEC. -, case (XXV)
THER. , heat (VIII)
THROMB-, clot (XXV)
THYM-, mind, strong feeling
(XXIII)
TOM-, to cut (III)
TON(US)-, a stretching, tension
(XXIII)
TOP-, place (XIV)
TOX-, poison (XXV)
TRI-, three (XVI)
TROP-, to turn (XII)
TROPH-, to nourish, grow (IV)
TYP-, stamp, model (XI)

U

UR-, urine (XXI)
UR-, tail (XVIII)
URG-, work (X)

X

XANTH-, yellow (XXII)
XEN-, stranger, foreigner (XIII)
XYL-, wood (XXV)

Z

ZO-, animal (XIII)

2017.10.16

16.95